UNMARRIED WOMEN
IN JAPAN

Akiko Yoshida addresses common misconceptions about single, never-married women, shedding light on the major social and cultural factors contributing to Japan's singlehood phenomenon. Through interviews with married and never-married women aged 25–46, she argues the increasing rate of female singlehood to be largely the result of structural barriers and a culture that has failed to keep up with economic changes.

Here is an academic book that is also reader-friendly and accessible to the general public. Alongside insightful analysis, Yoshida presents evidence from interview transcripts in rich detail. Important sociological concepts and theories are also briefly explained to guide student readers in making connections. Thus, this book serves not only to enlighten readers on current issues in Japan – it provides sociological perspectives on contemporary gender inequality.

Akiko Yoshida is Associate Professor of Sociology at the University of Wisconsin–Whitewater.

ROUTLEDGE RESEARCH ON GENDER IN ASIA SERIES

RELIGION, GENDER AND
POLITICS IN INDONESIA
Disputing the Muslim body
Sonja van Wichelen

GENDER AND FAMILY IN EAST
ASIA
*Edited by Siumi Maria Tam,
Wai-ching Angela Wong and
Danning Wang*

DALIT WOMEN'S EDUCATION
IN MODERN INDIA
Double discrimination
Shailaja Paik

NEW MODERN CHINESE
WOMEN AND GENDER
POLITICS
Ya-chen Chen

WOMEN AND THE POLITICS
OF REPRESENTATION IN
SOUTHEAST ASIA
Engendering discourse in Singapore
and Malaysia
*Edited by Adeline Koh and
Yu-Mei Balasingamchow*

WOMEN AND CONFLICT IN
INDIA
Sanghamitra Choudhury

GENDER, GOVERNANCE
AND EMPOWERMENT
IN INDIA
Sreevidya Kalaramadam

SOCIAL TRANSFORMATION IN
POST-CONFLICT NEPAL
A gender perspective
Punam Yadav

MOTHERHOOD AND WORK IN
CONTEMPORARY JAPAN
Junko Nishimura

GENDER, VIOLENCE AND THE
STATE IN ASIA
*Edited by Amy Barrow and
Joy L. Chia*

INTIMACY AND
REPRODUCTION IN
CONTEMPORARY JAPAN
Genaro Castro-Vázquez

POSTCOLONIAL LESBIAN
IDENTITIES IN SINGAPORE
Re-thinking global sexualities
Shawna Tang

UNMARRIED WOMEN IN JAPAN
The drift into singlehood
Akiko Yoshida

UNMARRIED WOMEN IN JAPAN

The drift into singlehood

Akiko Yoshida

LONDON AND NEW YORK

First published 2017
by Routledge
2 Park Square, Milton Park, Abingdon, Oxon OX14 4RN

and by Routledge
711 Third Avenue, New York, NY 10017

First issued in paperback 2018

Routledge is an imprint of the Taylor & Francis Group, an informa business

© 2017 Akiko Yoshida

The right of Akiko Yoshida to be identified as author of this work has been asserted by her in accordance with sections 77 and 78 of the Copyright, Designs and Patents Act 1988.

All rights reserved. No part of this book may be reprinted or reproduced or utilised in any form or by any electronic, mechanical, or other means, now known or hereafter invented, including photocopying and recording, or in any information storage or retrieval system, without permission in writing from the publishers.

Trademark notice: Product or corporate names may be trademarks or registered trademarks, and are used only for identification and explanation without intent to infringe.

British Library Cataloguing in Publication Data
A catalogue record for this book is available from the British Library

Library of Congress Cataloging in Publication Data
Names: Yoshida, Akiko, 1963- author.
Title: Unmarried women in Japan : the drift into singlehood / by Akiko Yoshida.
Description: Abingdon, Oxon ; New York, NY : Routledge, 2017. | Series: Routledge research on gender in Asia series | Includes bibliographical references and index.
Identifiers: LCCN 2016020988| ISBN 9781138860353 (hardback) | ISBN 9781315716503 (ebook)
Subjects: LCSH: Single women–Japan–Social conditions. | Women–Japan–Social conditions. | Japan–Social conditions–1945-
Classification: LCC HQ800.4.J3 Y665 2017 | DDC 305.40952–dc23
LC record available at https://lccn.loc.gov/2016020988

ISBN 13: 978-1-138-60470-4 (pbk)
ISBN 13: 978-1-138-86035-3 (hbk)

Typeset in Galliard
by Wearset Ltd, Boldon, Tyne and Wear

TO MY MOTHER
AND ALL WOMEN WHO SUFFER(ED) FROM THE
OPPRESSION OF PATRIARCHY

CONTENTS

List of illustrations	viii
Acknowledgements	ix

1	Introduction: the drift into singlehood	1
2	Decline of marriage age norm: cohort effects and anomie	17
3	Limited chances of romance and problematic men: structural barriers and gender ideology	42
4	Cohort contrast in marriages that surrounded women: impacts of linked lives	74
5	Women's ideas about gender roles: persistence of traditional gender ideology	106
6	Why aren't Japanese women getting married? Conclusion and implications	144

Appendices: research method	171
Bibliography	186
Index	202

ILLUSTRATIONS

Figures

1.1	Percentages of never-married women and men by year: Japan, 1950–2010	2
2.1	Median age of first marriages in Japan: 1950–2012	18
3.1	Changes in composition of love marriage and *miai* marriage: 1940–2009	45

Tables

1.1	Intention of marriage among single men and women aged 18–34: Japan, 1982–2010	4
3.1	How/where married couples met with each other	46
6.1	Summary: causes of singlehood for the boom and recession cohorts	152

ACKNOWLEDGEMENTS

It sounds clichéd, but the writing of this book was a very long journey and I have many people to thank. However, I would prefer to keep the acknowledgement section brief. Thus, please allow me to express my appreciation mainly by the mentioning of names. This brevity does not reflect the great level of gratitude I feel.

I thank (in alphabetical order) Drs. Loretta E. Bass, Ann M. Beutel, Thomas Burns, Elyssa Faison, B. Mitch Peck, and Martin Piotrowski of the University of Oklahoma (OU) for their valuable input, constructive critique, support, encouragement, and compliments during the time I worked on this project for my doctoral dissertation. I appreciate that my doctoral committee members (Drs. Bass, Beutel, Burns, Faison, and Peck) also nominated my dissertation for the University-wide award for doctoral dissertations, which I won for the year 2010. Winning this award led to a conversation with one of my former colleagues at the University of Wisconsin–Whitewater (UWW), Dr. Michael Oldani, who urged me to consider a book publication. I thank him for his encouragement.

I thank the OU Graduate College for funding my field research in Japan with a generous grant. I also thank the OU College of Arts and Sciences, and Department of Sociology, for funding my trips to conferences in which I presented part of the findings from this research. I thank (in alphabetical order) Dr. Richard C. Miller of the University of Wisconsin–Madison, Dr. Yoshimichi Sato of Tohoku University, and Dr. Noboru Tomonari of Carleton College (who served the Chair of the Midwest Japan Seminar in 2012) for inviting me to give a talk on this subject. The insightful comments and critiques I received from attendees of these conferences and talks were invaluable.

Many friends, colleagues, relatives, and students kindly read the near-final version of the manuscript, in part or in total, and gave me feedback and encouraging comments. Without them, my book would not have been as good as it has become. I thank (in alphabetical order) Tonya Bentel, Ron Berger, Rob Boostrom, Natalie Farell, Kasumi Kato, Leda Nath, Larry Neuman, Mayumi Suzuki, Marybeth Vaughan, Chandra Waring, 24 students – I'm sorry I cannot name all of you! – who took my "Gender and Family in Japan" course in Spring 2016, and the three anonymous reviewers provided by Routledge. Kasumi,

ACKNOWLEDGEMENTS

Larry, and Ron read the rough draft of the entire manuscript despite busy schedules. Kasumi's insight as a "recession cohort" Japanese woman was greatly helpful. Input and critiques I received from Ron and Larry – my senior colleagues at UWW – were constructive, and the conversations and debates I had with them enormously strengthened my theoretical arguments. I am very fortunate to have such true intellectuals as my colleagues!

This book, of course, would not have materialized without the cooperation of the 40 women who agreed to participate in my interview research, or without my friends and acquaintances who provided referrals to these women. Unfortunately, these individuals must remain anonymous in order to protect the interviewees' identities. I appreciate that my interviewees trusted me and shared life stories that often touched on very private, sensitive matters. I am still concerned by the distress and sadness expressed by some interviewees, and am wishing all of them happy lives. Some of my friends in Japan – who must remain nameless for interviewee confidentiality – went to great lengths to find interviewees and arrange meetings. They were busy with work and/or family and one was dealing with a health problem. I was moved to rediscover these enduring friendships so many years after leaving Japan.

In the midst of my work on this manuscript, my mother unexpectedly and very quickly died at the age 74 in January, 2015. She was never sick, was physically and socially active, and was always mistaken to be 10 years or so younger. *No one* – even her closest friend – suspected or knew that she was dying of colon cancer. *Everyone* who knew her, including myself, simply assumed this woman would live to be a centenarian. In mid November of 2015, I received the news that she was possibly at stage 4. I flew to Japan and spent a little over one month with her in December 2014 and January 2015. Her dying and death, which led to unfortunate conflicts with the rest of my family of origin, harmed my physical and psychological health. I had to put the book on hold and focus on recovery for about six months. I thank Simon Bates, the editor of Routledge, for his understanding and agreeing to extend the manuscript submission date. In this difficult time I went through, my very close friends – both from Japan and in the U.S. – provided an amazing level of support for me. They listened to my depressing stories with patience and compassion, lent me their shoulders to cry on, gave me kind words and advice, cheered me up, and never cast doubt upon me and my actions. I will keep most of them anonymous – they know I am talking about them – but I want to mention one particular woman Makiko Sagawa, a friend from my childhood, for the amount of help she offered me was beyond belief.

When I began my doctoral program at OU, my daughter Mia was a second-grader. She is now graduating from high school and taking off for college. In-between, I was always busy, sometimes gone for extended periods of time and unable to be there when she needed me, often stressed and fatigued, and also depressed from my mother's death. I know these issues caused difficulties for her, yet she came out to be such a beautiful young woman, inside and out.

ACKNOWLEDGEMENTS

There were many occasions when her big, happy smiles cheered me up. Thank you, Mia, for accepting your sometimes-unreasonably-grouchy mom and loving me back!

The support I received from my husband Brian is beyond anyone's imagination. I can't possibly find the words to thank him enough for everything he has done. As a husband, he was always my biggest advocate, believing in my abilities, listening whenever I felt discouraged or stressed, and on numerous occasions taking on extra chores and childcare. As a fellow sociologist with a deep understanding of the field, he always stimulated my thoughts and on numerous occasions gave me input on the research and book. An excellent writer, his guidance helped me become a better writer, and he read the entire draft of my book manuscript, patiently correcting errors (that I continue to make as a non-native English speaker/writer) and suggesting better wording. He left his career as a tenured professor in Oklahoma in order to give me the chance to have an academic career in Wisconsin. He was put in an extremely tough position when I was going through health problems caused by my mother's dying and death, but we stayed strong. He deserves that I dedicate this book to him, as I did my dissertation. But, as I explain below, I decided to dedicate this book to my late mother and other women in the same shoes.

Although I never questioned my mother's unconditional love for me, for most of my lifetime she and I were not very close. In my adolescence, she was very strict and unaccepting of me and I learned to keep my distance from her as a means of minimizing conflict. After I became a mother, I intentionally cultivated a friendly, civil relationship with her for the sake of my daughter. I visited her with my daughter once a year for several weeks each time, usually in the summer. She was always very happy to see us. Deep down, however, I was holding in lingering anger because I felt that my mother, along with many other things about Japanese society, damaged my self-esteem – damage that took decades to undo.

In her final days, my mother apologized for not having been a very good mother. We had several heart-to-heart talks, and the grudge I was holding melted down. But in the days I was taking care of my dying mother, conflicts broke out between me and my father and brother, and intensified after she passed. My visit, and the conflicts I had, made me face the deeply entrenched patriarchy in my parents' marriage and family relationships. Up until then, I naively believed that my elderly father was not as authoritarian as he used to be, and that my mother was generally managing to live happily. She had many friends, was involved in various activities such as English lessons and a workout club, and most of all – as many people remember – laughed often and very merrily. Only her very close friends knew the extent of her suffering, caused by my father, the patriarch.

I knew my father was an unreasonable man but was not aware of the extent of the control he exercised over, and demands he made of, my mother. The geographic distance, our infrequent visits, and the joy she expressed when we

ACKNOWLEDGEMENTS

visited obscured her problems, leaving me unable to assess them accurately. When I flew back upon hearing news of her illness, she was very accepting of her fate (i.e., death). She told me, however, that she knew she would die of cancer because of the stress caused by my father. She shared with me many stories – terrible things he did or said to her in the past – and said, "Your father had some good qualities, but I hated 90 percent about him." I even wonder if her acceptance of death came from the relief that she would no longer need to take care of my father. After her death, her close friends told me more stories. Eventually, it all came together in my mind. My mother's strictness towards me in my adolescent years was a spillover – triggered by her anger and frustration in marriage. The distant relationship I had with my mother – a relationship between two women – was, ironically, caused by patriarchy.

I realized this only after my mother passed. For a long time, I was unable to forgive myself (What kind of feminist and sociologist am I?). This took a serious toll on my health, but, in the end, this painful experience strengthened my book. I gained a much deeper understanding of gender inequality and a new approach to analysing the boom cohort's parents' marriages. It goes without saying that I would rather have my mom back than having a more academically sound book published.

I regret tremendously not having fought hard against the patriarchy in my mother's marriage, and for women in Japan. I know now that patriarchy short-ened my mother's life, but it is too late to fight for her. I can yet fight for many other women who are alive and continue to endure patriarchal marriage and family relations. As a start, I am hoping that my book helps increase social awareness and plays some small part in inspiring many women and men to work to undo this social injustice. With this hope, and my gratitude towards and apology to my mom, I dedicate this book to her and all women who suffer(ed) from the oppression of patriarchy. *Okāsan, hontoni arigatō soshite hontoni hontoni gomennasai.*

1

INTRODUCTION
The drift into singlehood

> I was learning new things at the job I got after graduating from college, and the job was getting kind of interesting.... I had a boyfriend from college but it didn't lead to marriage.... There were many other single women around, so I didn't feel much pressure [to marry]. I was kind of relaxed, not thinking much, and then found myself getting here [i.e., remaining single].
>
> (Tsuneko,[1] 43 years old, never married, marketing consultant)

On June 18, 2014, Tokyo Assemblywoman Ayaka Shiomura, from a minority party, was making a speech at an Assembly meeting. She was requesting more governmental support for women in the areas of childrearing and infertility when she was interrupted by heckling. Multiple men of the leading conservative Liberal Democratic Party shouted: "You should get married soon!"; "Can't you bear children?" Loud laughter followed. Assemblywoman Shiomura, a former TV personality and bikini model, was never married and had no children, and was just a few weeks shy of turning 36. Barely collecting herself, she completed the speech with tears and a shaking voice.[2] Publicly humiliating women for their single status, as observed in this incident, is hardly uncommon in Japan.[3] Shiomura later complained in one interview to the press that her hecklers were "insensitive to women who want to but cannot marry."[4] Indeed, politicians and the general public have been oblivious to the notion that women might in fact be *unable to* marry. Instead, never-married women have been objects of criticism and ridicule, particularly since the late 1980s when the number of unmarried women began to surge.

As in all developed nations, as well as many rapidly developing countries,[5] the number of never-married singles has increased dramatically in Japan. As Figure 1.1 shows, for women, the first significant rise was observed among those aged 25–29 between 1980 and 1990, when Japan's economy was booming at an unprecedented rate. In the early 1990s, the Japanese economy entered a severe recession, and still the never-married population continued to grow. The most recent statistics from 2010 show that 60.3, 34.5, 23.1, 17.4, 12.6, and 8.7 percent of women in age groups 25–29, 30–34, 35–39, 40–44, 45–49, and

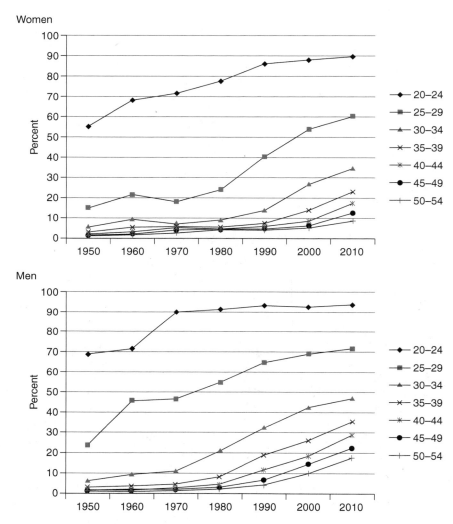

Figure 1.1 Percentages of never-married women and men by year: Japan, 1950–2010.

Sources: For figures in 1950, 1960, 1970, and 1980, Ministry of Internal Affairs and Communications, Statistics Bureau (2015b); for figures in 1990, 2000, and 2010, Ministry of Internal Affairs and Communications (2011).

50–54, respectively, had never been married – record highs for each age group. (Note that the corresponding figures were higher for men: 71.8, 47.3, 35.6, 28.6, 22.5, and 17.8 percent.[6]) Unlike unmarried people in many Western countries, most of these never-married singles in Japan were not cohabiting with partners.[7] Instead, the majority lived with their parents, and some lived on their

INTRODUCTION: THE DRIFT INTO SINGLEHOOD

own.[8] Also, whereas a growing number of unmarried women in the West have children outside wedlock, unwed motherhood is extremely rare in Japan.[9] These figures reveal Japan as one of the least-partnered nations in the world.

This phenomenon of increased singlehood (*mikonka*) has received political, social, scholarly, and media attention in Japan largely because of its direct association with Japan's "population problem (*jinkō mondai*)." Japan's birth rates declined sharply and have lingered far below replacement level (which is an average of 2.1 children per woman)[10] at the same time as the single population grew.[11] The total fertility rate[12] for 2014 was 1.42 (meaning that the birth rate of 2014 estimated an average of 1.42 children would be born per woman). Simultaneously, as in other nations, average life expectancies increased. Japan's birth rate has been one of the lowest in the world, whereas its average life expectancy has been one of the longest.[13] Together with a low level of acceptance of immigrants,[14] Japan has become the most *aged* country – meaning that the proportion of the population that is elderly is larger than is the case for any other country.[15] To illustrate, in 2013, one out of four (25 percent) residents in Japan was aged 65 and above. This rate is projected to increase to one out of three (33.4 percent) by 2035.[16] By comparison, in the U.S. the proportion of the population aged 65 and above was about one in eight (13 percent) in 2010, and is projected to grow to be one out of five (20 percent) by 2030, after which the growth rate of the elderly population should slow down.[17]

The Japanese government came to consider the changing demographic structure as a "social problem" and has implemented various social programs and policies to help married women balance work and family, with the intended goal of increasing birth rates.[18] These programs and policies, however, have had little effect because the single population continued to rise and never-married women rarely had children.[19] Women who do not marry have therefore been seen as the major obstacle to solving Japan's population problem, and this partly (or perhaps largely) explains why never-married women have faced harsh treatment by the public and government officials.[20]

Women's single status in Japan has often been assumed to be the result of personal choices and preferences. This assumption was made not only by many politicians but also by the popular media and some prominent social scientists. Coining the later popularized term, "parasite singles," Japanese sociologist Masahiro Yamada contended that many individuals chose or preferred to stay single and live with parents because they wanted to maintain luxurious, materialistic, carefree lives instead of marrying and taking on parenting and other family-related responsibilities.[21] On the other hand, some feminist scholars interpreted increased singlehood to be an outcome of women's resistance against (patriarchal) marriage or traditional gender roles/ideology.[22] Since the late 1980s, the popular media has coined stigmatizing labels for never-married women and propagated them.[23] These include: "Christmas cake," popularly used in the 1980s and meant to belittle unmarried women past age 25 as leftovers – like Christmas cake, which is no longer sought out after December 25;

3

INTRODUCTION: THE DRIFT INTO SINGLEHOOD

"parasite singles," Yamada's term suggesting singles were selfish, materialistic, dependent, and irresponsible; and "loser dogs (*make inu*)," taken from a book title by a never-married female author Junko Sakai and directly defining single women as "losers."[24] It is also very common for the mass media to frame women nowadays as unquestionably "choosing careers over marriage."[25]

This assumption that women chose or preferred to stay unmarried, however, is not grounded in empirical evidence.[26] As shown in Table 1.1, national surveys of single women (and men) have consistently shown that the great majority of single women in Japan – more women than men – wished to marry one day, and this statistic holds throughout the time of increasing single population.[27] Empirical studies have also shown that most Japanese, married or unmarried, take (heterosexual) marriage for granted as the "normal" life path to take;[28] this was the case even for and among gay men.[29] Never-married women are also significantly less happy and healthy than their married counterparts,[30] and struggle more economically compared to never-married men and married people.[31] Why, then, are so many more women in Japan unmarried today than in the past? This book aims to employ a sociological perspective to identify the true causes of increased singlehood among women in Japan.

Increased singlehood: a global yet undertheorized phenomenon

As mentioned above, the number of never-married singles increased in all developed, and many newly developing, nations. Despite its ubiquity across the

Table 1.1 Intention of marriage among single men and women aged 18–34: Japan, 1982–2010 (in percentages)

	1982	1987	1992	1997	2002	2005	2010
Women							
Intend to marry one day	94.2	92.9	90.2	89.1	88.3	90.0	89.4
No intention to marry	4.1	4.6	5.2	4.9	5.0	5.6	6.8
No answer	1.7	2.5	4.6	6.0	6.7	4.3	3.8
Total	100.0	100.0	100.0	100.0	100.0	100.0	100.0
Men							
Intend to marry one day	95.9	91.8	90.0	85.9	87.0	87.0	86.3
No intention to marry	2.3	4.5	4.9	6.3	5.4	7.1	9.4
No answer	1.8	3.7	5.1	7.8	7.7	5.9	4.3
Total	100.0	100.0	100.0	100.0	100.0	100.0	100.0

Source: National Fertility Surveys, National Institute of Population and Social Security Research (2007, 2011a).

Note
Single individuals include never-married, divorced, and widowed individuals.

globe, never-married singlehood has been relatively understudied in the West, and undertheorized in sociology. Existing sociological theories tend to lump different types of unmarried statuses (e.g., cohabitation, unwed motherhood, divorce, postponement of marriage, and lifetime singlehood) together, and attempt to explain all ("not married") as one phenomenon sharing the same cause(s). Whereas other forms of non-marriage – especially divorce, cohabitation, and unwed motherhood – have been studied extensively in sociology, never-married singlehood has received very little scholarly attention in the Western context.[32]

On the other hand, in the context of Japan, a fair amount of research has been conducted on never-married singlehood, and many of these studies indicate the inapplicability or inadequacy of current sociological theories of non-marriage/singlehood,[33] themselves built on observations of (a limited number of) Western societies.[34] Even so, Japanese studies have had little impact on theory-building, leaving existing theories limited in scope and explanatory power.

The most influential theories of singlehood come from the neo-economic perspective, which attributes the cause of singlehood to individuals' rational choice making in changing economic contexts. The focal variable is either the economic independence gained by women (according to Gary Becker[35]) or deterioration in men's economic prospects (according to Valerie Oppenheimer and her colleagues[36]). In these theories, individuals, especially women, are perceived to be calculating the cost and benefit of marriage (mostly in terms of its economy) and voluntarily choosing whether/when to marry, divorce, and so forth.

Other theories, the most prominent of which is the second demographic transition theory,[37] point to a shift in culture as the cause of increased singlehood/non-marriage. This line of theories views societies as progressing towards greater individualism and secularization, or moving away from tradition. The argument is that this change in cultural context allows individuals to seek or choose non-traditional forms of romantic relationships other than marriage (i.e., the conventional form). In other words, according to these cultural theories, non-marriage/increased singlehood is an outcome of greater personal freedom.

Generally speaking, both camps of theories are, in my estimation, severely flawed because they see individuals as agents who make choices freely and shape their life courses with few social or cultural constraints. Though Oppenheimer et al. consider the constraining impact of men's weak economic prospects, they continue to assume women's ability to choose not to marry, and fail to address the impacts of other forms of social inequality, such as those based on gender, class, and race. This neglect of inequality is rather strange considering that a basic tenet of the sociological perspective is that social and cultural structures, embedded with power and inequality, shape individual lives and limit choices.[38] Moreover, in the empirical world, people of disadvantaged statuses, such as the poor and highly educated black females in the U.S, are more likely to remain unmarried.[39] It would seem that more intricate examinations of culture, economy, and social structure in general are needed.

This book aims to fill the gap in sociological literature and singlehood theory with insights derived from my original research, conducted on women in Japan for the explicit purpose of identifying possible structural causes of increased singlehood. Put succinctly, the life story interview research I conducted suggests that persistent gender inequality, permeated within social and cultural structures, is one of the most fundamental causes of many Japanese women's inability to marry. As implied in the words of never-married interviewee Tsuneko in the beginning of this chapter, women *drifted into singlehood* unwillingly.

My study

My study begins with the assumption that most women in Japan did *not* intend, choose, or prefer to remain unmarried. The assumption is warranted because, as mentioned above, the great majority of never-married women in Japan reported the desire to marry throughout the time the single population increased, and marriage is still largely expected as the normative life path.

I wanted to reconstruct the social and cultural structure women have lived through, especially when they were in their prime marriage age, for my analysis. This should unfold through women's subjective lived experiences – what they perceived and lived as their "real" world – because that was the world that mattered to their lives. For this reason, I considered life story interviews the most appropriate and informative. I chose this data collection method also because I wanted to empower women by giving them voices,[40] and most studies on singlehood employ quantitative research methods.[41] Surveys and demographic data are limited in their ability to capture the intricacies of social and cultural structure and social processes. Because I deem existing sociological theories of singlehood that assume individual agency to be inadequate, my research is guided by a different theoretical framework, employing the feminist perspective, theory of anomie, and life course theory. Below I discuss my theoretical framework and research method in more detail.

Theoretical framework

Gender is embedded in everyday routines, culture (social norms, values, beliefs, ideology, traditions, and so forth), and social structure. It is much more than the social distinctions made between two sexes – female and male – or individual identities based on them. Gender is so pervasive that we often take it for granted. We tend to view gender differences as "natural" or fail to notice socially constructed aspects of gender. However, as Judith Lorber[42] succinctly stated, gender is simultaneously a social institution, part of the social stratification system, a social process, and permeated in our social structure. In other words, gender is a basis upon which to organize society. There are many examples of this: roles within marriage and other forms of kin relationships are typically allocated by gender (and age); not only are males more likely to occupy positions of power in societies, but the traits associated with masculinity (e.g., strength, independence, etc.) are also tied to power and privilege; we "do gender"[43] – interact with others in gender appropriate ways in everyday life to reinforce gender culture and perpetuate gender inequality. Thus, gender permeates culture and social structure to the extent that some feminist scholars, such as Barbara Risman, consider gender to *be* social structure.[44] It is also important to note that social location by gender intersects with other locations such as race, ethnicity, socioeconomic class, sexual orientation, (dis)ability, nationality, etc., and thus places persons of the same gender into different power locations.[45] From this perspective, researchers (and people generally) are urged to take critical views on society, social phenomena, social relations, etc., with a specific focus on inequality based on gender (and its intersection with other locations).[46] In coming to understand issues related to marriage, this outlook makes sense, as gender has been the basis for marital relation formation, and the decline of such relation formations warrants investigation into the relevance of gender.

As briefly mentioned above, in Japan the single population first soared during the economic boom and continued to rise after Japan entered a severe economic recession. I suspected the relevance of this dramatic – even rollercoaster-like – shift in the economy, and employed two social theories, the theory of *anomie* by Emile Durkheim and life course theory, to guide my research and analyses of data.

Durkheim predicted that rapid social change weakens normative constraints, creating a state of society he called *anomie*.[47] Norms are needed, not only to organize society, but to shape the daily conduct and life paths of individuals.[48] Thus, anomie – weak or absent normative guidance – could have detrimental impacts on individuals' lives. In contrast to individuals who simply follow the norms of their societies, people in anomic societies must navigate their lives on their own. While some may embrace such liberty, many may become lost and end up taking life paths they did not intend or desire to take. Single women in Japan wished to marry, but were in a sense left hanging by a society in the throes of rapid social change: a society unable to adjust – to settle upon norms, with regard to gender and marriage, that meshed well with new social realities. This anomic society – one that left women drifting unguided – may have played an important role in the phenomenon of increased singlehood.

Life course theory informs us that different historical contexts shape individual life courses differently. Particularly in rapidly changing societies, the life course varies significantly by cohort membership as the historical context changes during one's lifetime.[49] I therefore expected that causes of singlehood could differ between the two cohorts of women: those who spent their young adulthood during the economic boom, and those who reached young adulthood after the economic recession. This research thus includes women of two cohorts, which I call the "boom cohort" and "recession cohort," and compares their stories to assess whether and how social structure differed between the two, and thus caused singlehood differently.

In sum, my study critically examines the relevance of gender to the phenomenon, anticipates the impact of anomie, and analyzes the extent to which causes of singlehood differ between the two cohorts of women. These approaches depart significantly from existing theories of singlehood, which assume agency and choice-making by individuals.

My social location

I would like to share my background briefly here so that the readers can be aware of potential biases derived from it. This research was conducted for my doctoral dissertation,[50] which I completed in 2010 at the University of Oklahoma. I am a native of Japan, was born in 1963, and experienced Japan's economic boom of the 1980s in my mid twenties as a single woman. In other words, I belong to the "boom cohort," was one of the "Christmas cakes," and contributed to the rise of the single population along with some of my friends in Japan. I, however, moved to the U.S. in 1992 at age 28 to pursue a master's degree in sociology. In 1994, I married my husband, an American citizen, and have lived in the U.S. since. Many of my friends in Japan with whom I stayed in contact, on the other hand, remained single. I felt the move to the U.S. divided the fates of myself and my friends. None of my unmarried friends, about whom I care deeply, intended to stay single, nor were they happy about their single status. Thus, my own history and relationships obviously shaped my interest in this subject.

Before starting my doctoral study in 2006 in my forties, I had contemplated doing doctoral dissertation research on this subject for a long time. I was certain that the economic boom of the 1980s has some significance, but the single population grew even after Japan's economy deteriorated. I was very curious about the life circumstances and views of the younger generation of women that experienced the recession acutely, but knew few women of this generation.

I therefore had more intimate insight into life in Japan up to the economic boom, particularly as experienced by women of my own cohort, but not so much for the time after the economic recession and about women of the recession cohort. I was a sort of simultaneous insider and outsider. In conducting this research and analyzing the data, I found my unique social location more advantageous than disadvantageous. I was able to communicate with my interviewees with no cultural and language barriers, and understand much of women's lives in Japan through personal insights, but at the same time I could interpret their stories somewhat objectively from my Americanized, outsider's viewpoint. Nonetheless, as in any qualitative research, my interviews and data analysis cannot escape my subjectivity. I hope readers find this information helpful in identifying potential biases.

INTRODUCTION: THE DRIFT INTO SINGLEHOOD

Research method[51]

I conducted life story interviews with 40 never-married and married women in the Greater Tokyo Area between May and July of 2009. At the time of interviews, my interviewees were aged between 25 and 46 (i.e., born between 1962 and 1984). Based on their experiences of job search upon graduation, I classified 19 interviewees as members of the "boom cohort" (born between 1962 and 1971, or age 38 to 46 at the time of interview) and 21 as "recession cohort" (born between 1972 and 1984, or age 25 to 37 at the time of interview).[52] Among the boom cohort, 11 were never married and 8 were married; for the recession cohort, 17 were never married and 4 were married. Married women were included in the research for comparison. All women were recruited via purposive, convenience, and snowball sampling methods. They varied in terms of level of education, occupation, and income level. More detailed information on the study participants is provided in Appendix C.

Interviews were in-depth, open-ended qualitative interviews, semi-structured with the prepared interview guide and conducted face to face and one on one. The language used was Japanese, which was the first language for both myself and the interviewees. Interview questions were centered on interviewees' life experiences (with a focus on their romantic and work histories) and their views toward marriage/singlehood and gender roles. An English translation of the interview guide is provided in Appendix B and the original Japanese version is available upon request to the author. Note that I did not ask my single interviewees why they were unmarried. I believed such a question would put them in a defensive stance, and my main goal was to learn about the social and cultural contexts they were in, not women's own reasoning about their single status.

The length of interviews ranged from 40 minutes to 4 hours and 33 minutes, with an average of 2 hours and 13 minutes. All the interviews were recorded with interviewees' permission and transcribed by me. I analyzed the transcriptions in the original language (i.e., Japanese), along with field notes I took after interviews, using the grounded theory approach.[53] All interview quotes in this book are translations done by me. Appendix A provides more detail on the research method I employed. All my unmarried interviewees either voluntarily expressed, or indirectly but clearly indicated, that they never intended to stay single,[54] and all but one wished to marry at the time of the interviews.

Chapter overview

Chapters 2 to 5 present my research findings on four themes that emerged from this study. Chapter 2 concerns the relevance of *anomie*. The two cohorts' stories indicate that the traditional age norm regarding appropriate timing of marriage for women was strongly internalized among the boom cohort, but its enforcement weakened due to a labor shortage during the economic boom. On the other hand, for the recession cohort the traditional age norm became obsolete, and there was no socially shared age norm. The chapter illustrates this process of breakdown of a once-strong marriage norm, and discusses how Durkheim's concept of anomie helps us understand the singlehood phenomenon. The cohort difference in women's experiences was clear, affirming the relevance of *cohort effects* as predicted by life course theory.

Chapter 3 points out the most direct causal factors for increased singlehood among women in Japan. Many women had difficulties in meeting romantic partners due to structural barriers imposed by work/workplaces, and the interplay of these factors with beliefs in traditional gender ideology. Desirable men were also scarce. Together with the findings presented in Chapter 2, this chapter demonstrates that the fundamental cause of increased singlehood among women lies in the social and cultural structure, itself embedded with gender inequalities, as well as with other forms of power and social inequalities. Cohort differences, as well as similarities, were observed here.

Chapter 4 presents a sharp cohort contrast in views toward parent and peer marriages. The boom cohort almost invariably held negative views towards their parents' marriages, whereas the recession cohort was much more positive or had more flexible views towards marriage due largely to influences of their peers. Their stories indicate that the marital relationships differed sharply between the wartime generation (i.e., the boom cohort's parents) and the postwar democratization generation (i.e., the recession cohort's parents). This chapter describes this difference and discusses the possible impact of intergenerational ties – or *linked lives* in the language of life course theory – on the two cohorts' views towards marriage.

Chapter 5 delineates a cohort difference in gender role conceptions. The boom cohort almost uniformly held traditional ideas, while there were more variations in gender role views among the recession cohort. Generally, however, gender ideology remained quite traditional for both cohorts. This lingering, traditional gender ideology clashed with changing employment opportunities for young women during the boom, and for men during the recession. Many were unable to reconcile two competing devotions[55] – one to marriage/family and the other to paid employment.

The final chapter summarizes the causes of increased singlehood for the two cohorts identified in this study, and discusses the implications of this study for the sociological theory of singlehood, women's empowerment, and social policies. It concludes that women in Japan drifted into singlehood, and that their single status was an outcome of unfulfilled desires rather than women's rational choice making, search for non-traditional romantic relationships, or resistance against patriarchy. Thus, my study highlights the *lack of* human agency in a phenomenon (or population) that is often assumed to be associated with human agency or autonomy. This study underscores the notion that gender and other forms of power inequality, permeated in social structure and culture, are the fundamental causes of increased singlehood. The never-married population has

INTRODUCTION: THE DRIFT INTO SINGLEHOOD

grown, and is likely to continue growing, in many developed and developing nations. This book sheds critical light on this phenomenon from feminist and sociological perspectives that emphasize the importance of social forces and inequalities in understanding individuals' lives.

Notes

1 All interviewees' names are pseudonyms. Interviewees' ages are as of 2009 when the interviews were conducted.
2 Shiomura posted this incident on Facebook and the story spread quickly through it and Twitter. Soon news stations across the world covered the incident and broadcasted the video-recorded assembly session (e.g., Ripley and Henry, CNN 2014).
3 L. Nakano 2014.
4 I watched several examples of TV news coverage on-line after the incident. I have a vivid memory of Assemblywoman Shiomura, in response to questions from the press, asserting that the hecklers were insensitive to unmarried women who wished but were unable to marry. I could not locate that particular news clip on-line, unfortunately. Shiomura and her party demanded the Tokyo Assembly identify hecklers and take action in response to their sexist behaviors. Five days after the incident, Assemblyman Akihiro Suzuki of the Liberal Democratic Party identified himself as the (only) heckler and formally apologized at a press conference. At this conference, Suzuki stated that he lacked sensitivity towards women who were unable to marry for various reasons (*samazamana riyūde kekkon dekinai katagata e no hairyo ni kaketeita*) (*YouTube* 2014). From the video recording, it was obvious that there were multiple hecklers, yet the case was closed by the nominal sanctioning of Suzuki only.
5 See, Cherlin 2012; Jones and Yeung 2014; Lesthaeghe 2010; OECD 2015f; Raymo et al. 2015 for details.
6 Ministry of Internal Affairs and Communications 2011.
7 Cohabitation numbers somewhat increased but remain low in Japan. According to the National Fertility Survey (NIPSSR 2011a), only 2.1, 2.8, and 1.6 percent of never-married women aged 25 to 29, 30 to 34, and 35 to 39 (respectively) were currently cohabiting in 2010. According to the OECD (2015a), in 2011 the average rate of cohabitation for persons aged 20 to 34 for all OECD countries was 17.06 percent (excluding Chile, Finland, Israel, Japan, Mexico, and South Korea that did not have data; the rate for New Zealand was from 2013 and that of the U.S. was from 2010). According to Raymo, Iwasawa, and Bumpass (2009), in Japan approximately 20 percent of never-married women born 1970 and after have cohabited, but duration of cohabitation tended to be short and most preceded marriage. Four of my younger interviewees were cohabiting at the time of interviews. One was hoping to marry her partner and another discussed marriage with her partner (and later they married). One woman was cohabiting with her female partner – hoping but unable to marry, as Japan has not legalized same-sex marriage. The youngest cohabiting interviewee was 26 years old. Her partner was divorced and uninterested in marriage, according to her. Losing her mother after a long battle with terminal illness, this interviewee was ambivalent about marriage, though she wished her boyfriend wanted to marry her. Thus, cohabitating women in Japan do not seem to think of cohabitation as a permanent living arrangement. Cohabitation has not been widely accepted in Japanese society. My older interviewees did not approve it as a valid lifestyle and openly discussed and/or expressed negative views.
8 Approximately 70 percent of never-married women lived with their parents, and this figure has been consistent over time (Fukuda 2009; Raymo et al. 2015; Raymo 2015).

INTRODUCTION: THE DRIFT INTO SINGLEHOOD

9 Unwed motherhood remains extremely rare in Japan, unlike in many other developed nations, particularly in the West. The unwed birth rate has been around 1 to 2 percent of all births for the last 40 or so years (Ato 1994; Raymo 1998; Rindfuss et al. 2004; Tsuya and Mason 1995; Zaiki 2000). Moreover, some of the "unwed" childbirths were not strictly outside of wedlock. There was an increase in women who married socially (i.e., had weddings), but not legally (i.e., filing the marriage in the family registry system), with the purpose of retaining their surnames. Japanese law until very recently required that one party of a married couple change his or her surname to that of their spouse. Births by these women were counted towards the "unwed" childbearing statistics. In 2012, about 2 percent of all Japanese births were to unmarried mothers, and the corresponding figure for the OECD average was 38.7 percent (OECD 2015b). Hertog (2009, 2011), based on her qualitative interview research, provides an excellent account of why non-marital childbearing remains rare in Japan.

10 The lowest TFR, 1.26, was recorded in 2005 (Ministry of Health, Labor, and Welfare, 2014b).

11 Japan's birth rates actually started declining in 1976, but the government and media paid attention to the declining rates in reaction to the so-called "1.57 shock" of 1989. In this year, the total fertility rate (TFR) hit 1.57. This figure was significant because it was lower than a one-time drop in 1966, the *hinoeuma* year – the special year of the horse (in the Chinese zodiac) that comes once every 60 years – believed to be a bad year for girls to be born. Many people in Japan avoided having babies that year. A rate lower than this year was, therefore, a "shock." The government and media framed the declining birth rates as "*shōshika* (child shortage phenomenon) problem" (Roberts 2002).

12 The total fertility rate (TFR) indicates an estimated average number of children a woman would have in her lifetime. It is calculated based on the number of babies born in a given year.

13 According to the Population Reference Bureau (PRB) (2015), for 2015 the average total fertility rate of Japan was 1.4. In comparison, the rate was 2.5 for all countries and 1.7 for the "more developed" region. The average life expectancy (at birth) in Japan was 80 years for males and 87 years for females. The corresponding averages for all countries were 69 and 73 (respectively) and 76 and 82 for the "more developed" region. For the definition of "more developed" region, see PRB 2015.

14 The immigrant share of total population in Japan was 0.1 percent in 2013, which is one of the lowest among the OECD countries (OECD 2015e).

15 PRB 2015.

16 Ministry of Internal Affairs and Communications 2014.

17 Federal Interagency Forum on Aging Related Statistics 2016.

18 These include the Childcare Leave Law and the "Angel Plan (*enzeru puran*)." I discuss more about these policies and programs in Chapter 6, but for greater detail see Boling 2008; Gelb 2003; Ministry of Health, Labor, and Welfare 2010; Rebick 2006; Roberts 2002, 2005; and Takeda 2011.

19 According to the Ministry of Health, Labor, and Welfare (2003), increased singlehood accounts for almost 90 percent of the fertility decline between 1975 and 1990 and 60 percent of the decline between 1990 and 2000.

20 For instance, in 1990, then Finance Minister Ryutaro Hashimoto (who became Prime Minister in 1996) recommended that the cabinet reconsider the policy that encourages women to attain higher education – since higher education deters women from childrearing (Garon 1997). In 2003, then Prime Minister Yoshiro Mori opined that single childless women were unworthy of social security benefits because not having children meant they did not contribute to society (AtWiki 2009).

INTRODUCTION: THE DRIFT INTO SINGLEHOOD

21 Yamada 1999. His parasite singles hypothesis is not supported by empirical data (Genda 2005; Honda 2002/2005; Kukimoto 2005; Oishi 2004; Raymo 2003b; Shirahase 2005; Tanaka 2003).

22 Many scholars decisively described the phenomenon as women "deciding/choosing" to remain single or "rejecting/resisting" marriage/gender roles (e.g., L. Nakano 2010; Rosenberger 2013). Also common is the depiction of single women as "independent" (Iwashita 2001; Ueno 2009). Rosenberger (2013), however, hesitated to apply the concept of "agency" to single women in Japan, but still framed singlehood as "long-term resistance."

23 Brinton 1992; Creighton 1996; Dales 2015; L. Nakano 2014; Nakano and Wagatsuma 2004; Yoshida 2011.

24 Sakai (2003) did not intend to call single women "losers." She herself was unmarried in her thirties and the usage of the term was sarcastic. But the popular media and public picked up the word and used it to insult single women. Other stigmatizing labels followed and stuck. See, for instance, Yamaguchi (2006) for the term "*Onibaba* (Demon Hags)."

25 For instance, see *The Economist*, 2011.

26 The percentages of women who agreed with statements such as "Marriage is the source of happiness for women" in surveys have declined significantly in Japan since the 1980s. Some social scientists and the popular media interpreted this change as declined interest in marriage by women (e.g., Ohashi, 1993). The statement, however, is *not* a valid measure of women's interests in, or intent of, marriage.

27 National Fertility Surveys (NIPSSR 2007, 2011a).

28 Ato 1989, 1994; Ato and Kojima 1983; Ato et al. 1994; Dales 2015; Hertog 2009; R. Kaneko 1994; E. Nakano 1994; L. Nakano 2010; Nemoto 2008; Tokuhiro 2010.

29 Japan is observed to be "friendly" towards male homosexuality culturally (though there are various misperceptions about homosexuality), but marriage is still highly restricted to heterosexual relationships (see, for instance, Tamagawa 2015) and, at least until fairly recently, even gay men themselves expected to marry heterosexually (Lunsing 2001).

30 Raymo's (2015) study's primary focus is to compare self-reported happiness and health between living-alone singles and singles who live with their parents. His study, however, indicates a discernable difference in these measures between the married and the unmarried, especially among women.

31 L. Nakano 2014; Ronald and Nakano 2013; Tachibanaki 2006.

32 Klinenberg (2012) studied living alone singles (which included never-married singles) in the U.S., but his study focused primarily on the urban, middle-class, white population. His book was written in a popular style and thus lacks academic rigor. Klinenberg also helped Aziz Ansari, a comedian and actor, publish a popular book entitled "Modern Romance" (2015) on the subject of singlehood. This work, however, is clearly pseudoscience. Though he is a law professor, a monograph by Banks (2011) on middle-class African American women is the only extensive sociological study on never-married singles in the Western context of which I am aware.

33 For instance, Ohashi (1993) and Retherford, Ogawa, and Matsukura (2001) supported the women's economic independence hypothesis theorized by Gary Becker (1981/1991/1993). They argued that Japanese women came to avoid marriage due to their advancement in economic position. Both studies drew conclusions based on the simultaneous occurrences of two events – increased singlehood and another event, such as increased labor force participation by women/narrowed wage gap by sex for younger employees, or declined percentage of women who agreed with the survey statement, "Marriage is the source of happiness for women." They never established causal relationships between the two. Other studies from Japan (Ato 1994; Hiroshima 1999; Iwama 1999; Kamano 2005; Nemoto 2008; Raymo 1998, 2003a; Raymo and

INTRODUCTION: THE DRIFT INTO SINGLEHOOD

Iwasawa 2005; Tsuya and Mason 1995) did not support Becker's hypothesis. Rejecting Becker's theory, Oppenheimer and her colleagues contended that women's higher economic prospects increase the chance of marriage (Oppenheimer 1994, 1997; Oppenheimer, Blossfeld, and Wackerow 1995; Oppenheimer and Lew 1995) and it is deteriorated economic conditions among men that cause the decline of marriage (Oppenheimer 1988, 1994, 2000; Oppenheimer, Kalmijn, and Lim 1997). Sweeney (2002) pointed out that the impact of women's economic independence differs by cohort. Study findings from Japan are mixed on this line of theories. Cohort membership was the determining factor of marriage rate decline – i.e., women of the cohort among which singlehood increased remained unmarried regardless of their education, employment, or urban–rural upbringing (Ato 1994; Hiroshima 1999; Iwama 1999; Raymo 1998, 2003a; Raymo and Iwasawa 2005; Tsuya and Mason 1995). Highly educated women postponed marriage but married at the same rates as lower-educated women (Raymo 2003b), had higher single rates (Raymo and Iwasawa 2005), or always had higher rates of non-marriage and considering that, the increased single population was much more significant among the lower-educated women (Shirahase 2005). Brinton (1993) pointed out that college-educated women are much more likely to become homemakers than lower-educated women in Japan. The impact of men's earnings was irrelevant to the rise of the single population during the economic boom (Shirahase 2005; Tsuya and Mason 1995), though since the economic recession, men of lower income (Shirahase 2005) and those in casual employment (Piotrowski, Kalleberg, and Rindfuss 2015) were more likely to remain unmarried. Another theoretical camp points to cultural (ideational, attitudinal) changes as the cause of increased singlehood, or decline of marriage. The most dominant theory in this line is called the second demographic transition theory (Lesthaeghe 2010; Lesthaeghe and Neidert 2006; van de Kaa 1987) but some postmodern theorists such as Beck and Beck-Gernsheim (2005) and Giddens (1991) also made similar arguments. Attitudinal change, however, was found *after* the single population increased (Tsuya and Mason 1995), and most women (and men, including gay men), adhered to the (heterosexual) marriage institution in Japan (Hertog 2009; Kelsky 2001; Lunsing 2001; Nemoto 2008; Tokuhiro 2010). Arland Thornton (2005) criticized the second demographic transition theory for its ethnocentric presumption that all societies "develop" to take the same pathway, an idea he called the "developmental paradigm." Hertog (2009) and Tokuhiro (2010) echoed his criticism, backing their arguments with their studies on unwed mothers and single women (respectively) in Japan.

34 Some studies from the U.S. (e.g., Edin and Kefalas 2005) also argued the limited nature of existing theories of singlehood.

35 Becker 1981/1991/1993.

36 Oppenheimer 1988, 1994, 1997, 2000; Oppenheimer et al. 1995, 1997; Oppenheimer and Lew 1995.

37 For the second demographic transition theory, see Lesthaeghe 2010; Lesthaeghe and Neidert 2006; and van de Kaa 1987. Similarly, some postmodern theorists argue that individuals in the postmodern world are searching for "pure relationships" (Giddens 1991) or alternative ways to form egalitarian intimate relationships (Beck and Beck-Gernsheim 2005). Arland Thornton (2005) criticizes this line of thinking – which he called "developmental paradigm" – for its assumption that all societies develop in the same direction, or more specifically, that other societies, as they develop, follow the paths of Western ("developed") nations. I concur with his argument, and also contend that these theories are middle-class/elite academia-centric.

38 Rather than assuming ubiquitous patterns, some sociologists compare cross-national evidence and theorize that different cultural or institutional contexts affect associations between women's economic advancement and marriage differently. For

INTRODUCTION: THE DRIFT INTO SINGLEHOOD

instance, Blossfeld (1995) observed that the relationship between women's higher education and marriage rates was positive or insignificant in Sweden, West Germany, Hungary, and the United States, weak and negative in France and the Netherlands, and strong and negative in Italy. Blossfeld hypothesizes that cultural context affects the above causal relationships. In the least egalitarian societies, such as Italy, highly educated women marry less often because of difficulties in balancing family and paid work (i.e., higher opportunity costs for educated women). In more egalitarian societies such as Sweden, women's higher education has zero or positive effects on marriage because work–family balance is possible, or marriage poses little opportunity cost. Empirical support for Blossfeld's hypothesis is, however, mixed. Analyzing data from Sweden, the United States, and Japan, Ono (2003) found support for the effects of cultural context on marriage rates of highly educated women. The relationship between income (potential) and marriage was positive for Sweden and the United States but negative for Japan. However, other studies show mixed results regarding the association between education and marriage rates in Japan (Raymo 2003a, 2003b; Shirahase 2005; Tsuya and Mason 1995). I find Blossfeld's conceptualization of "egalitarian" societies arbitrary and problematic. By what criteria are France and the Netherlands judged less egalitarian than the United States and West Germany?

39 E.g., Banks 2011; Edin and Kefalas 2005; Edin and Reed 2005; Smock 2004; and Smock, Manning, and Porter (2005).

40 Feminist methodology encourages researchers to empower and transform the researched in the process of research. Giving voice to the disadvantaged is one example of such methods (Cook and Fonow 1986).

41 Holloway (2010); Le Blanc (1999); and Tamanoi (1990) discussed how most research conducted on Japanese society has not taken women's lived experiences into consideration, even when women were the subject matter. Research that employs interviews of women has increased since then, but most of this seems to be conducted by researchers trained outside Japan. Research on singlehood, in particular, is clearly dominated by quantitative researchers thus far.

42 Lorber 1994.

43 West and Zimmerman 1987.

44 Risman 2004. Patricia Yancy Martin (2004) made a similar argument but framed gender as a *social institution*.

45 Collins 1998.

46 Ferree 1990.

47 Durkheim 1951/1979. His theory comes from his analysis of suicide.

48 Durkheim (1951/1979) theorized that an excessive level of normative constraints is also detrimental to individuals' lives.

49 For more detail on life course theory, see Elder (1994, 1995); Elder, Johnson, and Crosnoe (2003); Elder and Pallerin (1998); and Settersten (2003). Glen H. Elder, Jr., a sociologist, is one of the prominent figures in the development of life course theory. The theory is a synthesis of historical, sociological, and psychological perspectives on life course development. The four major principles of this theory are: (a) human lives are embedded in historical time and geographic location; (b) the timing of lives, such as at what age people experience historical events, differentiate impacts of historical events on the life course; (c) linked lives, or to whom individuals are connected (e.g., family members) impact life course; and (d) individuals have agency in making decisions.

50 Yoshida 2010.

51 More details on my research method are provided in Appendix A.

52 The so-called "bubble" booming economy lasted roughly from 1986 to 1991, and the sudden, severe limitation on hiring young graduates – described as *shūshoku hyōgaki* (job placement ice age) – was first observed in 1993. The "ice age" lasted

INTRODUCTION: THE DRIFT INTO SINGLEHOOD

about a decade (called the "lost decade" of Japan) or until 2005 (Kurotani 2014; Tachibanaki 2006). My interviewee Midori (born in 1972) was on the job market in 1994–1995 and told me that it was the worst time to look for jobs. Another interviewee, Hitomi (born in 1973), identified herself as a member of the "post-bubble economy generation," frequently referring to women of the generation before her as having very different life experiences (from her and her generation). On the other hand, interviewees born in 1971 or earlier did not mention such hardship in job search experiences. Of course, timing of job search is not determined solely by birth year, as one may look for jobs after finishing high school, two-year college, four-year college, etc. Among my 40 interviewees, a cut-off based on the birth year 1971–1972 happened to work in classifying them into two cohorts.

53 Glaser and Strauss 1967.
54 Interestingly, a few *married* interviewees of the boom cohort said they planned to stay single when they were young. People's intentions, wishes, and attitudes are generally not good predictors of their behaviors (Kroska and Elman 2009).
55 The term "competing devotions" is borrowed from Blair-Loy (2003).

2

DECLINE OF MARRIAGE AGE NORM

Cohort effects and anomie

Yes! [Marriage] by 25! That was normal!... I was dating this guy [when I was in my early twenties], and believing that I would of course marry him!

> (Rumi, 45 years old, never married, vice president of a small company)

Of course I want to marry ... [but I don't need to marry] by any particular age. Well, but recently, well, if I'm going to have a child, maybe [I should marry] pretty soon.

> (Ran, 29 years old, never married, medical researcher)

Age norms are said to be strong in Japan,[1] and marriage has been the normative – socially expected – life path for all.[2] In much of Japan's modern history, women were expected to marry during *tekireiki*, which literally means appropriate or suitable age/time to marry. Age 22 to 25 was considered to be *tekireiki* for women, and when women of this age did not have concrete marriage plans, they were pressured to marry (or secure marital partners) by neighbors criticizing them for being unmarried, parents and relatives urging them to have *miai* (arranged meetings with potential marital partners through gobetweens), etc.[3] As Figure 2.1 shows, up until the mid 1980s, most women did indeed marry during, or not too many years after, *tekireiki* – indicating the strength of this age norm.[4] The average age at first marriage for women, however, rose constantly and significantly – and was 29.2 in 2012.[5] As discussed in the last chapter, since the late 1980s the number of never-married women in their late twenties began to increase, and the never married outnumber the married among women aged 25 to 29 today (See Figure 1.1 in Chapter 1). We must conclude that the traditional marriage age norm is no longer in effect in Japan.

When and how did this age norm lose its effect? This chapter presents stories, told to me by women of the boom and recession cohorts in the course of my research, indicating that the norm was strongly internalized among boom cohort women, but that its enforcement began to weaken during the economic

DECLINE OF MARRIAGE AGE NORM

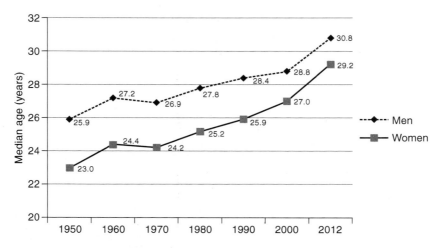

Figure 2.1 Median age of first marriages in Japan: 1950–2012.
Source: Ministry of Health, Labor, and Welfare, Population Statistics (2013a).

boom. By the time the recession cohort women grew up to be young adults (during the economic recession), the norm was completely obsolete.

Has the decline of this marriage age norm had any impact on women's life paths, and if so, in what ways? It is helpful to apply Emile Durkheim's concept of *anomie* in understanding the impact of the breakdown of norms on individuals' life paths. Anomie is a state of society, caused by rapid social change, in which (traditional) culture is weakened or absent and thus effectively no longer prescribes appropriate behaviors for individuals.[6] Though this societal condition could be seen as providing greater personal freedom and liberation from tradition, Durkheim argued that humans need some level of normative guidance to balance selfish urges, and that the absence of constraint provided by norms could have serious consequences for individuals (as well as society as a whole). Imagine if all of us had to drive without maps, directions, GPS, and traffic rules. We would have difficulty figuring out what paths we should take, how to navigate, how to avoid dangerous roads and accidents, etc. Some (or many) could end up getting completely lost – or inadvertently turn onto wrong paths and never reach the destination they originally planned/wished to reach. The impacts of the absence of social norms on life paths are more abstract and harder to imagine than this simple analogy portrays, but the basic argument is the same. If we are not clearly guided by socially shared norms, some or many of us may end up taking unintended life paths – such as lifetime singlehood.

The marriage age norm did not disappear overnight. It was well internalized among the boom cohort yet began to lose its power when boom cohort women were young adults, and was absent by the time the recession cohort reached adulthood. Life course theory informs us that different historical contexts shape individual life courses differently. Particularly in rapidly changing societies, the life course varies significantly by cohort membership as the historical context changes during one's lifetime.[7] As will be demonstrated below, the two cohorts' life stories indicate discernable differences in social and cultural contexts between the economic boom era (when the boom cohort women were young adults) and the economic recession era (when the recession cohort women were young adults). Thus, the impact of the (weakening) marriage age norm was not identical for the two cohorts.

This chapter presents the accounts of two cohorts of women – the boom cohort first and the recession cohort next – which illustrate the process of the breakdown of the marriage age norm and its impacts on young women. As we will see, realities of gender and gender inequality, as well as other forms of social inequality, permeated their life experiences and perceptions.

Boom cohort

Internalized tekireiki *norm*

My boom cohort interviewees were born between 1962 and 1971. When I asked them whether they had any ideas about the right age to marry when they were younger, many of them – both married and unmarried – gave me answers that indicated how most of them took the *tekireiki* norm for granted. Most envisioned, either explicitly or vaguely, that their future marriage would occur during *tekireiki*, as the following accounts by my never-married interviewees illustrate:

> *Author: When you were young, did you have ideas about the right age to marry?*
> Saori (45 years old, never married): [With no pause] Yeah, 24.
> *Author: How old were you when you thought so?*
> Saori: Around 21 or 22. I never imagined I'd be single at 25. I thought that I would automatically marry when I turned 24. With no logical reason.

> When I was in high school, in the home economics class, there was an assignment where we had to write about our future life course. I wrote I would marry at 24 or 25 [chuckle]. I now wonder why I thought so.
> (Teruko, 41 years old, never married)

> Yes! [Marriage] by 25! That was normal!... I was dating this guy [when I was in my early twenties], and believing that I would of course marry him!
> (Rumi, 45 years old, never married)

> Everyone else got married [when I was around 25], and I thought it was my turn.... I was the last one [to marry among my friends].... [When I started dating with this guy] "Now, finally it's my turn!" was what I thought. So it wasn't like I thought I would never, ever marry. I wasn't

thinking I would really want to marry, either, though. Just naturally, I thought, "Ah, now it's my turn to marry."

(Kozue, 45 years old, never married)

Marriage by/around 25 was viewed to be "normal," "natural" or even "automatic." Many women answered my question promptly, and their answers were mostly consistent – indicating that the marriage age norm for women was clearly shared among the women of this cohort when they were younger. As I discuss later in this chapter, this contrasted with answers given by the recession cohort interviewees. The same question did not yield such a clear, prompt, and universal answer from them.

The age 25 had a special importance to this cohort. Approximately half of boom cohort women clearly recalled they either wanted or expected to marry *before they turned 25*, or *by 25 at the latest*. This was probably because these women spent their teen years and/or twenties in the 1980s when single women past age 25 were called "Christmas cake." As mentioned in the first chapter, the term was used to tease or criticize women for staying single past the age of 25, indicating that they would not be pursued by men, like Christmas cakes after December 25. Several of my interviewees mentioned this term in discussing the *tekireiki* norm. For instance:

I believed that *tekireiki* was 22 or 23. You know, they used to say 25 is the 'Christmas cake,' didn't they? So I married during *tekireiki*.... I think I wanted to marry before I turned into [Christmas cake].

(Sonoko, 45 years old, married at 23)

One of my friends went to Australia for [a program called] Working Holiday when she was 25. I thought, "What are you thinking? You're 25!" You know, a woman of that age shouldn't [do such a thing]. Because it's "Christmas [cake]." I was saying that. Well, I ended up not marrying myself, but still [I was saying that]!

(Saori, 45 years old, never married)

When the older boom cohort interviewees were in their early twenties, single women past *tekireiki* were stigmatized. Some of my interviewees recalled episodes that illustrate such prejudice or their own negative views toward single women:

[When I was younger] I was actually wondering why some people aren't married.... When I was ... in college ... when I heard about women like my friend's aunt, who were single and in their thirties, I always thought there might be some serious problems with them.

(Natsumi, 43 years old, never married)

When I started working [at age 20 in the early 1980s], there was a woman who ... was called "*Okkasan* (Mamma, insinuating an old mother)." ... Only 27 or 28, but called "*Okkasan*."

(Kozue, 45 years old, never married)

People said Makiko-san, a woman in my department, gave up [on marriage].... People used to say that kind of thing about women who were over 30 and unmarried.

(Eri, 46 years old, married)

Rumi (45 years old, never married): It was normal to marry and quit [work] by around 25. There were women past 30 [in our office] but ... they were regarded as a bit weird.... I was only 20 back then, you know? I wondered what I should talk about with this woman [who was past 30]. I thought I shouldn't talk about dating and things like that. [laugh] I remember I felt really nervous when I faced this woman one-on-one because I didn't know what to talk about.
Author: So when women were past 30 and single, were they assumed to have no one to date?
Rumi: Yup! People assumed so.
Author: Without knowing that was really the case?
Rumi: Right, right, right! We don't talk about such private matters, you know? So I had absolutely no idea. Women who didn't marry past 25 were weird or old maids. It was that kinda time. When a woman was single at 30, back then, people said, "Oh, no!"

During the time of the boom cohort's young adulthood, it was considered normal for women to give serious thought to marriage prospects if they were still unmarried at the age of 25. When women were unmarried past age 25, they were viewed either to have given up on marriage or to have undesirable characters – and, in either case, as "weird." Indeed, to some of my married interviewees, age (around) 25 marked the next step, and they took action:

After I started working [as a non-tenure school teacher] and then three or four years later, [when I was 25 or 26], I wondered about my future. I had no secure job, living with my parents. I had a boyfriend, but didn't know if we were going to marry. Everything was like, pending. So, I thought, "What am I going to do?"

(Fujiko, 38 years old, married)

Fujiko confronted her boyfriend (i.e., her current husband) about whether he intended to marry her. They got married when she was 27. Similarly, after years of dating, Nozomi (40 years old, married) pressured her boyfriend to become engaged with her when she was 25 (though she later broke up with him and married another man at 29). Mari (38 years old) was unmarried when she was 27. When she first met her current husband, she made it clear to him that she would not date him unless he would seriously consider the possibility of marriage. In her words:

> Mari: Because I was already 27, immediately, ah, I, [laugh] I think I told him, "If you have no intention to marry, please don't see me. If you have no intention, I'd like to look for someone else, so, if you have no intention, please don't call me."
> *Author: Did he say he intended to marry you?*
> Mari: He is two years older, he was 29 already, so he was like, "Well, it's not like I have no intention" or something like that. So I started dating him.
> *Author: So you discussed the possibility of marriage fairly soon?*
> Mari: Yes. It was like, it was the condition (*jōken*) [to date]. [chuckle]

Men also took relationships with women passing *tekireiki* seriously:

> [I was dating] a boy two years younger than me. And I was 25 or 26. He thought he'd have to marry me soon, just because he was dating a woman of this age.
>
> (Tomomi, 39 years old, never married)

In contrast to the married interviewees above, who took action to marry in their late twenties, most of my single interviewees did not put serious thought into marriage when they were passing *tekireiki*, even though they grew up taking the age norm for granted:

> *Author: When you were 24 or 25, did you think you would have to marry soon?*
> Teruko (41 years old, never married): No, I didn't. Well, people were saying "Christmas," so I think the general climate was [I should marry soon]. But I wasn't dating anyone at that time, so I was just hoping to meet a nice guy.

> Rather than feeling I want to marry, well, I was going out [with the same man] since I was in college and we were continuing [our relationship] after I started working, so vaguely, I thought I might marry him one day. But we didn't. [laughs]
>
> (Tsuneko, 43 years old, never married)

> I believed I'd marry ... in my late twenties.... I was dating a college classmate ... I thought I'd marry him, and my parents thought so, too.... Looking back, I think I was only vaguely thinking that marriage comes in as a result of being in love ... somewhere down the road.... I wasn't thinking of marriage concretely.... I was like, one day I'd marry. Not like, I really want to marry now.
>
> (Natsumi, 43 years old, never married)

Unlike Fujiko and Nozomi who confronted their boyfriends, Tsuneko and Natsumi only vaguely envisioned marriage and did not pursue it with their boyfriends. Whereas Mari purposefully sought a man who would consider marriage, Teruko passively hoped and waited to meet someone she could marry. I commonly observed this passivity towards marriage among my boom cohort single interviewees. All of them wished to marry and some stressed, "It wasn't like I had no intention to marry when I was young." But they did not put concrete thought into marriage because, as I show below, other things occupied their lives and thoughts when they were passing *tekireiki*.

Economic opportunities create shift in social norms

Prior to the economic boom, young unmarried women were typically hired into dead-end, easy-to-replace clerical positions, commonly called OLs or Office Ladies. This gendered hiring practice was aligned with the societal norm that women should marry in their early 20s and resign from work to take care of home and children.[8] Young, unmarried female workers were also tacitly a pool of bride candidates for young male employees. Because employers typically awarded raises based on seniority, lengthy service by OLs, who took on only simple tasks, was not desired by employers. It was common that workplaces had or deliberately created an atmosphere that put pressure on OLs to resign around *tekireiki* or shamed them for staying on the job past *tekireiki*.[9] These sexist practices reinforced the traditional marriage age norm.

My older boom cohort women's experiences and observations indicate such practices were common in the early and mid 1980s. As we have seen earlier, colleagues talked negatively (e.g., "weird," "given up on marriage") about older single women behind their backs and teased them about their "old" age (e.g., calling them "*okkasan*"). But back in those days, older single female employees were rare. In the company Sonoko (45 years old, married) worked for as an OL, "every woman got married soon after she started working" and "all quit when they got married ... [or] after getting pregnant." The pressure to quit during *tekireiki* came largely from the fact that most or all female workers married and resigned during *tekireiki*, as illustrated in Rumi (45 years old, never married)'s words: "Rather than 'you have to quit,' it was just normal (*atarimae*) that we quit before we turned 25." Sonoko married and resigned from her job at age 23. Rumi and another OL, Saori (45 years old, never married), also quit when they were around 24. These two, however, did not have concrete plans for marriage. They left their jobs because they "felt awkward to stay in my job."

These discriminatory practices and this work atmosphere, however, began to change in the late 1980s. Another OL, Kozue (45 years old, never married), as mentioned above, initially witnessed a senior colleague being called *Okkasan* and felt pressure to marry after all other female workers of her age resigned for marriage ("It's my turn!"). But by the time she was reaching the *Okkasan*'s age herself, such negative treatment had vanished. Instead, her (male) supervisor encouraged her to stay employed. "He told me, 'If you're marrying, then quit, but if you're not marrying, please stay.'" The economy was booming and her company was growing. It was hiring many new workers and trying to retain as many good workers as possible, including clerical workers. Kozue continued to work because her marriage plan fell through due to her boyfriend's infidelity.

Likewise, though Rumi and Saori were compelled to leave their first companies, there were many jobs available and both of them found other full-time jobs with ease. Some other single boom cohort interviewees were hired into non-clerical positions or professional occupations, previously reserved for men, right after graduating from school. Such work histories reflect Japan's unprecedented level of economic growth in the late 1980s, which caused a severe labor shortage. This labor-scarce economy made many employers turn to a previously undesired population for needed labor: women in their late twenties, women with higher education, and foreign migrant workers.[10] Even clerical workers became hard to replace, and women were needed to fill positions that were traditionally taken by men.[11]

Here, I can share my personal experience and observations to illustrate the extent of labor shortage at that time. When I was searching for a job in my final year in college in 1985, I (and other college-educated female friends) struggled because women with four years of college education were not desired by most employers. High school or two-year college education was thought sufficient and preferred in women filling clerical positions. I took a job in a department store, one of a handful of employers that actively recruited women with higher education. I left my first job in 1989 when Japan's economic boom was in full bloom. Prior to the boom, there were hardly any full-time jobs available for women aged 25 and above. Yet in 1989, at age 25, I received immediate job offers from ten companies out of the eleven I applied for. This included one company in which the interviewer criticized me for not possessing the required office skills! Job ad magazines for new graduates (such as *rikurū to*[12]) were thick like large city phonebooks, and there were weekly job ad magazines designated specifically for (unmarried) women who wished to change their jobs. One such magazine was *trabāyu*, and the word *trabāyu* became a synonym for women changing their jobs (or *tenshoku*).[13] Women talked about thinking of "doing *trabāyu*," supervisors begged their female subordinates "not to do *trabāyu*," etc.

Another term commonly used during the boom was *chūto saiyō* – the hiring of people who were not new graduates, and in non-hiring seasons. Prior to the boom, most companies hired only new graduates in a set season each year, and *chūto saiyō* was typically practiced only in emergency circumstances, usually by small establishments. My second job was a large Mitsubishi-group company, and its personnel manager told me and several other new hires, all females, that it was the first time for this company to hire on the basis of *chūto saiyō*. This implies that there were urgent labor needs in this company at that time. The pay was much higher than the salary I would have earned at the department store, and when I told my supervisor of my intent to resign in 1991 to study abroad in the U.S., he insisted that I reconsider my plan and stay employed.

In those days, *kyaria ūman* (woman/women in career – a new, buzz word) were highly visible and often portrayed fashionably in the media. New magazines that targeted young working women, such as *Nikkei Woman* and *Hanako*, were largely circulated. Later labeled the "Bubble Era (*baburu ki*)," this was a time of optimism for young, unmarried women in Tokyo.[14]

Thus, though some employers continued to pressure women to resign, there were plenty of employment opportunities for women past *tekireiki* during the economic boom. The government's labor force survey shows that the labor force participation rates among women ages 25 to 29 rose from 47.5 percent in 1980 to 61.8 percent in 1992, and most of these employed women were unmarried.[15] My boom cohort single interviewees said they "felt okay to be single" in those days "because there were so many other single women working" past *tekireiki*.

All of factors mentioned above indicate that women were caught in social and cultural contradictions. On the one hand, women were made to believe they should marry by age 25. On the other hand, they were welcomed to stay employed past age 25 – and there were indeed many other single women working past this age. As presented above, some women considered the marriage age norm seriously and took action. But other women put marriage on the backburner partly because the alternative – delaying marriage – was more appealing to them at that time (more on this, below).

New opportunities: leisure options and stimulating jobs

In part due to the strength of the yen, their incomes allowed boom cohort single women to enjoy previously inaccessible luxuries and leisure activities. They spent their earnings on things such as travel and studying abroad, shopping for foreign brand-name goods, skiing, golfing, scuba diving, gourmet food, and drinking with friends. These were exciting days in the lives for many Japanese women of the cohort, as illustrated by Saori (45 years old, never married)'s words:

> Saori: It was so much fun ... there were other women [in my office] ... one older than me ... one the same as me, and ... two others joined – one a year older than me and another a year younger than me. It was like a school.... After work, we always went to drink. We probably went out to eat three nights a week.... [The next company I worked for] was also fun. I started when I was 26.... My hobby was traveling. I loved traveling more than men. So ... [I traveled] every year, twice or three times a year.
> *Author: Abroad?*
> Saori: Yes.... I went to Europe – Spain, Italy. I went to Korea twice. Spain, how many times did I go? Spain twice, Italy once. And Bali, Thailand. I don't remember, I went to many places. I spent most of my time [traveling]. Money and time.

Author: With whom did you travel?
Saori: My girlfriends from work.... So, I didn't date much. I was just having fun. It was really fun.... It was so much fun going to work. We played [a game called] twenty-five[16] during work. Isn't that silly? We did such a thing during work. That was totally leisure time. I didn't feel I had to have a boyfriend, not at all. It was fun every day. And I went to Hawaii [for my first trip abroad]. Oh, my, Hawaii was so much fun. Wow! I didn't know how fun it was to go abroad! So every year since then. I went to Hawaii, New Caledonia, and, I can't remember all. Well, maybe like 15 or 16 times?... I saw this woman on TV, she said, "I would go on a trip abroad as many times as my age." I thought, "That's it! So I would have gone 30-something times when I turned 30-something!" Wasn't I a fool? I wasn't thinking about men at all.

Karen Kelsky described single employed women during the period of Japan's unprecedented level of economic expansion in the 1980s as "one of the wealthiest groups in the world."[17] Of course her claim was not that these women were literally wealthy, like oil tycoons of the Middle East or billionaire CEOs in the U.S. What it means is that single, employed women in Japan during the boom had a large amount of disposable income and time to spend on luxury goods and leisure. The upward-surging economy and labor shortage led to higher pay even for clerical workers, and a strong Japanese currency provided great purchasing power for those who earned incomes in Japanese yen. Additionally, it was normative for single women to live with their parents until marriage,[18] and thus many could afford to spend most of their incomes on their own wants. Though single men of their cohort on average earned higher incomes than women, men were expected to work overtime and save money for future marriage. Married women of this cohort were typically staying home with no income. Thus, relative to men and married women of the same age group, single women of this cohort were the largest consumers of luxury goods and services in Japan.[19]

Interestingly, as related in Saori's story, men and relationships were perceived to be an impediment to the enjoyment of leisure activities. Mari, though she married at 29, said she had little interest in marriage and relationships when she was enjoying the fruits of the economic boom in her early to mid twenties:

For example, going skiing [with my friends] meant staying overnight. Men could make a fuss over it. That kind of thing is tiresome (*mendokusai*). I went skiing and traveled abroad with my [female] friends from work. I had a lot of unmarried [girl] friends, and I didn't want my friendship to be disturbed [by a boyfriend], either.... When I was in my early twenties, I didn't want to marry. It was much more fun to go skiing, golfing, traveling, that kind of thing [with my girlfriends].

So, leisure activities were much more appealing and relationships would inhibit the fun. Some women hung out with their female (single) friends and put off not only marriage but relationships as well.

For some single women, rewarding experiences came from jobs instead of luxurious consumptions and activities. Rumi (45 years old, never married) is one such woman. After graduating from a two-year women's college, she first worked for a large insurance company as a clerical worker (i.e., OL) for a few years. As mentioned above, when she was in *tekireiki*, she sensed that her services were no longer desired at her company. She changed jobs, taking a position at a small advertising company. For Rumi, this new job was a life-transforming event:

> Rumi: Gradually, I began to enjoy my work. First, it was only assisting. Well, when I was an OL, there was a manual. We just do work according to it, so we can do all the work without having any knowledge of insurance or studying it. In other words, a boring job.... But when I started to work for this [advertising] company, well, the pay was low and I had to work until really late at night, but I could make something out of what I thought of, or I could improve something with my own efforts, and I also loved photography and I could make use of it, and I started enjoying that kind of thing a lot. A lot of the time, I went home taking the last train, or couldn't go home and stayed at the company overnight.... When I was talking with my boyfriend, well, I will not forget this for the rest of my life. When shall we marry? Next year? We started talking about marriage concretely, and I was thinking that I'd want to work, and so we'd both work, right? And that was fine with him. But then he started saying things like, he wouldn't like it if I'd not be home when he comes home, or he has never run a washing machine. Then suddenly, the reality hit me. Well, how should I put it? I felt, ah, forget it! Uh, you know, I felt I didn't want to think about things like "I have to go home now," "I have to go to cook dinner," or "My husband would say this and that" when I'm working.... He was a real nice guy. I still think he was nice. We shared the same values and he was fun and I really loved him. But when I thought about life with him, I thought, well, marriage seemed just too much trouble, then my feelings [toward him] cooled down, then I had a crush on another guy, so we broke up.
>
> *Author: Do you think your new job influenced you a lot?*
>
> Rumi: [In a firm tone] The job changed me. So, if I didn't know anything, if I kept working for that insurance company, I'd probably have married him and divorced [laugh]. I'd probably have thought, boring [referring to marriage]!

Interestingly, although she was resistant to the idea that she would have to come home early enough to take care of cooking and other house chores, Rumi strongly believed that homemaking was the proper role of married women. This belief in traditional gender roles, as I will present in more detail in Chapter 5, was common among the boom cohort. For Rumi and other boom cohort women who wished to work, there was no cultural tool to reconcile their wants of employment and marriage (more on this in Chapter 5).

Other single interviewees who received a college education landed interesting jobs right after college. Like Rumi, many of them were excited about challenging jobs, which were also demanding and all consuming. According to Natsumi (43 years old, never married), who was hired by a prestigious advertisement company:

> I thought I'd learn all [I needed for the job] in three years. Everything was new and interesting at the beginning. My job required creativity, and I was placed in the section I was really interested in, and, um, I thought I couldn't do as well as others because I was just novice [so I kept working hard].... It took me about eight years to realize I shouldn't be so immersed into my job.... Also, I was working among experienced workers. They were in their thirties and talented so very interesting people. It was fun talking with them, learning their philosophies and stuff.

She said it was commonplace for her (and her colleagues) to work until past midnight and go home taking a cab (paid for by her company). Likewise, Izumi (46 years old), Tsuneko (43 years old), Teruko (41 years old), and other women who found career positions worked incredibly long hours. As mentioned earlier, some of these women were dating their boyfriends from school, but their relationships gradually dissolved without a clear moment of break-up. These women were too excited and/or busy with their jobs to put concrete thought into marriage. They were not aware, at that time, of the consequence of putting off marriage/relationships. After letting go of their boyfriends from school, many single women of the boom cohort found only rare opportunities to meet potential romantic partners – a subject discussed in the next chapter.

Thus it would appear that young, single women suddenly found themselves valued in the labor market during an economic boom, and faced little pressure in the workplace to marry and quit. For many women, staying employed (i.e., unmarried) led to rewarding experiences: interesting jobs and/or leisure allowed by good income. This contrasted with the previous generation of single women, harshly treated by staying employed past *tekireiki*. (Note that my boom cohort interviewees were *not* encouraged to marry and continue working.)

Little pressure from parents

Considering that the marriage age norm was strongly held among older generations of Japanese, I expected that the boom cohort women may have received pressure to marry from family members, especially parents. Contrary to this expectation, most of my single interviewees faced little pressure to marry from family. Only two women, Seiko and Tomomi, said their parents pressured them to marry by 25. Seiko (43 years old) said her father constantly nagged, noting that her late mother married at 24, and made her meet a man through *miai* (meetings with potential marital partners through third party mediation). Tomomi, 39 years old, recalled her mother complaining about her being single when she was 24 or 25.

For others, however, parents said little about such mid twenties singlehood. In these cases, parents began to nag or express sincere concerns when women remained single around 30. After that point, parents were quiet. Interviewees inferred that parents were "afraid to bring up" the subject to their daughters. The unmarried did not perceive parents' comments to be compelling in any case. These were just words, "not like she [my mother] would go and look for a *miai* partner." Also, some single interviewees, especially those in career positions, moved out of parents' homes and lived alone in order to cut commuting time – an adaptation to overtime work demands. This residential independence from parents allowed single women to escape parental nagging and pressure. As mentioned earlier, it was (and still is) normative for unmarried women to reside with parents until marriage, and most of my interviewees lived with their parents when they were younger (some still did at the time of interviews). But women's career opportunities allowed many to live independently, the potential effects of which should not be overlooked.

In some cases, boom cohort women received ambiguous messages regarding marriage from their mothers. Kazuko (45 years old, never married) was a professional artist and living with her parents at the time of interview. Her mother also studied art and worked part-time as an art teacher.

> My mother was always saying like, uh, "In the long run, it'd be easier if you're not single. But if you marry someone who doesn't let you do art, that wouldn't be good. So if you don't have anyone [you want to marry] right now, I guess you can't do anything about it."

Izumi (46 years old)'s mother had a teaching certificate yet gave up on becoming a teacher because she married at 24 and got pregnant soon after. Izumi perceived that her mother "wanted to work. So, she was sending me mixed messages, 'Have a good career,' and 'You should marry.'" Newly opened opportunities for young women during the economic boom may have influenced mothers to encourage daughters, though in uncertain ways, to aim high. In Izumi's case, however, her mother did not encourage her to have both career and marriage, and she herself did not perceive these two as compatible – a typical view towards marriage and paid work held by boom cohort women, as I discuss in Chapter 5.

Recession cohort's views and experiences

Absence of tekireiki *norm*

My recession cohort interviewees were born between 1972 and 1984. In contrast to the boom cohort, the answers given by the recession cohort women to my question regarding women's ideas about the right age of marriage were varied. But these women uniformly considered marriage in the early twenties "(too) early." Most of their mothers married in their early twenties, but such a life course was described with disbelief by my interviewees, as demonstrated by the words of these two women:

> My mother married at 22 or so. She graduated from high school, started working, married my father who worked at the same company, and quit [her job]. Then she had kids. [She married and had kids] so early.
>
> (Megumi, 31 years old, never married)

> I'm now 26. My mom was married and raising a child at this age. Unbelievable!
>
> (Maya, 26 years old, never married)

These two women once asked their mothers, "Why in the world did you marry so young?" Their mothers answered that it was normal and that there was no other alternative for women back then. But these two interviewees had difficulty imagining such a world. When speaking of these historical realities, they sounded as if they were sharing unbelievable, unusual stories with me. I told some of my recession cohort interviewees, including these two, that single women past 25 used to be called "Christmas cake," and explained the term's meaning. They reacted with disbelief – some laughed at the ridiculousness of it, others commented that it was "mean."

These stories and reactions clearly show that the traditional *tekireiki* (appropriate marriage age) norm was no longer shared or even known by this cohort. What the boom cohort (and the generations above, including the recession cohort's parents) perceived as the *normal* life course, only one or two decades before, was seen as a puzzling way of life to the recession cohort. In fact, a married woman of the boom cohort, Sonoko (45 years old, a mother of two high school age children), expressed her frustration towards this kind of "misperception" by the younger generation. As shown in the previous section, cognizant of societal expectations of *tekireiki*, Sonoko herself married at 23 in the 1980s. Yet "nowadays, [young people say] I married really early. I married during *tekireiki*!" She conformed to the societal expectations of her time, and now this socially appropriate choice was taken as foolish or ludicrous.

Interestingly, marriage in the mid twenties was thought to be "early" even by my married interviewees who married in their mid twenties (Rika at 24 and Kimi at 25). Rika (29 years old)'s marriage was a so-called *dekichatta kekkon* (marriage due to premarital pregnancy; the equivalent of the English expression "shotgun wedding"). She expressed regret for marrying "too young." She "didn't wish to marry at this age. Really, I think I should have waited until 32 or so, seriously. I wanted to have more romance (*renai*), have fun, and go to different places." For newly-wed Kimi (25 years old), the ideal age of marriage was 27, but she ended up marrying earlier because her boyfriend was going to be transferred to a faraway branch office in Kyoto.

What did recession cohort women think the proper timing of marriage was, then? A majority of my recession cohort interviewees set the ideal timing of marriage for women by age, such as "the late twenties," "by 30," or "no later than 35," but some said there is no such thing as a right age for marriage because it depends on each individual's circumstances. The way the recession cohort interviewees responded to my question was different from the boom cohort. Answers were given as their *own* ideas, not something expected as *normal* according to some *societal* standard. In other words, when explaining why they thought the age they mentioned was ideal, they provided their *personal* reasoning. The most frequently cited reason was a desire for children and (perceived) age limits for childbearing. For instance:

Author: Did you have an idea about by what age you want to marry?
Kimi (25 years old, newly-wed): Yes, 27.
Author: Any particular reason for the age of 27?
Kimi: Well, I was talking about this with my friends when we were in college. Uh, we had this [method of] "backward counting of ideal ages." It's best to have the first child before 30. So let's plan to have a child at 29. We want to have about 2 years of honeymoon period before having a child. Then [marriage at] 27.

Author: Do you want to marry by a certain age?
Ran (29 years old, never married): No, no particular age. Well, but recently, well, if I'm going to have a child, maybe [I should marry] pretty soon.

Author: So, would you like to marry?
Yayoi (31 years old, never-married): Yes, very much! I want to marry by 35 at the latest.
Author: Why by 35?
Yayoi: I want to have kids. I'm hearing from others of the higher the risks [of childbearing], the older you get. Also, you'd be 55 when your kids grow up to be adults [referring to the Japanese custom of "coming of age" at age 20]. I want to [live to] see my kids grow up to be adults.

Author: Do you feel you want to marry by a certain age?
Momoe (30 years old, never married): Uh, right away, or any time [laugh].
Author: Do you have ideas about by what age you want to marry at the latest?

Momoe: Uh, well, by 35. When I turn 35, I may be saying "by 40," though [laugh].
Author: Any reasons for "by 35?"
Momoe: I love children, I want three, if possible, or at least two. I've been told that I should have kids while I'm still young, I'd need stamina to raise kids.

Other considerations, such as financial conditions, were also important. Ryoko, a 26-year-old woman cohabiting with her 20-year-old boyfriend, was between jobs at the time of interview:

Author: Do you want to marry by a certain age?
Ryoko: Uh, now, uh, I'd like to have kids, so if possible, I'd like to have at least one by around 30, so.
Author: So, do you want to marry at 28 or 29?
Ryoko: Well, uh, hmmm, that's really soon, so that doesn't seem realistic. Uh, it'd be great if I can have one [child] by 30, uh, 32. [laugh]
Author: So you aren't planning to marry in the near future, correct? Is that because your boyfriend is young?
Ryoko: Yes, hmmm, uh, it [marriage] is not concrete yet. Well, I think any time is fine.
Author: So what determines the timing of marriage?
Ryoko: Hmmmm, good question. I think, that's probably when we have a prospect of making a living.

Some women had never set the timing of marriage by age. Akane (34 years old, married) who married at age 33 said:

When I was passing 30, I started thinking I want to marry.... But I was enjoying my life around that time. I had a boyfriend, too, so I wasn't thinking of marriage too much. I had a lot of freedom, I had time and income. But I started thinking of marriage seriously around 33. I had enough fun time and wanted to marry. So I asked my friend [to introduce someone to me] and met my current husband.

Junko (27 years old, never married) was in her current job for a little over a year. She had a master's degree, and studied in England for a year before taking the job. She still had "a lot of things I want to do, like, I want to become a teacher, I want to study abroad, so it [marriage] doesn't come up to the number one thing I want to do." But she wanted to have children one day. I asked if this desire sets the age limit for marriage. Her answer was "by [pause] 30 [pause] mid-thirties ... by late-thirties at the latest, probably ... late-twenties at the youngest." It seemed that she never thought concretely about age limits for childbearing (and hence marriage) before I asked her this question.

It appeared that the once-strong marriage age norm no longer guided or even existed for the recession cohort, and that no alternative societal norm had emerged. Instead, the right time for marriage was determined by each individual's life plan, perceived age limits for childbearing, and financial and other circumstances. Some women did not think concretely about the issue, instead only vaguely expecting marriage somewhere down the road. The latter is reminiscent of my observations of boom cohort single women.

Little social pressure to marry

We saw earlier that, during the economic boom, many workplaces stopped pressuring young, unmarried employees to marry and resign. None of my employed recession cohort interviewees felt such pressure from employers. This may indicate that it became normative for employers to refrain from placing such pressure on women – at least in Tokyo. This may be also, however, be due to the shift in occupations taken by women. Most of my recession cohort interviewees were not OLs, but worked in female-dominated occupations such as social work, retail, and elderly care. Many of these women in female-dominated occupations were full-time "regular" workers (*seishain*) – permanent workers with fringe benefits (as opposed to temporary, casual, or part-time workers[20]) – and were generally expected or encouraged to stay employed for a long time, possibly even after marriage.

The accounts of my OL interviewees, however, suggest that OLs were also encouraged to continue working, though not necessarily after marriage. For instance, Momoe (30 years old, never married) and Yuri (32 years old, informally engaged) said their male bosses did "recommend that they marry" in their late twenties, but such comments were perceived by them as a "fatherly concern" rather than pressure. Both of them said confidently their service was valued and that their bosses wanted to keep them in the company if possible. Note that these OLs were hired as regular workers. Although many more clerical positions came to be filled by irregular employees such as temporary staff or short contract workers since the economic recession, employers may have been somewhat committed to clerical workers who were hired on the regular employment basis, at least until they married.[21]

Similar to single women of the boom cohort, I observed parental pressure to be weak or absent among recession cohort women. Several said their parents began to express concern over their singlehood or started asking about the prospect of marriage when they were around 30 years old – more evidence for the decline of the *tekireiki* norm.

Does this mean that recession cohort women felt no pressure to marry at all? Many did when their friends began to marry, typically in their late twenties and early thirties. For instance:

33

I was desperate before I turned 30. Since when I was 28 ... 28, 29, everyone started marrying. I went to two or three weddings a month. [laugh] Oh, no, oh, no, I have to hurry!

(Megumi, 31 years old, never married)

Some single women in their thirties began to feel bad (*"yabai"*) about their single status. But this feeling was completely absent among those in their mid twenties. Singlehood in the mid to late twenties, a condition viewed negatively by the older boom cohort prior to the economic boom, was normal among the recession cohort. Single interviewees of this cohort were, however, similar to those of the boom cohort in one aspect. Despite feeling "bad" about their single status, many of them, especially those in their thirties, were having difficulties finding potential marital partners. This will be discussed in the next chapter.

Jobs and leisure not obstacles to marriage

Whereas boom cohort single women focused on jobs and leisure in their twenties, for many of the recession cohort interviewees, jobs were not perceived as a source of enjoyment, but rather something they "have to do," and leisure activities were very modest. Some even wished to quit their jobs, viewing them as painful burdens. For others, jobs were "okay" or "good enough," but not something they felt attached to and wished to retain for life. A 36-year-old single woman Hitomi, who labeled herself as "Post Bubble Generation" (i.e., the generation after the economic boom), said she got along with older people, so most of her friends were from the bubble generation, or what I label the boom cohort. She discussed the contrasting experiences of the two cohorts:

It is my impression that people of the "Bubble Generation" ... think in ascending terms. Well, they spent [their lives] in the best time when the economy was upward, and they were sailing through life with a favorable wind [*junpū manpan no jinsei*].... Those women who have good careers tell me they love their jobs.... I don't have that, so I'm really envious. I don't even understand why they can be so sure about their love toward their jobs. Is that because they got jobs at good companies when the economy was going upward? Our era was when no matter how hard we, every one of us, tried, we couldn't get jobs at good companies. So if we were born in that kind of time, and we found jobs we'd love to take, then we'd have had that kind of passion towards jobs, perhaps. If so, I'd be so envious. If I have to remain single and have to work for the rest of my life, it'd have been nice if I loved my job.

There were some women of the recession cohort who did love their jobs, or had strong career aspirations. But an interesting contrast with the boom cohort was that these recession cohort women did not view their love towards or desire for jobs as obstacles to marriage or dating. Ryoko, 26 years old, was cohabiting with her 20-year-old boyfriend, and thinking about changing her career from nutritionist to accountant:

> *Author: So, do you not want to marry yet because you have other things you want to do?*
> Ryoko: Nope. I think I can do whatever even after I marry.
> *Author: Do you not think you may not be able to do certain things once you marry?*
> Ryoko: Nope. Wait, would I not be able to? [laugh] Did you give up on something [due to marriage]?

Junko (27 years old, never married) just started dating a man. As mentioned earlier, she wanted to do many things, such as study abroad before marriage, but did not consider him to be in the way of pursuing these interests. Kyoko, a 29-year-old married woman (with no children), had been continuously working after marriage and was very proud of her exceptional ability at work. Her job was her "hobby," and she was very confident about balancing work and family.

Likewise, leisure activities were not seen by the recession cohort to be incompatible with relationships. Compared to the boom cohort, the lives of recession cohort members were centered around significantly more modest and inexpensive activities, such as going to events held in the Tokyo area, window-shopping, and eating out with friends at inexpensive restaurants and pubs (or *izakaya*). This may suggest that the quality of this cohort's relationships with men was different from romantic relationships experienced by the boom cohort, and/or the recession cohort's modest leisure activities may not have posed obstacles to relationships (unlike overnight skiing trips enjoyed by the boom cohort). Recession cohort women also talked about particular characteristics of the men of their cohort that are relevant to our understanding of singlehood. These will be presented in the next chapter.

Views towards older single women

When the older boom cohort women were young, single women in their thirties and above were scarce and regarded as "weird." In contrast, singlehood in women's thirties and forties was common when the recession cohort was growing up. I wondered if this commonality and visibility of women's singlehood had some impact on recession cohort women's views. For instance, might they see lifetime singlehood with less prejudice, or as a viable or even preferred lifestyle? I asked my recession cohort interviewees if they personally knew any women who remained single past their mid thirties and if so, what they thought of those women.

Not surprisingly, most women of this cohort personally knew at least one, or many, older single women. They were their senior workers or relatives.

Although views towards these older single women varied among interviewees, they were generally negative and even harsh – contrary to my expectation. The most favorable view was to assume that older single women chose singlehood, prioritizing career or some other worthy cause over marriage. The following accounts illustrate this view:

Well, probably, women of the generation above us, staying single and working, probably faced a lot of pressure to marry. So, someone who could push aside such pressures must have been in professional occupations.

(Midori, 36 years old, cohabiting)

Kimi (25 years old, newlywed): Well, there are many single women [in my company], from early thirties to late forties.... I can't really ask why, but, those women have careers, they have advanced their careers, and it's hard to balance work and family,... so thinking about their careers, maybe they had to choose either one [between work and family/marriage]. I'm wondering if maybe they decided that they wouldn't need to marry yet.
Author: Have you heard of them saying something like that? Or are you just speculating?
Kimi: Just speculating. [laugh]

For some other women, older single women served as negative role models whose path should be avoided:

Author: What do you think of them [referring to Shoko's co-workers who are older and single]
Shoko (29 years old, never married): They wouldn't marry.... There's one, she's 38, I think. She's been living on her own, you know? She has lived a long life spending all [her income] as she pleases, so she doesn't want to marry and have a family at this point.
Author: Is it what you speculate about her, or does she say that's the case?
Shoko: She says so. She doesn't care about [men]. I've never seen her having a boyfriend.
Author: What do you think of that kind of life?
Shoko: [with repulsion] What is she gonna do?! About the future! It's okay for now, but she'd be totally alone! She says she doesn't want to marry but wants to have a partner. Then, do something about it! I tell her so and that's what I think. She's not feminine at all. No make-up. I really don't want to be like her. [weak laugh] Well, I'm telling that to her, too.
Author: So, she's a negative role model for you?
Shoko: Oh, yes, a negative role model.... Now I'm almost 30, and many of my friends of my age are getting married and having kids.... Now I'm turning 30. I'm scared. What if I become like those *senpai* (older

co-workers)!... Would I become like them?! I don't want to, I don't want to, but! [stopped talking, covering her face]

Other interviewees did not mind what others did, but did not respect older unmarried women they personally knew. For instance:

Honoka (32 years old, never married): Oh, yeah, there were a lot of women like that [at my first job, referring to older single women].
Author: What do you think about them?
Honoka: Hmmmm, well, I didn't have much interest in their private lives myself. But thinking objectively, well, they had money, so they could do anything on their own. Rather than being fed by someone else, maybe they had time and money to do something more fun than dating. There were many women who had a lot of hobbies. For example, *okkake* (groupies). I knew someone who was following a figure skater all over the world. I also knew someone who was buying all the art work of this particular artist. Well, if you're into something like that, you can't be dating [laugh]. I saw a lot of real bad cases.

Honoka felt those women were "pathetic." Kyoko (29 years old, married) was angry at older single women at her workplace because she viewed them as dead weight, and yet they were paid better than younger workers:

Kyoko (29 years old, married): Some women chose not to marry. They love their jobs and devoted their lives. But there are those who gave up. They aren't enjoying the jobs, just being there because they have no other options.
Author: What do you think about that kind of woman?
Kyoko: Well, being there [at work] means they are earning income. But those women, I feel, you know, rather than paying salary to them, I wish [the company] would pay more to others. Women who are just barely doing their work are always old [single] women. How shall I put this? They're valued only because they've been there for long. It's not like people can't do a good job because they're young. There are people who are inexperienced but better at work. So I'm really frustrated [with those older single women].

Thus, some recession interviewees thought single women of the boom cohort had good reason to stay single, while others saw their lives as undesirable or counter-productive. Regardless of their sentiments and interpretations, none of the interviewees of the recession cohort looked up to their predecessors as role models. Though sympathetic to and understanding of the single status of older women, they themselves did not want to follow the same path:

Well, uh, I don't want to be like them, myself. But, uh, there are many [single women] among celebrities, you know? Really beautiful and doing well. So, that's not a lifestyle for me, but I don't see it negatively, I guess. If they really want to marry, and have done *miai* but still can't marry, I would feel sorry for them [laugh]. But if not, well, if those women worked hard to achieve their goals, I can now see that's admirable. I always thought everyone wanted to marry, so I was thinking [about those women], "Ah, they just can't marry." [laugh]

(Megumi, 31 years old, never married)

Junko (27 years old, never married): Ah, that's [referring to older single women at work] the image of my future self [burst to laugh].
Author: Why?
Junko: Because they're like me. They're so focused on their jobs. I think that's great! I feel I may end up like them, but at the same time, I tell myself, I've got to be careful not to end up like them. [laugh]
Author: So you think you may be like them but you don't want to be like them?
Junko: Yes, that's right.

Increased singlehood among boom cohort women does not seem to have led to a wide appreciation or acceptance of the single lifestyle by my younger interviewees, who strongly desired to marry. Older single women presented only a cautionary tale to single women of the recession cohort. Though the traditional marriage age norm was absent for this cohort, the norm of marriage remained strong.

Chapter summary and discussion

Through interviewees' life stories and views, this chapter illustrated the process of breakdown of the marriage age (*tekireiki*) norm, and its (ir)relevance to the lives and views of women of both cohorts. The interview data clearly indicate that, while the norm of marriage remained strong, the marriage age (*tekireiki*) norm for women weakened during the economic boom and came to be unenforced by the time the economic recession came around. Older boom cohort women's memories and experiences show that, prior to the economic boom, employment practices were aligned with the marriage age norm, and female workers were pressured to (marry and) resign from work during *tekireiki*. In those days, employers and workplaces played a large role in enforcing the age norm. But the economic boom in the late 1980s, which caused a severe labor shortage, pushed many employers to retain female workers past *tekireiki* and hire women to fill career positions previously reserved for men. Boom cohort women enjoyed the newly opened opportunities in their young adulthood and put marriage on the backburner. On the other hand, the subsequent (i.e., recession) cohort of women did not even know, or could not believe, that women were once socially expected to marry in their early twenties. It was observed that no alternative marriage age norm emerged among them; the right time to marry was determined by each individual's mind and circumstances.

The observed decline and disappearance of a social norm regarding the timing of marriage is well explained by Emile Durkheim's concept of *anomie*. He theorized that this state of society can be detrimental to individuals because humans need normative guidance in shaping their behavior, life paths, etc. We observed that some women were determined to marry and took action, such as confronting boyfriends, asking friends to introduce potential mates to them, or telling potential dating partners that marriage had to be considered if the relationship was to commence. These women married. But many other single interviewees were observed to be laid back – passively waiting to meet someone to marry, focusing on present enjoyments such as leisure and stimulating jobs, vaguely expecting marriage to come one day, etc. They were not rational calculators. This passive orientation may not serve actors well in anomic society (and indeed is a symptom of it), because when societal norms fail to guide and constrain, each individual has to take charge of navigating their own life.

Though (as the following chapters argue) the decline and disappearance of the marriage age norm is *not* the only cause of singlehood, I contend that many women in Japan drifted into singlehood, due in part to the absence of clear normative guidance. These women were like persons placed on rafts with no rudders. Though they wanted to take the marriage path, they let the current direct their way instead; they did not, and perhaps could not, actively steer themselves to the desired port. Boom cohort women knew they were supposed to marry in their twenties, but new opportunities, unavailable to women of prior generations, were too appealing to let go. The recession cohort, on the other hand, started young adulthood with no clear societal guidance on marriage timing. They had to figure out the correct path on their own. Some did, but others struggled, and may yet end up at an unwanted destination (i.e., lifetime singlehood). Evident cohort differences affirm the importance of considering cohort effects (as does life course theory) in identifying the causes of increased singlehood.

On a larger scale, anomie regarding marriage norms applies to many other contemporary societies. There are perhaps many women and men across the globe today uncertain of the best time to settle down – unlike their predecessors, who were compelled to marry based on an age (and other criteria) set by their societies.[22] Most people in the developed world, of course, embrace the notion that people should not be forced to marry for the sake of age (or other criteria). But sometimes, set deadlines help us settle on decisions – whether it be school assignments, job applications, house hunting, or other choices. How can we be sure that our current relationship warrants a lifetime commitment? In times and places with marriage age norms, people settled because it was time to settle down.

Moreover, in many societies today marriage itself has become increasingly optional. Should we marry or should we not? In the traditional world, the

39

answer was a definite "yes" for most people. Today, it is up to each of us – and of course we can welcome this increased personal freedom. But if this freedom brings with it uncertainty and anxiety, and many people are unable to attain what they wish to attain, anomie may be the culprit, and Durkheim's concept may be a helpful lens through which we can come to understand increased singlehood.[23]

The impact of gender stands out in interviewees' stories. Employment practices were highly gendered, perceived age limits for childbearing shaped women's views toward marriage age, etc. Other forms of social inequality are also relevant. Women in career positions worked excessively long hours, reflective of the general practice of extreme labor exploitation by Japanese corporations. These themes will emerge in the remainder of the book, and I will discuss issues of inequality more in the final conclusion chapter.

As mentioned in Chapter 1, all single interviewees wished to marry (currently and/or in the past), and saw the right time to marry to be when they met the "right" person (rather than at the "right" age). However, meeting the right person was a challenge for many because opportunities for romantic encounters were severely and structurally limited, and good men were scarce. As I argue in the next chapter, this is another important factor that led to the increase in Japan's single population.

Notes

1 Brinton 1992.
2 Ato 1989, 1994; Ato and Kojima 1983; Ato et al. 1994; Hertog 2009; R. Kaneko 1994; Lunsing 2001; E. Nakano 1994; Tokuhiro 2010.
3 Lebra 1984; *Miai* was the common way to arrange marriages between men and women up until the end of World War II, but its popularity declined rapidly in the postwar period. I will discuss the decline of *miai* marriage a little more in Chapter 3, but for more detail on the *miai* system, see for instance Applbaum (1995).
4 According to Brinton (1993), approximately 40 percent of new brides in 1987 were aged 20 to 24, and another 40 percent were 25 to 29.
5 MHLW (2013a). The corresponding figure for men was 30.8.
6 Durkheim 1951/1979.
7 Elder 1994, 1995; Elder, Johnson, and Crosnoe 2003; Elder and Pallerin 1998; and Settersten 2003.
8 For instance, see Brinton 1993, 2007; Iwao 1993; Kelsky 2001; Kerbo 2008; Kurotani 2005, 2014; Lebra 1984; Ogasawara 1998; Roberts 2007; Shirahase 2005; Sugimoto 2010; and Tokuhiro 2010. The other common labor force participation pattern for women in Japan is for married women to reenter the labor force as part-time or irregular workers after the last child enters school (Brinton 1993, 2007; D. Kondo 1990; Lebra 1984; Lock 1996; Ueno 1994; White 2002; Yu 2002).
9 See Brinton 1993, 2007; Kelsky 2001; Kerbo 2008; Ogasawara 1998; and White 2002. It was also not uncommon for (male) managers to assume a match-making role for their subordinates as part of their managerial tasks. They might have overtly discussed the need for marriage with female employees nearing *tekireiki*, or introduce someone to them (Iwasawa 2010; Lebra 1984).

DECLINE OF MARRIAGE AGE NORM

10 Ato 1989; According to Tsuya and Mason (1995), employment rates of female college graduates jumped from 65.7 percent in 1980 to 72.4 percent in 1985 and 91.0 percent in 1990, while there was little increase for male college graduates during this time.

11 Shirahase (2005) states that, before the 1980s, most women with four-year college educations became schoolteachers – or, put in another way, women went to four-year colleges primarily to become school teachers. In those days, women with higher education had to use family connections to be hired in the private sector and accept the same employment conditions as female workers with less education. However, since the 1980s, the types of jobs taken by female college graduates diversified, and a majority of women entered white-collar professional occupations. Only 20 percent or so became schoolteachers (Hiroshima 1999; Shirahase 2005). Also, the gender gap in first-year earnings narrowed so that, according to Ohashi (1993), on average women with college degrees earned 96 percent of the earnings of men with college degrees. This, however, should not be mistaken for the narrowing of the *overall* gender wage gap.

12 *Rikurūto* refers to job advertisement magazines published by Recruit Holdings Co. Ltd. The word was adopted from an English word, "recruit."

13 The word *torabāyu* comes from a French word, travail, which means painful labor. Due to proliferation of the magazine, the word became a buzzword in the 1980s in Japan and came to mean "changing of job by women" in Japanese.

14 Karen Kelsky's book (2001), *Women on the Verge: Japanese Women, Western Dreams*, provides detailed accounts of experiences and views of unmarried women who had international experiences during the Bubble economy era.

15 Ministry of Internal Affairs and Communications 2015c.

16 A bingo-like game.

17 Kelsky, 2001:85.

18 Fukuda 2009.

19 Similarly, Kurotani (2014), calling this cohort the "bubble generation," discusses how this cohort was the driving force of conspicuous consumption during the 1980s.

20 For the difference between regular and irregular employment, see, for instance, Fukuda (2013) and Piotrowski, Kalleberg and Rindfuss (2015).

21 The fact that many of my recession cohort interviewees were not working as OLs might reflect changes in hiring practices by large corporations since the economic recession. Many corporations practiced hiring freezes, particularly of new graduates (Genda 2005; Jung and Cheon 2006), and the number of "irregular" employees in temporary or part-time positions increased after the recession (Chang and England 2011; Fukuda 2013; Piotrowski et al. 2015; Tachibanaki 2006). Many clerical positions came to be filled by "irregular" employees. This might have led recession cohort women to seek full-time "regular" employment in non-clerical, female-dominated occupations.

22 This point was addressed in Aziz Ansari's *Modern Romance* (2015).

23 My co-author Brian M. Bentel and I argue that anomie is also one major reason most Americans adhere to the marriage institution. For this argument, see Bentel and Yoshida (2013).

3

LIMITED CHANCES OF ROMANCE AND PROBLEMATIC MEN
Structural barriers and gender ideology[1]

> I often hear about fateful encounters (*deai*), "We just met, and," but I never had that sort of encounter. So, why don't I have it, is what I wonder.
>
> (Teruko, 41 years old, never married, graphic designer)

> There are many, many more cases of women wanting to marry, but their boyfriends have no intention to marry.
>
> (Midori, 36 years old, cohabiting, copy writer)

> They're saying I don't want to marry, I'm devoted just to my career, ... They're saying I think men are stupid.
>
> (Hitomi, 36 years old, never married, marketing consultant)

> Single men in their forties appear old for their age. Single women are pretty and active, so they probably can't find a match.
>
> (Tamami, 45 years old, married, social worker)

According to the National Fertility Surveys of single women in Japan, "I have not met the right person" is the most frequent explanation provided by respondents for their single status.[2] Though this may come across as women being choosy, I observed that many of my single interviewees were not currently dating and/or had rather short romantic histories, and therefore suspected that they may simply not have had much opportunity to date (as opposed to being picky about potential partners). My analysis of interviewees' romantic and work histories indeed indicates that opportunities to date were limited, and that this was due largely to structural barriers imposed by work. Additionally, men that interviewees met or formed romantic relationships with were often problematic. Most of the structural barriers observed in my study were shared across the two cohorts, but some were more pronounced among one cohort than the other. Problems regarding men, on the other hand, sharply contrasted between the two. These findings again affirm the importance of cohort effects, as outlined by life course theory.

In this chapter, I first show how sparse my interviewees' romantic histories were, and present my data and analysis on how and why romantic encounters were structurally limited for the two cohorts of women. Next, through interviewees' accounts, I illustrate the problematic nature of the men of each cohort. In these findings, we will see how deeply gender – traditional gender ideology in particular – is entrenched in social structure and culture, and how other forms of power and social inequality are relevant as well. These discoveries have led me to contend that increased singlehood is a gendered phenomenon, and that its fundamental causes are structural and cultural and not the outcome of women's active, strategic, free choices to remain single.

Sparse romantic histories

I observed that many of my single interviewees, especially those in their thirties and forties, were not dating at the time of interviews. Out of 22 single interviewees of this age group, only seven were in relationships, including one woman who was having an affair with a married man. On the other hand, all six single interviewees in their mid to late twenties were in relationships at the time of interviews, with one engaged, three cohabiting, and two having been dating for a short time.

Most of the older interviewees who were not dating at the time of the interviews spent substantial proportions of their lives without having partners, and, for them, the last relationship they had had was several years earlier – in some cases, more than a decade earlier. For instance, Shizuka (34 years old, never married) "had a boyfriend up until my first year of work. But I got busy with my job and we became distant. I've had no boyfriend since then." She began working at the age of 20, after graduating from a two-year vocational school, so she had not had a partner for at least 13 years. Kei (35 years old, never married) also had only one boyfriend in her life and the relationship with him did not last long. Other women had more than one relationship in the past, but, generally speaking, women of this age group tended to have very short or limited histories of romantic, intimate relationships in their long years of being single.[3]

This sparseness of relationship histories observed in my research corresponds to the statistics collected by the National Fertility Surveys (NFS). The NFS has been conducted on nationally representative samples of single men and women in Japan since 1983, and, throughout the survey periods, high percentages of respondents (about 40–50 percent of single men and women aged 18 to 34) were not currently in relationships.[4] Some have interpreted these survey results as an indication of women's disinterest in forming relationships,[5] but all my non-partnered single women wanted to date. Rather than disinterest, they pointed to a lack of encounters (*deai ga nai*) with decent men as the reason for not being in relationships, as demonstrated in the following account:

I often hear about fateful encounters (*deai*), "We just met, and," but I never had that sort of encounter (*deai ga nai*). So, why don't I have it, is what I wonder.

(Teruko, 41 years old, graphic designer)

[I just want to meet] A man I can enjoy having a meal with … or who can cook well, who likes to go out to eat … someone I can enjoy as a person is welcome.… Single women of my age are very visible, they are everywhere, but we hardly see single men.… I wonder whether they really exist.

(Izumi, 46 years old, marketing researcher)

I want to meet a man who will be a partner I can stay with forever.… We respect each other, respect each other's work … cheer up each other … that sort of partner. [Where can I meet a man like that?]

(Kazuko, 45 years old, artist/art instructor)

I thought I wouldn't be able to marry once I turn 40, so [when I was in my thirties I thought] I'd have to marry soon. It wasn't like any man was fine, you know? I wanted to marry someone I would love. So I was looking for a man I'd love, but didn't meet any.

(Saori, 45 years old, clerical worker)

These women were living and working in the Greater Tokyo Area – the most populated conglomerate of the world with the largest single population in Japan. How is it possible that they "hardly see single men" and wonder "whether they exist?" Why was it so difficult for them to meet someone pleasant to be with – someone they could love and respect mutually? Before diving into my analysis of the cause of this state of affairs, let me first identify where people commonly meet their romantic partners in Japan.

Common locations of romantic encounters

In order to figure out why many single interviewees faced difficulties having romantic encounters, I first wanted to find out where my married and engaged interviewees met their marital partners. Among 12 married and three engaged interviewees, four met their husbands/ fiancés in a four-year college, four through work, three through friends, one at a school reunion, one at a membership gym, one through an amateur radio club, and one at a music event. Thus, most interviewees met future marital partners through either a social organization they belonged to, with colleges and workplaces the most common, or via a personal (friendship) network. Only one interviewee was casually approached by her current fiancé in a public location (i.e., at a music event). None of my interviewees met their husbands or fiancés via *miai* – the

LIMITED CHANCES OF ROMANCE AND PROBLEMATIC MEN

traditional arranged marriage system in which mediators introduce potential marital partners.

This pattern roughly corresponds to the findings of the NFS conducted on married women and men. As shown in Table 3.1, between 1987 and 2005 the most common ways to meet spouses were through work and introduction by friends or siblings; meeting casually in public places was rare.[6] Figure 3.1 shows the change in percentage shares of *miai* marriages and "love marriages" between 1940 and 2009. The dramatic decline of *miai* marriage indicates a loss in popularity of this traditional mate selection system in Japan.[7]

I also wanted to understand where my interviewees, both married and unmarried, met current partners and people with whom they had past relationships. More than one third of their current and past relationships were formed while interviewees were in school. Other common ways to meet romantic partners were through work, friends, or social groups they belonged to (such as a golf club).[8] Some of my older interviewees had *miai* or *miai*-like mediated meetings, but, as I will discuss later in this chapter, none of these meetings developed into relationships. Casual approaches in public places rarely happened in interviewees' lives.[9] This rarity of casual encounters in Japan was reflected in Natsumi (43 years old, never married)'s fascination with American sit-coms, in which such encounters were portrayed as commonplace:

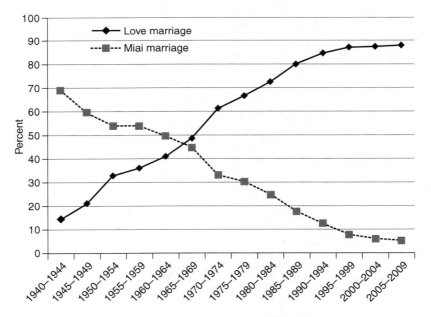

Figure 3.1 Changes in composition of love marriage and *miai* marriage: 1940–2009.
Source: National Institute of Population and Social Security Research (2011b).

Table 3.1 How/where married couples met with each other (%)

Year of Survey	Love Marriage							Miai	Others
	Through work	Through friends/siblings	School	In town/while traveling	Club activities	Part-time work	Neighborhood		
1982	25.3	20.5	6.1	8.2	5.8	–	2.2	29.2	2.5
1987	31.5	22.4	7.0	6.3	5.3	–	1.5	23.3	2.7
1992	35.0	22.3	7.7	6.2	5.5	4.2	1.8	15.2	2.0
1997	33.5	27.0	10.4	5.2	4.8	4.7	1.5	9.7	3.1
2002	32.9	29.2	9.3	5.4	5.1	4.8	1.1	6.9	5.2
2005	29.9	30.9	11.1	4.5	5.2	4.3	1.0	6.4	6.8
2010	29.3	29.7	11.9	5.1	5.5	4.2	2.4	5.2	6.8

Source: National Institute of Population and Social Security Research (2011b).

For instance, Westerners (*gaijin*[10]), well, I know only from TV and sitcoms, but you see something like she's sitting in a park, a guy talks to her, and then from there, a relationship develops, you know? That may be only in fiction, but in Japan, even those kinds of stories are absent, and that's because those kinds of situations are absent, don't you think? If that sort of thing is usual, what should I say, women in Japan would have more opportunities, we can meet someone more casually, not like we have to make efforts to meet someone.[11] ... I was always thinking, watching foreign sit-coms, there were many episodes ... that romances unfold from casual chats, and that means those kind of encounters are frequent.... We [Japanese women] are concerned about what kind of jobs the men have and that kind of thing, right? We prefer that we belong to the same company, or same group of some sort, right? But that doesn't seem to be the case in other [Western] countries. For instance, a fast food restaurant worker and a normal OL [female company clerical worker] could start a relationship if they get along. But in Japan's case, neither has the guts to go for it.

This scarcity of, or skepticism/fear towards, casual encounters implies that, if women did not meet potential romantic/marital partners when they were in school or at workplaces and develop such encounters into marriage, options were limited only to *miai* or turning to their friends and family members. As Natsumi continued:

Unless we have *gasshuku* (overnight trips – commonly practiced by school clubs) or camps, or we worked on the same project spending a long time together, unless we have those kind of things [in our adulthood, there are little opportunities] for others to learn about me, for me to learn about others, unless we are in school or in the same company, we have [few opportunities] to get to know each other. We have no other option but to accept going for *miai*. I think unmarried people are all having this problem.

Natsumi's words imply a hesitance to use *miai*. Note that, at the time of my research in 2009, online and other commercial dating/match-making services were still in their infancy, and most of my single interviewees looked down upon the use of such services, were skeptical of their effectiveness and legitimacy, and/or were afraid of potential victimization or losing money. This may have changed since then, but people in Japan may still be hesitant to use this kind of service, relative to their Western counterparts.[12]

Hence, work provided one of the most crucial sites for romantic encounters. Yet many never-married interviewees, of both cohorts, claimed it was difficult to meet potential partners through work. Some expressed the regret, painfully, that if they had known how hard it would be to meet romantic partners after they began working, they would have looked for more occasions to meet single men (such as *gō-kon*, or mixed-gender party for singles) while they were in school, or pursued marriage with their former boyfriends from school. These three interviewees' words reflect such sentiments:

> I wish I went out more [when I was younger].... I was mostly hanging out with my female friends when I was a student and also when I started working. I should have gone to *gō-kon* and that kind of stuff.... My life may have been different.
>
> (Kei, 35 years old, clerical worker)

> I turned down all the *gō-kon* with sport club members when I was in college.[13] I should have gone to all those. It's much easier to get to know men in college, you know? I'd know which college they go to and know that they belong to sport clubs. I'd know all that beforehand.[14]
>
> (Momoe, 30 years old, clerical worker)

> [I] wish I could go back to the time I was with him [referring to her boyfriend she had when she was in a vocational school] ... it would have been fine [if I married him].
>
> (Shizuka, 34 years old, clerical worker)

Why was it so difficult for the two cohorts of women to meet potential marital partners once they began to work? My analysis of interviewees' work histories, discussed below, suggests that work and workplaces played several roles in inhibiting romantic encounters and the development of romantic relationships for the two cohorts.

How work/workplaces limited chances of romance

Horizontal, vertical, and spatial gender segregation

The first obstacle to romance I observed was gender segregation at work. Many single interviewees were working apart from single men due to either *horizontal* or *vertical* gender segregation. Horizontal gender segregation refers to gender segregation by occupation. More than half of single interviewees were working in female-dominated occupations such as social work, elderly care, department stores and other retail that involved women's products (e.g., women's clothing), nursing, pharmacy, teaching, and nutrition or cooking-related occupations.[15] These women reported that "all" or "most" of their co-workers were women. They were also typically working in small establishments with small numbers of employees, and their clients were women, the elderly, children, etc., – not single men. This horizontal segregation limited these women's chances to encounter eligible bachelors through work.

LIMITED CHANCES OF ROMANCE AND PROBLEMATIC MEN

Women were also vertically segregated by gender – meaning that they typically occupied lower-level positions while men occupied higher-level ones.[16] As
discussed in the previous chapter, it was common for employers to hire women
for dead-end clerical positions (i.e., Office Lady/OL positions) and to place
men in career positions as management candidates.[17] Eight single interviewees
(two boom cohort and six recession cohort women) were working as clerical
workers at the time of interviews and five married interviewees (three boom
cohort and two recession cohort women) used to work as OLs before they
married. Recall that OLs were tacitly bride candidates for male employees of the
same company. One might imagine that OLs would have good opportunity to
find dates/marital partners through work. Interestingly, however, some of these
OL interviewees hardly saw single male workers at work because their companies segregated workers *spatially* by gender and age. Young, unmarried, clerical female workers were often placed in sections that consisted only of women
and older married men.[18] In other words, vertical gender segregation meant
spatial segregation of single workers in some cases.

For example, Kei (35 years old, never married), an interviewee of the recession cohort, worked for a company that hired more males than females, but was
placed in a small branch office located far from company headquarters. Her
office dealt with tasks such as bookkeeping. She was the only new hire in her
branch office when she got the job, and all her co-workers were older women
and middle-aged, married men. She said there seemed to be many unmarried
male workers in non-office work positions, such as the sales division, but they
belonged to other offices (in other locations), and therefore, she never had
opportunities to interact with them.

A married boom cohort interviewee, Chie (45 years old), described her first
job in a similar way. After she graduated from high school, she worked as an OL
for a company that was affiliated with a large, construction-related corporation.
There were 400 or 500 employees in her company and a majority of employees
were male, but like Kei's company, her office was separated from other offices
where many single men worked (though they did have offices in the same
building):

> Male workers in my office [which dealt with billing, etc.] were mostly old.
> Young men drew plans for A/C, plumbing, and electricity [in other
> offices], and supervised construction workers at sites. I rarely had a chance
> to see them.

There is an interesting cohort difference in corporate experience, however.
Despite the spatial segregation, Chie – a boom cohort woman – married her
senior worker, whom she met in her early twenties, in the mid 1980s. She was
approached by him on an annual company-sponsored trip for employees (*shanai
ryokō*). Prior to the trip, she knew him only briefly by receiving receipts from
him, which her office processed for reimbursements. After they married, her

husband told her that he, who was several years older than her, was encouraged by his seniors to think of her as his bride, saying "grab her [Chie] soon before other young guys get her." He was about to be transferred to a smaller affiliated office – a common corporate practice called *shukkō* – where there were no single female workers. The company trip was an opportunity, of which his seniors told him to take advantage, in order to approach and spend time with her. The two began dating and later married.

Prior to the economic recession, it was common for Japanese companies to sponsor trips and other social events (such as sport tournaments) to integrate employees across offices. Whether companies intended this or not, these company-sponsored events allowed young employees to intermingle occasionally and hence provided opportunities for romantic encounters. This may have changed, however, after the economic recession. Kei's company did not sponsor any such events. Kimi (25 years old), newly wed to a member of her *dōki* (her cohort at work), made an observation about the bank where she had been working for about three years:

> *Shanai kekkon* (marriage between coworkers) may have become rarer now. [Among older male employees at my bank] it's common that their wives also worked for this bank. I heard that there used to be sport events (*undōkai*) or company trips (*shanai ryokō*), but we don't have them now. My boss says there are fewer opportunities [for single employees] to meet now because of that.

During the economic recession of the 1990s, many companies slashed budgets, with social events a likely target for cuts. If this was the case, those budget cuts must have played a major role in reducing single workers' opportunities to meet, get to know each other, date, and marry.

Japan's recession may have further limited opportunities for women to meet young, single males at work. The conversation I had with Megumi (31 years old, never married), another clerical worker, illustrates the relevance of the hiring freeze:

> Megumi: When I got hired [to this company at age 22], most others were older. There was only one [employee] who was in my age group.
> *Author: Were there single men?*
> Megumi: No, hardly any. It was the time that companies refrained from hiring new graduates, so my company wasn't hiring any new graduates for some years. Office workers, well, women quit for marriage, right? So they were hiring replacements [only for women]. The youngest man was 29.

Her story suggests that newly graduated females were sometimes hired to fill clerical positions, as they tended to have higher turnover rates, whereas the same company strictly froze hiring for the career-track, typically designated for young males. This gender imbalance in hiring may have resulted in some young women, like Megumi, working among older (married) employees, making it hard for them to meet potential dates and marital partners through work.

Long work hours and other corporate demands

The above findings suggest that gender segregation at work – horizontal, vertical, and spatial – imposed obstacles upon some women who might have hoped to meet single men through work, and that the economic recession exacerbated the situation for some of the recession cohort. There is another aspect to Japan's employment practices that is relevant to missed opportunities for romance. As documented by many scholars, Japanese corporations commonly expected their (male) employees to express loyalty through work devotion, and white-collar male workers – "salarymen" – were notorious for working excessively long hours.[19] Interestingly, whereas men's overtime work was mentioned by almost all married interviewees in reference to their husbands' absence at home, the majority of single interviewees did not relate this fact to the unavailability of men for dating. Men's overtime work was so normative and taken for granted by women that they missed it as one obvious reason they "hardly saw single men" around.

Some single interviewees did address men's busy work schedules in relation to the dissolution of past relationships. For example, speaking of her former boyfriend, whom she dated in her early thirties, Izumi (46 years old, never married) said:

> He was like, staying overnight at work, or had to go somewhere immediately if something happens, and really, we couldn't make an arrangement to meet.... I probably should have married him. He was the one now I think I'd have been happy to live with. But at that time, he was too busy to see me ... and the relationship just dissolved before going anywhere.

Yayoi (31 years old, never married) expected to marry her boyfriend, whom she met in college and dated since she was 20. To her, he "was like my clone," getting along with her in every way. When she was 27 or so, however, he suddenly broke up with her:

> I really don't know, I still don't understand why [he broke up with me]. Hmmm. He got really busy with work. He didn't seem to have any days off. Maybe he got exhausted physically and mentally. He was out of contact with me for about half a year, and then he emailed me saying he wanted to break up. He wrote that it wasn't like he came to dislike me. He said his mind came to be occupied with his job, and he felt distant from me. It's

not like he didn't love me anymore. There was no problem with me, he said. I really wanted to see him in person and ask, but [he made no contact since then].

This is her version of the story, so we cannot discern his true motive for ending the relationship. He may have used work as an excuse, and it is also possible that he lost interest in her, gained it for another woman or man, suffered from mental illness, etc. But if what she said he said was true, he lost his feelings toward her because of his job and busy work schedule. It is intriguing that Yayoi thought she was still in the relationship with him during the time he was "out of contact" for six months! This may be an extreme case, but it implies it was not unusual for couples to be too busy with work to contact each other for extended time periods.

In another episode told by Yayoi, who liked cycling and watching soccer games, a friend of hers introduced her to a man with the same interests. They dated once, and Yayoi thought:

He seemed nice and I wanted to see him a few more times to see if this works out. But he was also really busy with work. At the beginning of the week, he said he may be able to see me this day, and then in the middle of the week, he told me he couldn't. I couldn't leave a whole week open for him, you know?

They could not manage to arrange a date at all, even though they were mutually interested in meeting again to see if they wanted to continue dating (at least according to Yayoi). The relationship ended before romance could unfold.

Mutsumi (32 years old, never married) briefly mentioned the possible effect of another common corporate practice in Japan: frequent job relocation (*tenkin*). She made this observation about her male co-worker at a company where she worked as a temporary staff worker:

There is a guy, a manager, who's single in his fifties. This company transfers men a lot. I believe he was unable to marry because of it. I feel sorry for him. He's not bad-looking or anything. Very normal and nice.

Men were not the only ones who worked long hours. As mentioned in the last chapter, during the economic boom, career-track positions opened up for women. Several single women of both cohorts were in career positions or professional occupations, and these women worked incredibly long hours, either currently or in the past. They regarded going home at 9 p.m. "early," many would often "hop on the last train" (which means going home past midnight), and some even reported they would "work through the night (*tetsuya*)." Natsumi (43 years old, never married) recalled that, in her first job in advertising, she regularly missed the last train. This was the time of the "bubble" booming economy (in the 1980s) and her company paid for a taxi that "cost more than my salary!"

Women who dealt with clients in marketing, advertising, etc. said their work hours were not only long but highly unpredictable because they were affected by clients' demands. They could not make plans for after work "because I can't tell what time I can get off work." Rumi (45 years old, never married), who was running a small advertising company as a vice president, discussed how the unpredictability inhibited her from finding a date or developing romantic relationships:

> Before going steady or anything, just to go out for dinner, I just can't even make any solid plans for a date (*yakusoku*). "I can probably meet you but if work comes up, I'd have to cancel the date at the last minute (*dota-kyan*)." Men don't like that. I also don't like to ask my subordinates [to take over my work] so I can date. I'd get so worried about my work during the date. So I have to find someone who can really understand my work demands and who won't get discouraged by a last-minute cancellation [implying such men are scarce].

Midori (36 years old, copy writer, cohabiting for eight months), who often worked until 3 or 4 a.m., felt that one of the reasons her past relationships did not last was that she "was so busy with work ... and I had little chance to cook dinner for my boyfriends like other women do." (Note that these two women's words reflect gendered social expectations that men do not appreciate women's devotion to work, and that women are expected to cook for their boyfriends.)

Due to working such long hours, these women had little time and energy for socializing after work. Honoka (32 years old, marketing consultant, never married) described her typical weekday:

> When I can go home earlier ... I have time and energy only to make dinner, go to *sentō* [public bath], and read books. On busy days, I go home on the last train. I eat *kappu rāmen* [instant ramen noodles in cups] at work and work continuously.

The way these overworked single women spent their days off was not so glamorous, either. All of them said they spent at least one day of the weekend alone in order to recuperate, to take care of chores such as cleaning and laundry, and/ or just to enjoy time for themselves after days of stressful work. There were also women who worked on weekends as their work demanded. The issue was not just time constraints. Izumi (46 years old, marketing researcher, never married) was unmotivated to get together with men during her spare time because men were typically overworked as well:

I don't like to see male friends on weekends because they're also busy ... really tired. So if we get together, we're both tired [laugh], so it's not fun.... I want to spend my weekends without talking about how hard we work. But [with those men] I'd have to listen to their nagging. I don't want that.

Again we see the notion of gendered expectations – in this case that women are listeners, and that men can complain but women cannot.[20]

Some of these women in career positions mentioned negative health effects of overwork. Honoka (32 years old) "got asthma when I turned 30." She attributed her health problem to "eating out (*gaishoku*) all the time" due to overtime work. In order to force her to develop a healthier diet, she began to "get vegetables by delivery service and ... this forces me to make *o-bentō* (boxed lunch) every day [to bring to work]" and cook meals at home on weekends. This, however, kept her from socializing with others over lunch and during weekends. Tomomi, a 39-year-old, never-married social worker, worked until 11 p.m. regularly in the job she used to have. She "began to have problems like pain in my hand and blood in my sputum" so she switched her job. Her current job, which dealt with bureaucratic tasks pertaining to elderly care services, required little overtime work. But her office consisted mostly of female employees, married with children.

Two other never-married interviewees, Natsumi (43 years old) and Teruko (41 years old), also quit their first jobs due to excessive work demands. Both found corporate jobs too stressful and started working freelance. At the time of the interviews, Natsumi was an established freelance illustrator and Teruko had just started her own business as a graphic designer. Though Natsumi was very happy with her job and flexible work conditions, she said she hardly had the chance to interact with single men through work. Teruko was having an affair with a married foreign man she had met at a business seminar. She wished to marry him but said the chance of that was "zero," as he was content with his current marriage.

Overtime work demands motivated some interviewees in managerial or career-track positions to purchase a small one-bedroom or studio *manshon* (condo). They needed to live closer to work, and small condos were all they could afford in Tokyo, where real estate values were high. Two women, Izumi (46 years old) and Rumi (45 years old), each talked about the same psychological effect the purchase had on them. It made them feel as if they had made a commitment to lifetime singlehood, though at the time of purchase, they were convinced by realtors that it would be a good investment for future marriage. Izumi also said that she began to work even harder since she bought her condo. She couldn't "afford to risk losing my job, so I do whatever my company demands."

Prejudice against career women

Women's career-track positions (as opposed to lower-status/clerical jobs) not only occupied their time and energy but also disadvantaged them in another way. My single interviewees in career-track positions concurred that their competence at work turned off men:

> I, well, win against men.... I talk a lot, am very sociable, and am good at work. Men can't take me. They get jealous. They say, "You can live without men, can't you?"
>
> > (Yoko, 36 years old, section manager)

> I work overtime, even throughout the night (*tetsuya*), I'd never say I can't do it. And men think I'm *kawaikunai* (unfeminine, not cute). They don't like women who never say "I can't." They think I'm too strong. That's why they don't want me. Men think they can't nag to women like me. They think we'd scold them. [laugh] There was a young girl at my client company, who went, "[in a childish high-tone voice] Oh, no, I got confused, *ufufufufu* [feminine chuckle]." What an idiot, I thought, but to men, she's probably cute (*kawaii*).[21]
>
> > (Rumi, 45 years old, vice-president)

> Yeah, guys tell me, "You can solve everything on your own." ... [They think] I can live by myself without their help. I'm independent.... Younger men are different. They say "I respect you for this." ... But for men [of my age] ... it's probably strange that women work.
>
> > (Izumi, 46 years old, marketing researcher)

> I was told by my [unmarried male] senior worker. Girls should pretend to be stupid ... or no men would approach them.
>
> > (Seiko, 43 years old, accountant)

These accounts show that, when women have the ability to take on tasks independently or exhibit their intelligence, competitiveness, strength, eloquence, or willingness to take overtime work as demanded, they are perceived by men as intimidating, unfeminine (*kawaikunai*), and uninterested in men, romantic relationships, and marriage.

Interestingly, while being frustrated with such prejudice, these interviewees labeled themselves "unwomanly (*onna rashikunai*)" because they "can't show my weak side" and "leave nothing for men to protect or support." Their crafting of selves as "unwomanly" indicates that these women accepted such traits as mental strength, competence, and independence as inherently masculine – rather than questioning or challenging such notions as sexist. Instead, by interpreting and labeling these traits as "unwomanly," they were *doing gender*[22] and reinforcing gender differences/inequality.

55

One of the career-track single interviewees, Hitomi (36 years old, marketing consultant), on the other hand, articulated that her true nature was "feminine," and discussed the dilemma that her real self would never be seen and understood by her male colleagues:

> They [men at work] don't tell me directly, ... but I know they're saying I don't want to marry, I'm devoted just to my career. I know they're saying I think men are stupid. [laugh] ... They say I'm exceptionally smart and good at work.... I tell my [male] boss that my ultimate dream is to become a housewife, to quit my job receiving a flower bouquet,[23] but no one believes it.... I don't think I could have *shanai renai* [romantic relationships with co-workers].... I come to my company to work, not to have love relationships. I think I'm a very different person when I'm "on" and "off" [the job].... I'm very different when I'm in love relationships. That's the real me. But when I'm in the "work mode," I probably look like a devoted career woman. So men can't see me in the "love mode." I think I'm sealing up my feminine side [at work]. So I can't possibly get into love relationships with anyone at work.

Hitomi pointed out this disadvantage faced by career women – the pressure to suppress femininity in career-track jobs that require a strong focus on work. But here again, like other interviewees, Hitomi associated devotion to work with masculinity. She also related femininity to her desire to become a housewife, and to a different self she would exhibit when in the "love mode" (later in the interview she implied this had to do with her sexual expression). Thus, like others, she did not reject gender dichotomy in roles and traits, even as she complained about its unfair impact on her image. Indeed, as I will discuss in later chapters, hardly any interviewees expressed the idea that women should not be considered lacking in femininity due to having careers and exceptional abilities at work.

In Nemoto's study,[24] highly educated single women in professional occupations (in Tokyo), whose age group roughly corresponds to my recession cohort, also reported that they were seen "unfeminine." She interviewed single men as well, and most of them expressed negative views toward women in career positions and preferred to date or marry women with traditional feminine traits.[25] Thus, unlike clerical workers and women in female-dominated occupations, women in career-track positions were *not* segregated from men at work, yet they were disadvantaged in romance due to the link between career-track jobs and masculinity/ lack of femininity.

Additionally, older single interviewees in clerical positions told me that they were also viewed as "too strong," "unfeminine," and "uninterested in marriage" by men. This suggests that women's singlehood in older age was associated with a lack of femininity as well (because it signaled lack of interest in the nurturing role). Thus, boom cohort women were deprived of romantic opportunity regardless of occupation.

Not enough good men to marry?

So far I have discussed how women's opportunities to meet romantic partners were limited by factors related to work. Another important obstacle I observed was the problematic nature of men, which contrasted between the two cohorts. Below, I start by presenting issues with reference to men discussed by the boom cohort, followed by observations related to the same topic provided by recession cohort interviewees.

Boom cohort: one-dimensional, boring men

As briefly mentioned earlier, several single women of this cohort had *miai* or *miai*-like experiences. *Miai* is a mate-selection system in Japan, in which a single man and woman are introduced, through a mediator, as potential marital partners. Men introduced via *miai* are those in "good standing,"[26] typically exceptional in terms of job, education, income, and sometimes wealth (such as property-holding). In other words, these men are so-called *sararīman* (salarymen) in elite, white-collar, corporate jobs. My interviewees wished to marry men in white-collar occupations, yet invariably expressed negative views toward men they met through *miai*:

Tetsuko (43 years old): [The men I met were] My sister's husband's company's boss's something. They said, "There's a single man so why don't you meet him?" I met a few in that way, but they didn't appeal to me (*nanka pin to konai*).
Author: What didn't appeal to you, miai meetings or men you met?
Tetsuko: Ah, well, men I met. ... Men who work at banks, places like that, looked much older even when they were the same age, and also ... were too square (*okatai*). I felt they were living in a different world.
Author: Have you dated any of them?
Tetsuko: No. No common interests. Not interesting to talk with.

Izumi (46 years old): My friends told me there were a lot of [single] men in research jobs in private companies, so I met several but they were not interesting (*omoshirokunai*) at all.... They were working in research institutes in the mountains and commuting by car, so they just go back and forth between company and home. Because they drove, they didn't go out to drink [after work].... I don't think it'd be fun living with this type.
Author: Do you think they had no hobbies?
Izumi: They may have hobbies like computer or cars, but they don't go out to cities.
Author: Do you feel their world is too small?
Izumi: Their life sphere (*seikatsu-ken*) is small.... We [single women] always hold passports so we can go abroad as soon as we find cheap tours.

But they [these men] move around in a small area. I hate to say this but we're active and have much more experience. We're aggressive in finding interesting things [but they are not].

Seiko (43 years old): [I had *miai*] Once. He worked for a bank.... My father's friend's son or something.... He was uninteresting (*tsumaranai*).
Author: He wasn't your type?
Seiko: Well, ah, by hearing him talk, I could tell he had no personal time. So, it was impossible [for me to take interest].
Author: Was he like someone who devoted his life to work?
Seiko: Rather than devoted to work, he was pressed by work so he did only work.... No hobbies.... I asked him what he does on days off, but he was mostly working. And if he had some free time, he drove. I asked him where he would drive to. He said he drove to Kichijōji [a town in Tokyo] and drove back home. [laugh] ... We had no common hobbies or anything. He was uninteresting (*omoshirokunai*).

Another reason the single men these women met through *miai* were considered "uninteresting" was that they lacked the ability to communicate eloquently or talk about things other than work. To illustrate:

He [a man she met through *miai*] wasn't trying to communicate actively. He hardly talked and the mediator also hardly talked. It was painful. I made efforts and asked him questions, and he answered, but it didn't lead to conversations. "Oh, I see (*ā sōdesuka*)" – that was it.

(Hitomi, 36 years old)

I just couldn't talk with them [her *miai* partners]. They're thinking only about money, and can't talk about anything cultural.... Well, they're very different in how they spend time. I asked what he [one of the *miai* partners] liked to eat or where he liked to go. I thought that'd lead to some conversation. But whatever I asked, he was like "*iyā* [ah]." I felt, "What's this guy thinking? He's boring." ... They're probably very serious, just focusing on the job. Those kind of men should marry women who want to support that.

(Teruko, 41 years old)

As discussed in the previous chapter, this cohort of single women had rich social and cultural experiences such as travel (domestic and abroad), brand name goods shopping, study abroad, skiing, and gourmet food eating. They had discerning tastes, and expected men to be even savvier than themselves:

For the second date [with a man I met through *miai*], he said, "Let's meet for lunch" and we met in Ochanomizu. What kind of [fashionable] place was he going to take me!? I was excited, you know? It turned out that he took me to Mansei [a chain restaurant] in *ekibiru* [a shopping mall adjacent to a train station]. He insisted he wanted to go there.... What!? I came all the way to Ochanomizu for this? [laugh]

(Saori, 45 years old)

Single older women wanted men to act "smoothly (*josai naku*) ... not like looking at magazines intently [to search for nice places to go] or something like that" (Teruko, 41 years old). By not knowing where to take women, my interviewees viewed these men as having "had no dating experience before" and rejected them. None of the *miai* meetings my interviewees mentioned led to serious relationships.

The mismatch between single men and women of the boom cohort was observed by married interviewees as well:

Mari (38 years old): My single girlfriends ask me to introduce them to someone, so I asked my husband and brother to find someone for them. But they said single men past 30 were guys who never had a girlfriend and were unattractive. They were leftovers, they said. They said they can't introduce those guys to my friends. [laugh]
Author: But your girlfriends are not "leftovers?"
Mari: My single girl friends are cute and beautiful.... By thinking about my single friends, yeah, I couldn't introduce those guys to them. They [those guys] are kind of old for their age (*ojisan-kusai*).

Single men in their forties are old for their age (*ossan-kusai*). Single women [in their forties] are pretty and active, so they probably can't find a match.

(Tamami, 45 years old)

Kimi (25 years old): Single men past 40 at my bank are a little strange. They may not be suited for marriage. Some are selfish. Also the way they treat women. Others [employees] are saying, "What's up with those guys!?"
Author: How do they treat women? Do they look down upon women?
Kimi: That, too. Also, well, they brown-nose people above but are rude to their subordinates. Those kind of men are [short pause] single. [laugh]
Author: How about single women past 40? Are they also rude to subordinates?
Kimi: No. They are actually very beautiful. One woman is gorgeous. I wonder if she remained single because she was too gorgeous when she was young and not approachable.... Men working at banks are usually popular. Women think they have good education, good income, and are dependable (*majime*). My friends ask me to introduce them to someone [from my work]. So, men who work at banks and remain single are, you know [chuckle]?

By women's accounts only, I cannot conclude whether many single men of this cohort were indeed selfish, arrogant, and/or disrespectful towards women and subordinates, or whether they were merely exhausted, inexperienced in dating, and lacked social and communication skills due to excessive work hours. I am inclined to think that the latter is at least a possibility for some men, considering the social and cultural context, and the conditions these men worked under. Men in Japan worked so many hours, as mentioned earlier, at least partly because dedication to work was an expected element of culturally idealized, or *hegemonic*, masculinity.[27] This form of masculinity, labeled *salaryman masculinity* by Dasgupta, prescribed that for men to be successful, they should graduate from college, take white-collar jobs in elite corporations, work hard, and provide for families consisting of a stay-at-home wife and children. In the 1950s and 1960s, salarymen were called "corporate warriors (*kigyō senshi*)." As the word "warrior" implies, what was expected of salarymen paralleled expectations held of *samurai* warriors of the feudal period, and soldiers of the early twentieth century: self-sacrifice, stoicism, and loyalty and devotion to masters (i.e., their company, feudal master, or country). In other words, working long hours was indeed expected of successful men, while eloquent communication with women was not.

The descriptions of men introduced in *miai* suggest that these men of elite status indeed worked long hours and had very little personal time. They were also probably working among men. Is it not somewhat harsh to reject these men for lacking the rich cultural knowledge and social skills needed to communicate smoothly with women? Understand that prior to the economic boom, this type of man was sought out in the marriage market, possibly highly so, simply due to his high status. Then, the economic boom led to a huge rift in cultural fluency between men and women.[28]

While I could understand why my boom cohort interviewees found these men unappealing, I felt sympathy towards single men molded into "uninteresting" one-dimensional persons by virtue of doing the "right" thing. They were, ultimately, victims of corporate exploitation used in the pursuit of profit. Even without eloquence and cultural fluency, some (or possibly many) may have possessed redeeming qualities. I asked some interviewees who experienced *miai* if they might at least give this type of man a chance – perhaps getting to know them more rather than immediately rejecting the possibility of a relationship. I also suggested that women might guide such men in the pursuit of cultural knowledge. However, desirous of men who were savvy and ready to take the lead, interviewees refused such suggestions.

Though I am hesitant to draw conclusions with regards to the (un)desirability of boom cohort men, as an advocate of gender equality I most definitely found problematic another aspect of men of this cohort that emerged from my interviews. More than half of single boom cohort interviewees had had at least one affair with married men, in the past or currently.[29] In most cases, these women hoped, wished, believed, or were made to believe that their partners

LIMITED CHANCES OF ROMANCE AND PROBLEMATIC MEN

would eventually divorce their wives and marry them. All but one, who was currently having an affair, regretted their past involvement with married men. There were also incidents of infidelity, physical abuse, verbal abuse, cruelty, and gambling problems by men in women's past or current relationships (including marriages). Unfortunately, I was unable to explore these subjects in depth in my research. It is, however, important to keep in mind that such incidences of gender injustice were likely to occur, and no doubt impacted women's life paths in important ways.

Recession cohort: uninterested, indecisive men

My younger single interviewees addressed very different problems with men. Many women of the recession cohort felt that it was men who lacked interest in marriage, and kept them or their friends from getting married. For instance, Midori (36 years old, never married) said:

> I have never met a woman who doesn't want to marry. There are many, many more cases of women wanting to marry, but their boyfriends have no intention to marry. So I think the problem [of non-marriage] is in men's mood.

Midori's boyfriend was one such man. She had been cohabiting with her boyfriend for eight months and was frustrated with his ambiguous attitude towards marriage. She wanted to marry and have children. Her wish to marry was especially strong, she said, when she was passing age 35 – the age she perceived as the limit for childbearing. But her partner's intent was never clear. He seemed content with the relationship but never discussed marriage. Other women of the recession cohort shared their experience with uninterested boyfriends, past and present. Still others shared their observations of uninterested men they knew, such as their friends, boyfriends of friends, and co-workers. Note that this subject was never brought up by my boom cohort interviewees.

I asked my recession cohort interviewees why they thought these men were uninterested in marriage. Some thought it had to do with men's lack of economic security. Three women shared their observations of friends or friends' boyfriends:

> Junko (27 years old, never married): There are quite a lot of men who want to marry, but can't marry with their salary.... I hear this from my friends. I tell them, go ahead and marry.
> *Author: Your male friends say they can't marry?*
> Junko: They do.
> *Author: Even when their girlfriends say they both can work?*
> Junko: When they say so, men, maybe they're only saying it to make themselves look cool, but they say they want to provide [for the family].

61

Author: What if you were in that kind of relationship?
Junko: If I love him and that's the reason [of non-marriage], I'd tell him, don't worry, I'd work, too.

Ryoko (26 years old, cohabiting): There are quite a lot of men who don't want to marry, or don't want to marry yet. There are many couples like that.
Author: Do you know why?
Ryoko: I think they [men] want to be free, for now.
Author: Is it also that they can't afford to marry?
Ryoko: Ah, I think that's the reason, too. Boyfriends are temp-workers. Probably boys are thinking they'd take on [financial] responsibilities [in marriage]. They're taking [marriage] more seriously than girls, in my opinion. Especially in terms of finances. Girls are thinking they [wife and husband] can both work, but boys aren't sure about it.
Author: Do you think boys feel they have to provide for the family?
Ryoko: I think that's how they think.

Kyoko (29 years old, married): I saw boys changed their jobs and other parts of life, and girls were very sensitive about it, and said, "I don't feel secure, I can't see a future with you," and broke up after dating for so many years.
Author: Did you say boys change their jobs often?
Kyoko: Yes, many. I think they feel insecure about their jobs so they think about changing them. I think they [women] should be patient and wait.
Author: Some say there are more men who are not interested in marriage. Do you know that kind of man?
Kyoko: I don't think they have no intention to marry.
Author: Do they feel they can't afford to marry, for example?
Kyoko: Yes. Also, hobbies and other things they [men] want to pursue, so they can't think about family yet. I saw that kind.... Girls fell in love with them [boys] who were chasing their dreams, but once they [girls] started thinking about marriage, it became obvious that the goals [of marriage and dreams] are not compatible.

However, Midori and Megumi (as well as some other women), felt the reasons for men's hesitation were not limited to insufficient income and job insecurity:

Midori (36 years old, cohabiting): Well, part of the reason may be income. [laugh] I think in marriage, couples can share financial burdens fifty–fifty, but there are many men who think they can't afford to marry with their salary level, I think. Even when men earn enough to feed themselves, a lot of men, probably, think, "If I marry, I'd have to have this much income." I also think there are a lot of men who think, "I prefer to keep my present lifestyle so I can spend all my money on my hobbies."

Author: Does this apply to your current boyfriend?
Midori: I don't think not enough income applies to him. I've been living with him, and I know he's not someone who wants to be fed by me. He can spend his money on his hobbies, though. I don't know. Maybe it's that he may not have much adherence to marriage. We're living together, so maybe he's thinking we don't need to marry.

Megumi (31 years old, never married): Among my friends who married recently, men were indecisive and women pushed for marriage. In the past, I think, men probably said, "Let's get married."
Author: So, are you saying that it's not because men don't earn as much today?
Megumi: Not just that.
Author: How about your [male] friends?
Megumi: I don't think that's the case. They have jobs. No timing, no trigger to push, maybe. There are many who are cohabiting, you know? Maybe they are happy there, no marriage. But when women are turning 30, that should be the push, don't you think? I don't understand why they wouldn't say ["Let's get married"].

In a similar manner other women, based on frustrating past relationships, talked about the indecisive nature of men. For example:

Shoko (29 years old, never married): [They're] Like girls. Wishy-washy. Always like, "Where shall we go?"
Author: Do you not think it's nice that he'd let you decide where to go?
Shoko: Well, that's nice, but when it's so often, I get annoyed. I have to make decisions. That's no good. "Whatever is fine" means it doesn't have to be me [to date]. When they say "Whatever is fine," I hear "I don't care [much about you]."
Author: Do you not hear "I'd love to go anywhere you want to go?"
Shoko: That's different. Every time we had a date, I asked, "What do you want to eat?" "Anything is fine." That's "I don't care." It's different from "I feel like Korean BBQ today, so let's go to a BBQ restaurant." "Anything is fine" is "I don't care." That's feminine.

He [my most recent ex-boyfriend] was younger, six years younger and, it [our relationship] became like counseling. Well, I've been working since I graduated from [two-year vocational] school [at age 20], but he went to college and graduate school, so at age 26, he had only a year or so work experience. I have long work experience, right? So I was listening to his troubles, and gradually, I started thinking, why am I listening to his troubles without being paid for it? ... I had to make plans for him. I do that for my clients. I've always been making plans for others. But I do that [for my clients] because I get paid for it. But why do I have to make plans [for my boyfriend] without getting paid? I wanted him to make plans for me, too.

(Honoka, 32 years old, never married)

Other women of the recession cohort shared similar stories about "men these days," who they perceived lacked the ability to make decisions – not just in reference to marriage, but in general.

There is some evidence that indicates the passive nature of men of the recession cohort.[30] I am, however, a little cautious of my interviewees' observations that "men these days are indecisive." In 2009 when I was conducting this research, "herbivorous men (*sōshoku-kei danshi*)"[31] – referring to men who have little interest in dating or marriage and spend time on grooming themselves – was a buzzword, and young men's wishy-washiness was frequently talked about in the popular media and by people generally. This may have colored my interviewees' perceptions. It is still interesting, though, that only my recession cohort women discussed this aspect of men's nature when describing men of their own cohort.

As already mentioned, the economic recession of the 1990s – commonly called the "lost decade of Japan" – caused serious job insecurity issues among men and women who graduated from schools during that time. According to some studies,[32] Japanese corporations practiced hiring freezes much more commonly than layoffs of existing workers as they tried to commit to the employees who were already hired on the premise of lifetime employment. This resulted in massive unemployment and underemployment among new graduates during those years.[33] Many young people (i.e., the recession cohort) had no other choice but to take casual, low-pay, low-skill jobs with little job security,[34] and even after Japan's economy recovered, many of them remained underemployed because Japanese companies preferred to hire either new graduates or skilled workers.[35] Some of my interviewees' accounts above indicate the prevalence of job insecurity issues among men (and women) of this cohort.

Underemployment is likely to reduce men's chances of marriage. One recent quantitative study shows that, in Japan, more men in irregular jobs postponed marriage than those in regular jobs.[36] Whether or not men of the recession cohort were less interested in marriage (relative to the cohorts above) is, however, unclear. National Fertility Surveys (NFS) of single men show that "finance (*kekkon shikin*)" was the most frequently listed obstacle to marriage in 2010, but this was always listed the most common reason throughout the time the surveys were taken (since 1987), and there was little fluctuation in the percentages of men who chose this answer between 1987 and 2010.[37] The same surveys[38] and other studies[39] suggest that single men of this cohort found marriage burdensome, but as shown in Chapter 1 the great majority of men of this cohort wished to marry one day, and most never-married men in their thirties intended to marry within a year. I hesitate to conclude that men of the recession cohort were *less* interested in marriage than the previous cohort.

LIMITED CHANCES OF ROMANCE AND PROBLEMATIC MEN

My recession cohort interviewees' accounts suggest to me that many men of the recession cohort preferred to have traditional marriages. Men observed by the interviewees were not responding to their girlfriends' offers to share the provider role, and/or were talking about the need and want of high, stable incomes that would allow them to be sole providers. In qualitative work by Hidaka,[40] Tokuhiro,[41] and Nemoto, Fuwa, and Ishiguro,[42] single (salary)men expressed that they preferred that their future wives take full responsibility for domestic tasks, and for themselves to take the breadwinning role. Surveys indicate that traditional views toward gender roles are generally persistent in Japan, particularly among men.[43] Taga's interviews of young (single) men, on the other hand, show signs of change toward men's acceptance of wives' employment. Yet men who were open to wives' employment still expected to take the primary provider role.[44] Though this remains speculative, I tentatively conclude that many men of the recession cohort strongly adhered to traditional gender ideology. Midori's cohabiting boyfriend avoided the talk on marriage perhaps because she was working full-time and until late ("3 or 4 a.m."). For him, this was probably okay in cohabitation but not acceptable in marriage. Men's sentiment towards marriage as "burdensome," observed in some of the above studies, may reflect increased difficulty fulfilling the provider role and hesitance to participate in domestic tasks.[45] Further research on these male attitudes and orientations – and their possible association with increased singlehood – is required before more confident conclusions can be drawn.

Chapter summary and discussion

This chapter points out the most direct causal factors for increased singlehood among women in Japan. Many women remained single, despite their wishes and intentions to marry, because of difficulty finding marital partners. Romantic encounters were structurally limited, and men they met or had relationships with were often problematic. Here, I summarize the findings and discuss how employment practices, which were partly consistent and partly changing in the contexts of economic boom and recession, and traditional gender ideology were the two key factors that created structural limitations and made men unmarriageable.

The gendered nature of Japan's employment system, which designated the career track to men and the clerical track to women, has been well documented by numerous Japan scholars. My study indicates that men and women were not only segregated in this vertical manner, but also separated spatially and horizontally.[46] Female clerical workers were often working spatially away from single male workers, and many women were also horizontally segregated by working in female-dominated occupations. Prior to the economic recession in the 1990s, however, female clerical workers in male-dominated companies were able to meet single men, at least once in a while, despite the vertical, spatial segregation, because employers sponsored social events to integrate workers from different sections. Additionally, according to Iwasawa, in the 1960s, 1970s, and early 1980s it was common for supervisors at workplaces to assume the matchmaking of subordinates as a work responsibility.[47] This may have provided not only female clerical workers in gender-integrated workplaces but also women in female-dominated occupations with opportunities to meet potential marital partners.

As we saw in Chapter 2, the labor shortage due to the economic boom led supervisors to encourage female workers to continue working. In this economic context (in the late 1980s and early 1990s), many supervisors may have refrained from matchmaking their female subordinates because women's marriage usually meant resignation from work.[48] Also discussed in Chapter 2 was how, during the economic boom, many single women enjoyed new opportunities that came from employment, and felt relationships would interfere with the enjoyment of these. Even if supervisors tried to match them with someone, women may not have responded. Thus, though employer-sponsored events were still common during the economic boom in the 1980s, and this allowed vertically, spatially segregated men and women to intermingle, women of the boom cohort may have foregone opportunities to meet romantic partners through work when they were in their twenties.

The economic recession of the 1990s severely reduced unmarried workers' opportunities for romantic encounters through work. Hiring freezes and budget cuts on company-sponsored social events decreased the number of young, single employees and eliminated opportunities for workers to meet potential partners. Although a good number of recession cohort interviewees were in clerical positions, only a couple of them were OLs in sizable corporations, and others were in small establishments (with a small number of single male employees) or working as temporary workers (with little job security). This cohort was also more often than the boom cohort to be found working in female-dominated, care-related services, such as social work and elderly care. Hiring freezes practiced by large corporations may have pushed many women to take these jobs that provided fewer opportunities for cross-gender encounters. Thus, spatial and horizontal gender segregation was more likely among the recession cohort than the boom cohort, and, therefore, I argue that this was one of the primary reasons that recession cohort women drifted into singlehood.

Corporate practices further limited romantic opportunities for both cohorts by demanding great devotion to work. Many of my interviewees had limited time and opportunity to meet potential partners, or develop romantic relationships, due to men's and/or their own long work hours. Japan's corporate culture, which demanded demonstration of employee loyalty through overtime work,[49] has been criticized for its negative effects on workers' health, family life, and women's career opportunities.[50] My study shows that long work hours might have had detrimental effects on yet another aspect of individuals' lives: their opportunities for intimate relationships.

LIMITED CHANCES OF ROMANCE AND PROBLEMATIC MEN

Traditional gender ideology permeates these corporate practices. Gendered employment practices designated and confined many women to lower status/income jobs and, as many scholars have pointed out, this clearly inhibited gender equality in terms of pay and access to positions of power in Japan. More subtly, this gendered division of labor minimized women's and men's romantic opportunities because devotion to employment was strongly associated with masculinity.[51] I contend that this association between work devotion and masculinity had three major impacts on increased singlehood. First, as already discussed, many men worked incredibly long hours and this made men unavailable for dating and developing romantic relationships. Additionally, as you will see in the next chapter, many married men were rarely at home, and, in hearing married friends' complaints about their husbands' absence, some single women were skeptical of the possibility of happiness in marriage. The issue of long work hours was a problem shared by the two cohorts.

Second, work devotion shaped many men in elite occupations into one-dimensional, boring persons who lacked cultural fluency and the skills needed to communicate with women. My research also suggests that these men were likely to be spatially segregated from women at work,[52] which probably contributed further to their poor communication skills.[53] Thus socially, economically, and culturally privileged, elite white-collar workers (i.e., "salarymen"), ironically, did not excite women romantically, since women of the boom cohort expected their men to be culturally savvy. The mismatch in cultural fluency was, however, relevant only to the boom cohort.

Third, since the economic boom more women entered career positions previously reserved for men. By taking such jobs seriously, performing well, and working many hours, women in career-track positions were viewed as masculine/ unfeminine. My research and other studies[54] suggest that men were disinclined to consider these women as potential dates/marital partners, finding them intimidating, unattractive, and uninterested in marriage and family (i.e., the traditionally feminine domain). Women also tacitly accepted the association between work devotion and masculinity. This acceptance was shared by the two cohorts, but boom cohort women faced the same prejudice even when they were in clerical positions. Women's single status in older age was another trait interpreted as indicating a lack of femininity.

A couple of other, related factors may contribute to the phenomenon of increased singlehood. Though this remains speculative, men of the recession cohort, many of whom were deprived of well-paying white-collar jobs, may have believed in traditional marriage (in which men take the breadwinning role and women take the domestic role) and felt reluctant to marry due to being unable to maintain such a marriage financially. Also, some boom cohort women were unable to marry because of sexual exploitation by married men, as well as victimization in abusive relationships.

What can we conclude from all of the above? Persistent, entrenched, traditional gender ideology permeates and is intertwined with corporate practices, marriage, family, intimate relationships, and people's beliefs. Along with the cohort effects observed, this salient characteristic of Japanese society sheds some light on the mystery of singlehood. (Chapter 5 explores cohort differences in women's conceptions of gender roles in depth). In addition to *gender* inequality, it is clear that exploitative use of labor by corporations, itself a serious issue, had considerable impact on the phenomenon of increased singlehood by siphoning away time and energy from young workers.

Recall that, in Chapter 2, my boom cohort single women reported putting marriage and relationships on the backburner, focusing on leisure activities and/ or jobs. I discussed how their postponement of marriage was due to rewarding experiences and optimism at the time. But they may also have procrastinated due to ambivalent views they held toward marriage. The next chapter presents how women of both cohorts perceived their parents' and peers' marriages. The views contrasted sharply by cohort, and, in general, boom cohort women were deprived of good images of marriage. This may have indirectly influenced women of the boom cohort to put off marriage, which may result in a lifetime of singlehood for many of them.

Notes

1 Part of the findings and arguments presented in this chapter appeared in my earlier publication in *Contemporary Japan* (Yoshida 2011).
2 NIPSSR 2011a. In this survey, each respondent was allowed to choose up to three reasons from prepared response categories for "why they cannot marry." In 2010, 51.3 percent of never-married women aged 25 to 34 chose "I have not met the right person yet (*tekitōna aite ni meguriawanai*)." This was also the most frequently chosen reason among women aged 18 to 24 (35.1 percent in 2010) and men (31.0 percent for the age group 18–24 and 46.2 percent for the age group 25–34 in 2010). This survey report provides corresponding data from the same surveys taken in 1992, 1997, 2002, and 2005, and this reason had been listed most frequently throughout these years, and by about the same percentages of women and men of each age group. NIPSSR does not provide statistics for the age groups 40 and above, though the surveys were conducted on unmarried women and men aged 18 to 49. Also, the surveys included all types of "unmarried" persons of the said age groups (i.e., divorced and widowed are included in the surveys), but the above statistics are only for never-married singles.
3 One might wonder how these women's sexual needs were met. According to the National Fertility Survey (NIPSSR 2011a), in 2010, 29.3, 23.8, and 25.5 percent of never-married women of the age groups 25–29, 30–34, and 35–39 (respectively) answered that they had never had sexual intercourse. The corresponding figures for men were 25.1, 26.1, and 27.7 percent respectively. These figures indicate it is not unusual for adult women and men to have limited (or no) partnered sexual experiences. Discussing sexual activities, especially those outside marriage and intimate relationships (such as masturbation and use of commercial sex services), is generally taboo, particularly for women, and the absence of interpersonal sexual experiences may be a very sensitive issue for single women in Japan. I decided that my one-time (i.e., cross-sectional) interview research would not build enough rapport with my interviewees to allow comfortable discussion of such socially inappropriate and potentially sensitive subjects. For this reason, I did not ask my interviewees questions pertaining to sexual activities/experiences unless they voluntarily brought up the

subject. A handful of married and unmarried interviewees actively (though briefly) discussed either their current or past interpersonal sexual experiences. Most single women implied having had sexual experiences within intimate relationships, at least in the past. A few single women gave me the impression that they had never had sexual intercourse. My data on single women's sexual experiences are, however, clearly too limited to analyze.

4 NIPSSR 1983, 1998, 2004, 2007, 2011a.

5 The popular media often interprets fewer incidents of relationships, sex, and marriage as lack of interest in, or attitudinal changes toward, these areas. For instance, "The flight from marriage" in *The Economist* (2011) argues for disinterest in marriage among women in Asia, including Japan. "'Sexlessness' wrecks marriages, threatens nation's future" in *The Japan Times* (Arudou 2011) frames married couples in Japan as less interested in sex than their Western counterparts. "Why have young people in Japan stopped having sex?" from *The Guardian* (Haworth 2013) featured Japanese persons expressing disinterest in sex. A woman who provided sexual services to clients overgeneralizes when she claims that young people feel an aversion to interpersonal sex. These articles lack scientific interpretation of survey and interview responses, and thus make invalid generalizations.

6 NIPSSR 2011b.

7 NIPSSR 2012.

8 Note that not all the interviewees were willing to disclose thorough information about past relationships. This count, therefore, is not as precise as my count of encounters by married and engaged interviewees.

9 One exception was one interviewee who approached her current partner at a lesbian bar. Approaching potential partners in public locations is probably the norm among sexual minorities due to small pools of potential partners.

10 The Japanese word *gaijin* literally means "outside people/person" and is usually translated as "foreigner(s)." However, the word has come to connote (white) Westerners. I translated the word to "Westerners" as Natsumi was clearly referring to people she saw in American sitcoms and movies.

11 In the year I conducted the interview, the word *konkatsu*, coined by Japanese sociologist Masahiro Yamada (who earlier coined the phrase "parasite singles"), was a buzzword. In his pseudoscientific book, *Konkatsu jidai* (The Age of *Konkatsu*) co-authored with journalist Momoko Shirakawa (2008), Yamada argues that single people in contemporary Japan need to actively engage themselves in marital partner search activities (which he refers to by the term *konkatsu*), much like graduating students do for a job search. The latter is called *shūkatsu*, a shortened word from *shūshoku katsudō* (job search activities by graduating students). *Kon* in the term *konkatsu* comes from *kekkon* (marriage) – equivalent to the English "gamy" (e.g., mono*gamy*). The Japanese media picked up the term *konkatsu* and, along with businesses, promoted singles to use matchmaking services, etc. When I was conducting interviews in 2009, some of my single interviewees, including Natsumi, bristled at or expressed repulsion towards the term and the expectations it implied.

12 In his humorous (pseudoscientific) book on singlehood, Aziz Ansari (2015), a comedian, actor, and now author, wrote that the young people he interviewed in Japan were much less open to the use of online dating services compared to Americans.

13 One single interviewee, Saori (45 years old), expressed her regret about not going to four-year college. She went to a two-year English-language vocational school with a mostly female student body. She also graduated from an all-girl high school and thought the absence of co-ed experience left her with poor communication skills when it came to men. It was common for Japanese of these two cohorts to attend single sex high schools. Further research is needed to explore the effects of gendered schooling on singlehood and romantic relationships.

LIMITED CHANCES OF ROMANCE AND PROBLEMATIC MEN

14 Momoe belonged to a tennis club in college and preferred to date/marry a man who played sports, seeing it as a sign of self-discipline.

15 Labor Force Surveys indicate a high percentage share of women in the retail and service industries (particularly health care and social work) (Ministry of Internal Affairs and Communications 2015a).

16 According to the Gender Equity Bureau Cabinet Office (2016), women's share of mid level managerial positions in private companies increased but remains low. In 2014, only 14.9 percent of *kakarichō* (lowest-division chiefs), 7.9 percent of *kachō* (section managers), and 4.9 percent of *buchō* (general managers) were women.

17 See for instance Brinton 1993, 2007; Kelsky 2001; Kerbo 2008; Ogasawara 1998; Sugimoto 2010; and Tokuhiro 2010.

18 Spatial segregation by sex – e.g., in schools, workplaces, and general social life – was the norm until the end of World War II (McLelland 2010). In prewar Japan, when women's chastity was deemed important socially and politically, companies that hired a large number of unmarried young women from rural regions made deliberate efforts to keep young maidens from intermingling with single men, even after work hours (Faison 2007). It is possible that the spatial segregation practiced by my interviewees' companies is a leftover from this time period.

19 According to Sugimoto (2010), the average overtime work hours by employees in Japan come to over 100 hours per year, but because many employees voluntarily take overtime work, the official statistics reported by the government are likely to underestimate the actual average. This problem is also documented in Kitanaka (2012) in relation to the epidemic of depression and deaths caused by overtime work among Japanese corporate workers.

20 Long (1996) succinctly discusses how the nurturing role expected of women in Japan includes avoidance of conflict and maintenance of harmony. Allison (1994)'s work on hostess clubs also discusses the wifely role hostesses take in entertaining corporate male workers, which includes listening and not confronting.

21 *Kawaikunai* means "not *kawaii*" where *kawaii* refers to child-like cuteness. It implies "sweet, adorable, innocent, pure, simple, genuine, gentle, vulnerable, weak, and inexperienced" (Kinsella 1995: 220) as women's positive qualities. *Kawaii* femininity is one dominant form of femininity in Japan. Some women "perform" in order to appear cute, especially in the presence of men, by, for instance, using a high-pitch nasalized voice, elongating syllables, etc. (Miller 2004). Women who act in this manner are condemned by other women as being or doing *burikko* (fake child or phony girl) – a term first coined by female comedian Kuniko Yamada in the 1980s. The "young girl" my interviewee Rumi was referring to was either naturally *kawaii* or, more likely, *burikko*. Rumi expressed her repulsion toward this type of "fake cute" woman, and her frustration with men who would find such women "adorable."

22 *Doing gender* is an idea first discussed by West and Zimmerman (1987). They contest the idea that construction of gender ends at gender socialization, arguing that individuals actively recreate and reconstruct gender through everyday interactions that involve gender-appropriate behaviors, interpretations, etc. *Doing gender* refers to such gendered social interactions that reinforce gender differences.

23 It is common for companies in Japan to announce the retirement of female employees quitting work for marriage, and congratulate them by handing them flower bouquets (Ogasawara 1998). Hitomi was referring to this common ritual – obviously practiced in her company.

24 Nemoto 2008. She conducted qualitative interviews on 26 women in Tokyo in 2006.

25 Nemoto was the interviewer, but this piece was published in her co-authored piece (Nemoto, Fuwa, and Ishiguro 2012). Nemoto interviewed 25 single men in Tokyo,

most of whom were in middle-class occupations. These men viewed women in career positions as selfish and unfeminine, and preferred women who would take a home-making role and be submissive, small in size, and good looking.

26 Applbaum 1995.

27 *Hegemonic masculinity* is a concept developed by Connell (1995). Dasgupta (2003, 2010) discusses that salaryman masculinity is Japan's version of hegemonic masculinity, or at least was until recently. See also Hidaka (2010) for salaryman masculinity.

28 Mathews (2003, 2014) conducted qualitative interview research on men in Japan in 1989–1990 and reinterviewed some of them approximately 20 years later. In both sets of research, he observed that men, especially of older age groups, did not consider emotional connectedness with their wives as part of the husband's role. Women were, on the other hand, increasingly expecting emotional closeness in marriage, and this gender gap in expectations was causing unhappiness in or breakup of many of his interviewees' marriages. Therefore, it is highly likely that many men of the boom cohort did not even consider that they needed to effectively communicate with women, and, therefore, this was one factor that contributed to increased singlehood among this cohort. Though Mathews (2014) attributes this change in expectations to the economic recession, my data indicate that the initial catalyst was the economic boom of the 1980s, which opened up leisure and job opportunities for young women.

29 Lebra (1984) mentioned that *uwaki* (extramarital affairs) were common in Japan. Many of the unwed mothers interviewed by Hertog (2009) had babies conceived in affairs with married men. According to Bumpass and Choe (2004), nearly 50 percent of men aged 25 to 39 surveyed in 1994 agreed with the statement, "A woman should forgive her husband's sexual unfaithfulness." These studies imply the commonplace occurrence of extramarital sex/affairs in Japan.

30 Kotani 2002.

31 The term was paired up with "carnivorous women (*nikushoku-kei joshi*)." See the *New York Times* (2009) for more detail.

32 See Brinton 2011; Genda 2005; Jung and Cheon 2006; and Tachibanaki 2006 for the impact of the economic recession on hiring practices in Japan.

33 According to Tachibanaki (2006), new graduates' employment rate improved in 2006 when the Japanese economy was recovering. According to Mathews (2004), some young men purposely chose casual employment, refusing to work for corporations that demanded sacrifice of personal time.

34 According to Tachibanaki (2006), NEET (Not in Education, Employment, and Training) and so-called *furītā* (those in casual employment with no or little job security) increased, especially in the late 1990s and early 2000s among men and women in their twenties and early thirties, but most *furītā* wished to have stable, regular jobs.

35 See Genda 2005; Rebick 2006; and Tachibanaki 2006.

36 According to Piotrowski, Kalleberg and Rindfuss (2015), among Japanese men born between 1970 and 1973, those in non-regular jobs were much more likely to postpone marriage than those in regular jobs. Marriage rates are also lower among poorer people in the U.S. (e.g., Edin and Kefalas 2005).

37 NIPSSR 2011a.

38 It is important to note that, in NFS, respondents are asked to choose up to three concerns from prepared response categories, and therefore, men may *not* necessarily be concerned about what they chose. In 2010, among never-married respondents aged 18 to 34, 48.7 percent chose "whether I can maintain my own daily routines and lifestyle," 46.7 percent "whether I can freely spend my time for leisure and pastimes," and 46.1 percent "whether I can freely spend money" as their concerns over life after

marriage. These were also the top three concerns chosen by women of the same age group, and the percentages were actually higher for women than men (60.5, 51.1, and 46.5 percent, respectively). NIPSSR does not provide data for respondents above age 35 in the report, though the surveys were taken from unmarried men and women aged 18 to 49.

39 For instance, in Nagase (2006)'s survey on men (and women) in their twenties and thirties in 1997, which included 21 single employed men who lived in Tokyo as well as non-metropolitan areas, words chosen by single men to describe the image of marriage included "constraint" and "responsibility and duty." Similar views toward marriage were also observed by Nemoto et al. (2012), who conducted qualitative interview research on 25 never-married men in Tokyo. Note that all the single men in Nagase's study and 23 out of 25 single men in Nemoto et al.'s study were employed in large firms and/or earning high incomes.

40 Hidaka 2010.

41 Tokuhiro 2010.

42 Nemoto et al. 2012.

43 For instance, see Bumpass and Choe 2004.

44 Taga 2003.

45 There may be several reasons for more men of this cohort to perceive marriage as "burdensome," compared to men of older cohorts. In addition to provision, in Japan, married men are increasingly expected to be involved in childcare and develop emotional connectedness to their wives and children (Mathews 2014). Highly educated, single men in Nemoto et al.'s (2012) study expressed disinterest in marriage and relationships partly because long work hours limited their personal time. They judged that dating and marriage would take away their already-limited free time. These men thought marriage was unnecessary, as sex and meals were attainable through commercial services. These reflect the sexist/patriarchal view held by men that the primary role of wives is to provide sex and meals, and that women's desires for emotional connectedness within relationships and marriage are a nuisance.

46 Kubo, Kawasaki, and Hayashi (1993) examined the never-married rates among male workers of different divisions in an electronics company, and found that male-dominated divisions such as engineering had much higher shares of never-married male workers than the divisions that included female workers.

47 Iwasawa (2007, 2010) discusses that, in the 1960s, 1970s, and 1980s, many unmarried young people migrated into urban areas for employment, and this led employers and supervisors to introduce their subordinates to potential marital partners. As a result, coworker marriages were very common during this time. Since a third party was often involved in the mate selection process, some coworker marriages had *miai*-like elements (Lebra 1984, Tokuhiro 2010, Yamada and Shirakawa 2008).

48 Nemoto et al.'s study (2012) indicates that supervisors refrained from matchmaking their *male* subordinates in recent years. I assume this workplace practice is very uncommon today, because in addition a large number of supervisors themselves are unmarried.

49 See Sugimoto (2010) for more detail on corporate assessments of employees.

50 In terms of effects on workers' health, Kitanaka (2012) provides detailed accounts on the association between overwork, depression, and suicide among corporate male workers in Japan. Also, there are numerous studies (e.g., Iwasaki, Takahashi, and Nakata 2006) on so-called *karōshi* (lit. deaths caused by excessive work). Examples of studies on the impacts on families include Allison (1994) and Kotani (2002), who discuss the negative impacts of husband/father absence on wives/children. Difficulties experienced by women attempting to balance work and family/life and the association of this with slow career/economic/political advancement by women have been studied extensively (e.g., Creighton 1996).

LIMITED CHANCES OF ROMANCE AND PROBLEMATIC MEN

51 In the 1950s, 1960s, and 1970s, in promoting economic recovery and growth, the Japanese government deliberately propagated the traditional gender role model – male breadwinning and female homemaking – as ideal. For the postwar development of masculinity and femininity in Japan, see Dasgupta (2003, 2010) and Ochiai (2004/2006).
52 Kubo et al. 1993.
53 Nakamura and Sato's quantitative study (2010) found that the odds of having romantic partners were lower among men who rarely spent time with friends, compared to those who socialized with friends at least once a month. Using time spent with friends as a proxy for communication skills, they argue that poor communication skills by men reduced the chances of marriage for men, and tentatively concluded that spending time with friends – even male friends – would help single men cultivate communication skills and increase their chances of romance and marriage.
54 Hidaka 2011; Mathews 2003; Nemoto et al. 2012; Tokuhiro 2010.

4

COHORT CONTRAST IN MARRIAGES THAT SURROUNDED WOMEN

Impacts of linked lives

My father is a man of the old days.... "Pass me the salt," like that. Watching my father acting like a feudal lord, I feel disgusted, really repulsed.... And I question my mother, too, for allowing it to happen.

(Tomomi, 39 years old, never married, social worker)

They had a *miai* marriage. My father is seven years older, so he adores her. My mother doesn't like housework but he tolerates everything.... Yeah, I'd like to have a marriage like them.

(Junko, 27 years old, never married, secretary)

One set of interview questions I prepared yielded a clear cohort contrast regarding the nature of the marriages that surrounded the interviewees. I included questions that asked about the women's views towards parents' and peers' marriages in order to understand their ideas about gender roles. These questions prompted a veritable opening of Pandora's Box for the boom cohort. Many negative stories were told about their parents' marriages, sometimes angrily, and contrasted with answers given by the recession cohort. Images of peer marriages held by interviewees also contrasted by cohort, but not necessarily in terms of quality of marriages. This is because peer marriages were largely "invisible" to boom cohort single women, while the recession cohort was exposed to them more openly.

According to life course theory, *linked lives*, or other people's lives to which individuals are closely connected, have profound impacts on, and consequences for, their life courses.[1] Women's experiences and observations of marriage through their parents and peers may partially explain why some or many of them drifted into unmarried life paths. In this chapter, I present my findings regarding cohort differences in parents' and peers' marriages, and discuss how images of marriage – constructed through lives these women were linked to – may have affected women's life paths. Note that, for the analysis of parents' marriages, five interviews were excluded because, due to a variety of circumstances, they did not generate sufficient data.[2]

Cohort contrast in parents' marriage

Boom cohort: patriarchal, conflict-ridden, emotionally distant marriages

At the time of the interviews boom cohort parents were elderly, with some deceased. None of my interviewees' parents had been divorced. In other words, all interviewees of this cohort had parents who stayed married, or had one widowed parent. The absence of divorce may suggest that these women grew up in happy, stable families, but their stories indicate otherwise. Out of the 16 boom cohort interviewees included in this analysis, 12 overtly expressed negative views toward parents' marriages. Only one woman Sonoko (45 years old, married with two children), said her parents' marriage was "ideal," and attributed it to her father being helpful around the house. Three women – Kazuko (45 years old, never married), Sumire (45 years old, never married), and Nozomi (40 years old, married with one child) – did not have much to say about their parents' marriages, describing them as "hardly the ideal" but "not bad."

In the stories told by those women who expressed a negative perception of their parents' marriage, a recurring theme was disgust towards fathers' dominance coupled with mothers' submissiveness. For instance:

They [my parents] were classmates from high school.... A typical pattern – a salaried man (*sararī man*) and a housewife. My father took it for granted that my mother did everything [around the house]. She had to cook for lunch and dinner, so when she went out, she was always mindful of returning home early enough to prepare dinner. It was like working around my father's schedule, and I didn't like that at all. I prefer that people are independent and take care of themselves. I don't know, maybe they're alright. They're still together and go on a trip, while still complaining. They're really complaining about each other, all the time.... Even when my mother had a cold, he just sits and expects her to wait on him.

(Izumi, 46 years old, never married)

[My father] is a man of the old days.... He doesn't answer the phone even when it's ringing right there [by him]. "Pass me the salt," like that. Watching my father acting like a feudal lord (*otonosama*), I feel disgusted, really repulsed. I really hate men making women work. And I question my mother, too, for allowing it to happen.... My father is really short-tempered.[3] Really short-tempered. A kind of father who'd throw a [dining] table [referring to the old-fashioned father portrayed in an old TV drama,[4] famous for throwing a dining table, out of rage, during dinner].

(Tomomi, 39 years old, never married)

My parents' marriage? Well, now that my father passed, my mother dares to say she had a happy marriage. [cynical laugh] Back then, my dad often came home, really drunk. My mother really hated it. When he came home drunk,... he said [to her], "Drink!" He wanted her to drink with him.... He banged on doors and stuff, too, and she complained.... She was always complaining, "I hate it." I told her many times, "If you hate it so much, get a divorce." She said she wouldn't be able to make a living [if she divorced]. I said we could make a living. Well, at that time, she wasn't working. She started complaining when I was around high school age. I said, "We can make a living. I don't want to hear your complaints all the time, so why don't you get a divorce." Then I felt disgusted. Disgusted towards women who aren't independent. Disgusted with her complaining all the time.... Yes, yes, I think this has to do with why I don't marry. Because she can't be independent, she can't make a living [on her own], she'd have to put up with it all and keep on living [with him]. Yuck. So I disrespect my mother a bit for being that way. I think kids would disrespect mothers for saying that kind of thing. If you can't do anything about it, keep your mouth shut. She couldn't find a solution, only complained. I told her [what to do], but she just came up with excuses for not doing it. What did she want to do then!? I hated it.

(Rumi, 45 years old, never married)

These three women's descriptions clearly show the patriarchal nature of parents' marriages. Their fathers assumed the position of head of household, directing their wives to work like servants. Some of them intimidated the rest of the family by throwing tantrums, and expected their own wants and needs to be catered to, regardless of others' wishes. While some parents were observed to be sharing time together, interactions demonstrating love, caring, and other warm feelings were absent. Mothers were seen as dependent, unhappy, and most of all powerless. They complained, but never stood up to husbands or pursued divorce. Important to note is that while these women perceived their mothers' submissive positions as unfair and wrong, they expressed little sympathy towards them. Rather than being concerned for or allying with mothers, interviewees directed frustration at them for allowing these unfair relationships to continue, and even expressed feelings of disrespect or disgust towards their own mothers. For Tomomi and Rumi in particular, I sensed emotional distance not just between their mothers and fathers but also between their mothers and the interviewees.

One interviewee had a mother who was more independent in terms of earning power, and yet lacked the power to form an equal relationship. Eri (46 years old), a married interviewee, grew up with an employed mother. Her mother was in a professional occupation – a lawyer – that provided higher earnings than her father. This is a rather unusual case for this generation of women in Japan. Career-wise, Eri's mother was exceptionally successful, especially for a woman of her time. Growing up, Eri said her mother constantly preached about the importance of women's careers and economic independence. She said her mother "has a very strong influence on me." But ironically, the strongest impression left on Eri was *not* the glory of women's occupational success. It was the "apparent" impossibility of a woman's career to coexist with a happy marriage. As I will discuss more in the next chapter, despite her career success and high income, Eri's mother took responsibility for all "women's tasks" – i.e., housework and childcare – and her parents were always fighting:

> *Author: Did your father do any housework?*
> Eri: No, not at all.
> *Author: So your mother did everything?*
> Eri: Yes, yes.
> *Author: What do you think of your parents' marriage?*
> Eri: Well, when I was a kid, when I was living with my parents, I was wondering why they were staying married. They were always fighting. My father didn't help around the house at all, so my mother was doing all so hard, and he would just come home late, drunk. To a kid's eyes, he looked like he was only fooling around. So, I asked her why she married him. Uh, "He gives me money for living, however little it is." I asked why she wouldn't divorce him. She said she wouldn't get it [money] if she divorces, so she wouldn't divorce. [cynical laugh]

Eri's father refused to relinquish the male privilege of ignoring domestic work, despite (or possibly because of[5]) his wife's greater economic contribution. Her mother may have fought against that, but was unsuccessful in gaining her husband's cooperation. Observing the stress and hardships her mother went through, Eri recalled how cognizant she was of minimizing her mother's workload during her childhood. To Eri, women's economic independence, the importance of which her mother constantly preached, only added difficulties to the lives of married women and their children. When she was young, Eri wished to attain a career as her mother preached and thought she should forgo marriage. Ironically, she married at the traditional age and became a full-time housewife.

Frequent fights and lack of emotional closeness were other common themes mentioned by boom cohort interviewees when describing parents' marriages. These women described their parents' relationships as "*nakaga warui* (not getting along or in a bad relationship)" and some also mentioned a lot of fighting (*kenka*), which could mean either verbal or physical conflict. Emotional distance may have extended to all relationships within the family, as in the case of Kozue (45 years old, never married):

> My older sister was chronically ill and often hospitalized. So ever since I was little, because my sister was hospitalized … my mother was always with my

sister. My father was busy [with work] so he wasn't around much. I was often playing by myself outside.... Family, [pause] about family, how shall I put it? I haven't felt family is nice in my life. When I was an adolescent, they [my parents] were fighting (*kenka shiteta*) over the shop [which her father began as a family business]. I saw my mother trying to leave us, too. It was also shocking. Once, she also asked me, "Which one [mother or father] would you choose if we divorce?" That was really a shock.

Despite the talk of divorce, Kozue's parents remained in a disharmonious, cold marriage.

Notice that the word "divorce" was mentioned several times by interviewees when speaking of parents' marriages, though none of their parents actually divorced. Divorce was indeed rare for the boom cohort's parents' generation.[6] Instead of divorcing their husbands, interviewees' mothers endured unfair, abusive, cold, stressful, conflict-ridden, and/or unhappy marriages. Though these mothers may have thought of themselves as sacrificing for children, their ostensibly altruistic acts may have had detrimental effects on their daughters in terms of marriage prospects. The negative image of marriage acquired through their parents seems to have profoundly affected interviewees' views toward marriage in general. Some stated explicitly that their negative feelings toward marriage were due specifically to their parents' example. Parents remaining in disharmonious marriages could have given children the impression there is no way out of bad marital relationships. In the words of Natsumi (43 years old, never married):

They [i.e., my parents] were fighting (*kenka shiteta*) all the time. But divorce was out of the question in those days when we were kids, you know? As I grew up, I felt, I don't need to marry. I don't want to get into this kind of situation.

Additionally, one interviewee, Chie (45 years old, married), thought her mother was unhappy in her marriage because she had to work. Chie assumed that was because her father, who was a truck driver, did not earn enough to support the family. Her mother also took in her elderly parents and provided care and economic assistance. In speaking of her parents' marriage, Chie, whose father had recently become bed-ridden, became emotional:

I feel my mother had such a hard life, compared to me.... She was always working. I think she was in a situation where she had to work. I never talked about it, but growing up, I always thought she was having a hard life.

As I discuss more in the next chapter, Chie (as well as most women of this cohort) took traditional gender roles for granted. She felt very sorry for her mother, whom she loved dearly and respected, because she could not afford to stay at home. She loved her father as well, and did not describe her parents' marriage as conflict-ridden or disharmonious. Still, she did not describe her parents' marriage positively because her mother took on both employment and most of the responsibility for domestic tasks (with some help from Chie, and her grandmother when she was not ill). Chie's mother never had a break, and Chie was sad for her mother and expressed guilt feelings because she herself was able to be a full-time housewife.

Recession cohort: emotionally close marriages

In a sharp contrast to the patriarchal, emotionally distant, and/or hostile marriages described by the boom cohort, most recession cohort interviewees judged their parents' marriages positively. More precisely, 15 out of 19 interviewees used in this analysis described their parents' marriages as such, using the term "*nakaga ii*" (close, getting along, in a good relationship) – which is the antonym of "*nakaga warui*," used frequently by the boom cohort. Among recession cohort interviewees, nine women considered their parents' marriages as a model, describing them as their "ideal (*risō*)," and reporting they were "envious (*urayamashii*)" and wished to have marriages like that of their parents. For instance:

> Yeah, yeah, I envy their marriage. Real good relationship. I've never seen them fighting. Really close (*nakaga ii*). They're my ideal.... They're always together. They hold hands together.... Really ideal. Really close (*nakayoshi*).
>
> (Shoko, 29 years old, never married)

> They had a *miai* marriage. My father is seven years older, so he adores her [my mother]. My mother doesn't like housework but he tolerates everything.... My father's crazy about her. [laugh] ... Yeah, I'd like to have a marriage like them.
>
> (Junko, 27 years old, never married)

> They're very close (*nakaga ii*). They go on trips often and do everything together. [laugh] They're like two bunnies. If one gets weak, the other would also get weak.... I heard they met at work. I envy their marriage.
>
> (Shizuka, 34 years old, never married)

These accounts contrasted night-and-day with those of the boom cohort. Not a single boom cohort interviewee described her parents' marriage so fondly. Closeness, however, should not be conflated with equality in power: power inequality and traditional gender roles were common for parents of the recession cohort. However, as reflected in Yoko (36 years old, never married)'s account, recession cohort mothers were not observed to be powerless or miserable:

Yoko: [My parents have a] Really good relationship. They are my ideal. They had a *miai* marriage, but they take a bath together. They sleep in the same bed (*futon*). They go out together on weekends.... My father's like, I'm the head of the household, but my mother steps back very tactfully. My father's stubborn but she keeps the relationship smooth.... My mother had parents who were fighting all the time and she hated it as a child. So she decided she'd never fight in front of her kids. So I've never seen them fighting. I told her it's amazing that they never fight. She said she's mad inside. She started telling me, after I grew up, about the pathetic (*nasakenai*) things about my father, and things like that.... only after I grew up.
Author: What makes them ideal? Because they're close (nakaga ii)?
Yoko: Yes, because they're close. Also, she makes my father feel good, makes all of us respect him, and always allows him to make the final decisions about everything. My father feels good, but in reality, my mother's controlling him, so things are going well.
Author: That is your ideal?
Yoko: That's my ideal. My mother gets a lot of free time. She goes out on her own.
Author: Is your father not too authoritarian (teishu kanpaku)?
Yoko: No, not really. He's not very verbal, but he's kind, my father. He's really stubborn and hard to deal with, but my mother. Once, I heard her saying, "I'm really glad I married your father."
Author: Did she tell you why she was glad?
Yoko: No, she didn't.... But don't you think it's great that she can say it? After all those years of marriage? She thought she was glad that she married this man. Ah, I envy her.

Gender hierarchy clearly existed in her parents' marriage, and there is indication of her mother's frustration towards her father as well. But Yoko accepted this gender order as proper. She was impressed by her mother's cleverness in managing male authority and gaining control over her own life by keeping her father happy. Her parents, as well as other parents of this cohort, were observed to be emotionally and physically close and expressive, and free of open conflicts and hostility. This clearly contrasts with the boom cohort's experience.

Some recession cohort women attributed their parents' good marital relationships to the break from housework enjoyed by their mothers. As in the earlier quote, Junko's father tolerated her mother's slacking on housework. Other women said their fathers were involved in household chores:

My father did a lot [around the house]. He got groceries and cooked when my mother was late from work.... They didn't leave any room for me to do housework.... My mother was very active outside home, and my father spent a lot of time at home. They seem to get along well because of that.

(Akane, 34 years old, married)

Megumi (31 years old, never married): My father lost his mother young, so he did cooking and stuff since he was little. So he likes to cook. He doesn't do laundry and stuff, but he was cooking often. He still does.
Author: After coming home?
Megumi: On days off.
Author: Does your mother do all the other housework?
Megumi: Well, when he lived alone in Kobe for three years after being transferred (*tanshin funin*), I think he was doing everything. He can do anything on his own, I think. I went to see him, and he kept the place clean. [laugh] Maybe it was cleaner than our house. [laugh]
Author: What do you think about your parents' marriage?
Megumi: Nice. Yes. They're close (*nakaga ii*).

Six other women did not find their parents' marriages ideal and worthy to emulate, but described their parents' marriages as good, using the same term, "*nakaga ii* (close)." Some of these women observed their parents fighting in the past, but these fights were understood as "a normal part of relationships," understandable considering "how stubborn my father was" or "because my father didn't give enough respect to the work of housewife my mother was doing." In contrast to the boom cohort, these interviewees took the side of their mothers. In general, descriptions seemed to imply fights observed were less intense and hostile than those the boom cohort was exposed to, and/or that recession cohort women had closer relationships with their mothers or families, compared to women of the boom cohort.

Although positive stories were much more likely among this cohort, not all my recession cohort interviewees grew up with happily married parents. For two never-married women – Kei (35 years old) and Mutsumi (32 years old) – parents' marriages were similar to those of the boom cohort's parents. Kei said:

They insulted each other.... My father was close to his siblings, but my mother had a hard life. Her father died when she was little. She was poor and had to take care of her younger sisters. That's why she got the license to become a pharmacist. So she doesn't want to get involved with her siblings. But my father insults her, 'that's not how siblings should be.' I don't know why they do this, but I don't like them insulting each other.... I've seen a lot of conflict between them.... We didn't have much happy family time (*danran*) together.... I saw my mother's hardship. My father was doing [business] with his brother and they were sloppy with money. I heard that. It wasn't like we fell into poverty, but my mother took another job at some point. He worked, but was a bit too relaxed [with money]. I saw the suffering of woman from this. So I'd never, ever marry a man who doesn't take care of money right.

Mutsumi's parents were emotionally distant and her father used to be very authoritarian:

Author: Then, is it not a role model for you?
Mutsumi: No, probably not. It's not like really bad. They go out to eat together, too. Not like they're hostile, but, it's like they're not interested in each other much.
Author: Do they not talk with each other much?
Mutsumi: Like that. If TV is on, they may say something about it, but they don't talk much. Only when they want to ask something to the other.
Author: Is your father authoritarian (teishu kanpaku)?
Mutsumi: Not so much these days.
Author: Was he in the past?
Mutsumi: Oh, yeah. They fought, well, mother got scolded unilaterally. Very often.

Note that though these two women expressed dislike of their parents' marriages, similarly to the boom cohort, Kei and Mutsumi's words reflect feelings of empathy and respect towards their mothers, contrasting with feelings expressed by boom cohort interviews about their mothers.

Two other women – Hitomi (36 years old, never married) and Yayoi (31 years old, never married) – witnessed parents' separation and divorce in their childhoods. Both of them experienced high levels of conflict and tension between their mothers and fathers during the long years of separation and subsequent divorce. During and after parental separation, both interviewees lived with their mothers, both of whom worked full-time to provide for their families and never remarried. Neither of their fathers was involved in their lives. Yayoi had no clear memory of her father ever living with them. Hitomi shared a painful memory of being sent to her father's to collect child support. She helped care for her younger brother but her mother took care of the home adequately. Hitomi respected her mother greatly and seemed to have a fairly close relationship with her. On the other hand, Yayoi, an only child, "thought she [my mother] didn't like me very much. She was working, and looking back, she probably had too much to shoulder, but [back then] she was always irritable at home." Yayoi said she had developed a better relationship with her mother over the last few years. Not surprisingly, Hitomi and Yayoi rated their parents' marriages very poorly.

Parents of wartime vs. postwar democratization generations

Although there are exceptions, overall the views toward parents' marriages contrast between the two cohorts: very negative versus very positive. The observed cohort contrast may not be generalizable given my small sample of cases, but considering the historical context there is reason to think the two cohort's differential experiences quite representative. Whereas parents of the boom cohort were born before or during World War II, most parents of the recession cohort were born after the war. Japan underwent tremendous social, political, and cultural changes due to the wars[7] and U.S. Occupational Reform subsequent to defeat in World War II. These included changes in ideologies and practices with regard to family and gender.

From the late-nineteenth century to the end of World War II, the so-called *ie* (house) ideology was the official and dominant family ideology in Japan. The ideology was deliberately developed by the government as part of its efforts to "modernize" Japan, and permeated the family (or *ie*) system, which was defined officially in the Civil Code enacted in 1898.[8] Heavily influenced by Confucianism and values of the warrior (*samurai*) class of the Tokugawa feudal period,[9] hierarchies and division of labor based on gender and age were defined as proper.

More concretely, under the law the head of the household, always male, was granted absolute authority over his household (*ie*), including such matters as decision-making about whom each family member should marry. The eldest son was the designated heir of the house (i.e., the future head of the household) and had the right to inherit everything the family owned – family home, land, businesses, and other assets, family name, ancestral graveyard, etc. – as well as the duty to take care of all of these. The eldest son and his wife were expected to reside with his parents and obligated to look after them in their old age. Women's status was lower than men's, and generally older persons were higher in status than younger. Marriage was defined as a union of two houses rather than of two individuals, and was usually arranged by the household head or a mediator appointed by the head. Marriage was viewed as a pragmatic institution, its main purposes procreation, maintaining family lineage, and economic support.[10] While a husband had the liberty to divorce his wife for adultery, infertility, personal traits and demeanors deemed unsuitable to the ways of his *ie*, etc., it was difficult for a wife to initiate divorce. Children belonged to their *ie*, and therefore, in case of divorce or separation, custody of children went to the father.[11] The *ie* ideology went hand in hand with another official ideology of the time, called the *ryōsai kenbo* (good wives, wise mothers) ideology – which I will discuss in more detail in the next chapter – that assigned to women full responsibility for domestic tasks.

This meant that in the first half of the twentieth century, it was common that a woman "entered" another house (*ie*) upon marriage (arranged by a third party), occupied the lowest status in the new house, and was expected to obey her husband and parents-in-law (as well as her eldest son), take care of household chores (according to the rules of the *ie* under the authority of her mother-in-law), and bear at least one male child (i.e., the heir). If she was married to an eldest son of the house, she was obligated to look after her elderly parents-in-law. Further, as a mother, she was responsible for raising her children wisely, preparing her eldest son for the role of household head, and nurturing her daughters to become good wives and mothers.[12] These were the norms and common family practices throughout the first half of the twentieth century – during which the boom cohort parents spent their childhoods. Additionally, the *ie* and *ryōsai kenbo* ideologies were heavily promulgated through education curriculums and war propaganda during this time period.[13] Thus, parents of the boom cohort not only grew up in the *ie* system but were bombarded by the idea of its appropriateness through schooling and propaganda.

This dominant ideology related to marriage and family was, however, radically altered due to the post-World War II U.S. Occupational Reform. With the two major goals of democratizing and demilitarizing Japan, the U.S. Occupational Force identified the *ie* ideology and related practices as undemocratic, and worked to dismantle the *ie* system.[14] The Civil Code was revised to define marriage as a union of two consenting (heterosexual) adults, to eliminate the authority bestowed on heads of household, and to make other aspects of family relationships (such as inheritance and divorce rights) equal by gender and age. The constitution was also rewritten to include gender equality in the political, economic, and social realms.[15] These changes were not ushered in merely through the rewriting of laws and the constitution, but also via cultural means. Movies, music, fashion, and other cultural media from the U.S. were introduced to Japan in order to "democratize" male–female relationships.[16] American G.I.s, who publically displayed affection toward wives and Japanese women they dated, also made an impression on the views of young Japanese. A historian, McLelland, discusses how romance-based marriage as well as romantic gestures (such as kissing and holding arms and hands) came to be equated with democracy, civilization, and modernity during this war-torn time in Japan.

Most boom cohort parents married in the late 1950s or 1960s – after the Occupation Period – yet their marriages seem heavily influenced by wartime family ideologies and practices.[17] On the other hand, marriages of the recession cohort's parents, most of whom married in the 1970s or early 1980s, seem to reflect the impact of the Occupational democratization of love and marriage, despite the fact that they probably grew up in patriarchal households. Japanese family sociologist Ochiai points out that the 1970s was the era of "New Family," in which friend-like marital relations (*tomodachi kekkon*) were idealized.[18] The recession cohort's parents' marriages are indeed characterized by companionship, friendship, and romantic expression between partners.[19] The fact that two of my recession cohort interviewees experienced their parents' divorce – while no parents of the boom cohort divorced despite the coldness of marriages – may reflect this cultural shift to the idea that love and happiness are the foundations of marriage. But this cultural shift, clearly observed in the 1970s, hardly touched the marriages of the wartime generation.

These details suggest that, although childhood experiences have profound impacts on individuals' views and attitudes toward marriage, these impacts are mediated by the social and cultural context of the time period in which individuals spend their young adulthoods. Remember that the mother of Yoko (of the recession cohort) deliberately refrained from fighting with her husband in the presence of her children because she had witnessed bad fights between her parents during her childhood. Yoko's father was portrayed as somewhat authoritarian but lenient about his wife having free time. Yoko observed her parents to be very close, and happy in marriage. Judging by her mother's words, it is clear that Yoko's mother's (and probably father's) childhood was not free from the influences of the wartime family system. But her parents' marriage reflects adoption of the "New Family" culture that was popular during their young adulthood. On the other hand, many boom cohort mothers did not shield their daughters from fights, complaints, and absence of emotional closeness in their marriages. These mothers were probably resentful of their authoritarian husbands (and thus fought), as they too experienced the postwar democratization. But their husbands held on to positions of dominance, defined as proper in war time. The "New Family" culture of the 1970s hardly affected the dynamics of marital relationships of this generation.

Since the 1970s, romance-based marriage became increasingly desired and eventually mainstream among the younger generations (as mentioned in the previous chapter).[20] In this changing cultural context, it is understandable that my boom cohort interviewees expressed strong resentment towards, and disapproval of, their parents' outdated, patriarchal marriages. The fact that many of these women, in their adolescence, wondered why their mothers would not divorce when their marriages were apparently loveless, cold, and/or abusive suggests that the idea that marriage should be based on love was internalized strongly among these women. Some of the boom cohort women wished to marry but expressed their wishes in rather ambivalent ways. The negative marriage model had impacts on their views. Also, not a small number of boom cohort interviewees were distant from their mothers. They lost respect for their mothers because, for reasons interviewees were unable to understand, their mothers remained in undesirable marriages.

It is helpful to apply life course theory here. According to this theory, an individual's life course is shaped by *linked lives* and *period and cohort effects*.[21] *Linked lives* refers to the way people's lives are closely connected, for instance though family. *Period effects* are the impacts of characteristics of the specific time period individuals lived through. This means that people who lived in the same time period (and in the same geographical location, as well as the same social locations such as age, gender, race and ethnicity, and socioeconomic class) tend to follow similar life courses. When society is undergoing rapid change, similarities in life courses among members of the same birth cohort – people who were born in the same time period – and *differences between* different birth cohorts are sharp. Hence, cohort membership also affects life course (summarized in the concept, *cohort effects*). Life course theory predicts the sharp contrast I discovered in the (perceived) quality of marriage between the two parental cohorts: the wartime cohort (i.e., boom cohort's parents) and postwar democratization cohort (i.e., recession cohort's parents). In turn, through lives linked via family, the images of marriage held by daughters of these two cohorts contrasted sharply. It is thus no surprise that many boom cohort women put off thinking seriously about marriage when they were given new opportunities during the economic boom (as discussed in Chapter 2).

Along these lines, parents' marriages influenced women's general views towards marriage, and their life paths. But I observed that peer marriages also had strong impacts on women, and that this also differed by cohort. Next, I present the cohort contrast in how single women viewed peer marriages.

Cohort contrast in peer marriage

Boom cohort: "invisibility" of peer marriages

In asking what single interviewees thought of their married friends' marriages, Natsumi (43 years old) raised an interesting point:

> I don't know their husbands' faces, well, I don't know their husbands, you know? So I can't see their relationships. I'm not saying they're having bad relationships. I just can't see how my friends are doing in their marriages.

Natsumi seems to be saying that, since single women do not see their married friends with their husbands, these marriages are effectively invisible. Boom cohort women could not judge the character of their friends' married lives, not even whether or not these marriages were happy. This is partly due to the gendered social lives of the Japanese. Males and females tend to socialize separately, and this applies to married couples. Husbands spend time with their own friends, and so do wives.[22] Because of this, single women of this cohort got to see their married female friends only in the absence of their husbands, making these marriages invisible. Both single and married interviewees of this cohort confirmed that this was the most typical way for them to socialize with friends.

Another reason for the lack of opportunity to observe peer marriage was that friends often grew apart after marriage. All interviewees said they rarely met with friends whose marital status was different from their own (i.e., the married meet with married friends, and the unmarried with unmarried friends). Women of both marital statuses cited incompatibility in time schedules and interests as reasons that friendships grew apart. Married women could not make themselves available at night when single women were off work, and vice versa. Also, women of different statuses did not enjoy each other's company because their interests differed. Married women were frustrated about not being able to talk about children and family with single friends, whereas single women complained about "dull" talks about "kids and stuff" with married friends.

When boom cohort women did have a chance to get together with their married friends, they typically heard only negative stories about marriage. For instance:

Author: What do you think about your friends' marriages?
Tomomi (39 years old, never married): Huh? By seeing their marriages? [pause] I've never thought much about them. Well, I'm happy for them. [pause] There're some friends I feel sorry for.
Author: Because?
Tomomi: Well, for instance, she doesn't agree with her husband on the education of their children, and they have big fights. Also, when the mother is scolding [their child], her husband says something to undermine what she said. Another one has a mean mother-in-law.
Author: Do your married friends complain a lot?
Tomomi: Well, ah, they're busy, and. When they're really stressed, we'd get together, and they'd tell me a lot. In humorous ways, though.
Author: Do you hear stories about them being happy?
Tomomi: Every one of them wanted to marry so badly. And yet they tell me I shouldn't get married. I tell them, I haven't done it [married] yet [so don't tell me such a thing]. But everybody says I don't need to [marry].

Such negative talk was common, probably for different reasons. Some married women were indeed unhappy and frustrated in their marriages, so that was all they could talk about (see below for their accounts). Married women also rarely had the chance to gather with friends, and thus saw such meetings as opportunities to let off steam. Common complaints can foster in-group camaraderie; married women may feel closer to each other by complaining about their husbands and in-laws. In the Japanese context, it is also likely that women were discouraged from talking about positive aspects of their marriages due to the virtue of humility. Culturally, the Japanese are expected to refrain from complimenting their immediate family members.[23] It is not uncommon to hear them say degrading things about their own family members (e.g., "my stupid son" – even when the son is adored).

One of the married interviewees, Chie (45 years old), agreed with my observation that married women tend not to talk about happy aspects of their marriages with friends. Although she admitted there had been some major bumps in the road during her 21 years of marriage, she was happy with it in recent years. Chie now liked to tell others how wonderful her husband was, but when she did, they teased her as if she was a newlywed in the honeymoon phase, subtly suggesting that her behavior was immature or socially inappropriate. In response, she stopped expressing these positive evaluations. To share my personal observation, when I complimented my close friend's husband for being friendly, she immediately responded with negative comments (e.g., "He is full of problems.") In Japan, it would be inappropriate for my friend to reply, "Thank you, he is wonderful," even if she sincerely felt so. It is thus difficult to decipher the true meanings of negative comments regarding family members, and single women may accurately or inaccurately interpret their friends' marriages as unhappy.

Additionally, limited close contact with married friends itself shaped single women's impressions of peer marriage, leading them to view these marriages as "restrictive." All interviewees of this cohort – both unmarried and married – concluded the advantage of singlehood to be "freedom/autonomy (*jiyū*)," suggesting a lack of such freedom as the disadvantage of marriage.

Another characteristic of peer marriage pointed out by one single interviewee, Teruko (41 years old), was the loss or absence of romantic relations. She considered such absence typical of Japan and compared it to her observations of married couples in Paris, where she spent a year in her early thirties:

> Teruko: They [married couples in Paris] maintain such a [romantic] relationship forever. Even when they have kids, they leave kids behind and spend time [as a couple]. I'd like [to marry] a man who thinks in that way. But the Japanese are always going out as a family or just watching kids.
> *Author: Do you mean Japanese couples become just "dad and mom (papa mama)?"*
> Teruko: That's right! I don't want that.
> *Author: How about your married friends? Do they seem happy?*
> Teruko: I guess...
> *Author: Are there couples that remain romantic?*
> Teruko: No, there aren't any couples like that. For one of my friends [who is a designer], her husband is also a designer and they work together. So they're not just "dad and mom." ... For the rest [of my friends], husbands work hard and have money, and wives are alone at home. I don't want to be like them. I feel sorry for them.

It is of course unlikely that all married couples in Paris were happily married and romantically involved. But Teruko's reaction indicates how unusual it is for married couples in Japan to relate to each other in romantic ways – at least in public. It is, however, interesting that, as presented earlier, the generation above the boom cohort – the recession cohort's parents' generation – was observed to be emotionally close by their daughters. Though a detailed analysis of the nature of boom cohort marriage is beyond the scope of my research, the question of the degree to which such marriages were influenced by parents' marriage models is an interesting one.

Thus, to single interviewees of the boom cohort, peer marriages were largely invisible, and the limited glimpse available left only negative impressions:

COHORT CONTRAST IN IMPACTS OF LINKED LIVES

"unhappy," "restrictive," and "unromantic" were common descriptors. Because marriage was not the focus of my research and I included married interviewees only for the purpose of comparison, my data on boom cohort marriage are limited. Still, stories shared by eight married interviewees of this cohort tend to confirm observations made by single interviewees. Out of eight married interviewees of the boom cohort, only Chie (45 years old) and Nozomi (40 years old) described their marriages positively. As mentioned above, Chie admitted hardships and unhappiness experienced during 20-plus years of marriage, but felt content in recent years to the extent that she wanted to "boast" about it. At her beautiful house, Nozomi – a stay-at-home mother of an elementary school aged son – appeared genuinely happy and in love with her husband, though she referred to him as "*papa* (daddy)." She told me with a smile, "I shouldn't complain at all. He [her husband] gives me all I want." Her husband worked in the public sector and came home much earlier than his private sector counterparts. He drove to work, so rarely went out to drink after work. She described her husband as understanding and highly involved in raising their six year-old son. She expressed gratitude for his abilities as a provider, reflected in the construction of their new house in Tokyo.

Both Chie and Nozomi, however, limited their social activities. They felt hesitant or inappropriate about going out on their own during times their husbands were not at work, such as evenings and weekends:

> Even before I had my child, I was still conscious of time, knowing *papa* was waiting at home.... Even when he said I could go out, knowing he was waiting at home, I felt, oh, "I probably shouldn't go home late, it's probably bad," and worried about time. I didn't worry about time at all [when I was single], so that was really nice.

Nozomi felt she needed to be home when her husband was home, even though her husband approved of her going out. This is quite like this cohort's parents' marriages, in which husbands overtly or tacitly demanded that wives stay home and cater to them, but these women *felt* bad about not being at home. This was the case for other married interviewees as well. The belief in physically being there for the family, which Long[24] discussed as one of the distinct characteristics of married women's expected role in Japan, was strongly internalized and often embraced by boom cohort women, as I discuss more in the next chapter. In any case, this belief apparently restricted married women's social activities, which fed into single women's perceptions of peer marriage as "restrictive."

In response to my questions regarding their own marriages, the remaining six married boom cohort interviewees brought up only complaints. Granted, they may have refrained from boasting about their marriages' happy aspects due to cultural expectations. But I observed these women's expressions of frustration, anger, sadness, etc., to reflect genuine unhappiness in their marriages.

Eri (46 years old)'s husband had been living separately from her and their three children for several years due to his job transfer, and visited the family once a month or less. This type of job transfer, called *tanshin funin* (single-posting), is a common practice for large Japanese corporations, and thus separate living itself would not indicate marital discordance. Eri, however, said she would have been divorced long ago if they did not have children. After the long years of taking a full-time housewife role, she was working at her mother's law office part-time and studying to become a certified accountant. She insinuated she would divorce her husband after landing a full-time job. Tamami (45 years old) was working full-time and raising two children – one in high school and another in preschool. In reference to her own marriage, all she talked about was her frustration with her husband caused by his low level participation in domestic chores and childcare. She said she was too occupied with daily needs (i.e., work and childcare) to think about the quality of their relationship as a couple.

The accounts of three women – Mari (38 years old), Sonoko (45 years old), and Harumi (39 years old) – show concretely the emotional distance between couples. For instance, Mari said:

> My husband lets me do anything, so. [pause] Well, I have no complaints now. [pause] Well, it doesn't need to be my husband. I may have been just okay with any man as long as he doesn't complain. I may not love him [my husband] or anything like that. [laugh] I can do anything I like. I do sewing, I'm involved in kids' extracurricular activities (*sākuru*), I'm doing PTA, . . . as long as I take care of our home, he would say I can do anything, so. . . . We don't cling to each other. We're like, each of us does whatever we like to do. . . . For example, he has many days off during the "Golden Week" [referring to the weeks of vacation typically taken by corporate workers at the end of April and in May] but kids are in school. We're two of us, but we do things separately [laugh], and that doesn't bother me. So it's easy. Well, as a married couple, it may not be good, but. [laugh]

Mari said she was on the verge of divorce when her children were babies because her husband was hardly ever at home (due to his work). Her parents lived far away so she received no help raising children, causing her great stress. But by the time of the interview, she seemed resigned. She coped with a loveless marriage by shifting her focus to activities centered on her children.

Sonoko (45 years old) and her husband, who had been married for over 20 years, seemed equally distant from each other. Their children were teenagers and no longer interested in hanging out with their parents, so they ceased even to be "just dad and mom":

> Sonoko: Recently, he's kinda changed about how he spends weekends. He goes out on his own. He's into his own hobby, and that's not fair. He's

COHORT CONTRAST IN IMPACTS OF LINKED LIVES

into amateur radio operating [this couple met through an amateur radio club]. Also, once, what was that, something to do with his work, he went to college and took some seminars. He gets together with people from those seminars. With all these things, he's not around much on weekends. Also, he started doing PTA at school. [laugh]

Author: Your daughter's [school]?

Sonoko: Yeah. And he'd go, "I have a meeting today, and after the meeting we're having a party [konshinkai].

Author: I've never heard of fathers doing PTA. Is it common now?

Sonoko: No, he's the only guy and others are all mothers. I got so mad the other day. He went there on our anniversary. Would anyone do that? I understand about going to the meeting, but not the party afterward! He asked, "it's this [anniversary] day, but is it okay that I go?" I was like, "What!?" [laugh]

She did not strike me as unhappy about the lack of love between the two of them. Her husband prioritizing the PTA meeting over their anniversary seemed strange – was he cheating on her? – yet Sonoko did not seem concerned about this possible scenario. Her main complaint was that her husband started a life on his own once their children came to require little family time, and he was enjoying his hobbies while she was unable to. She complained that she had to work part-time at a book store to supplement the household income, which required working one weekend day. She wished they could afford for her to be a full-time housewife so that she could enjoy her favorite pastimes – baking and gardening. Sonoko was not bothered by the lack of romance in her marriage – a state of affairs Teruko would "feel sorry for" – as if that was a taken-for-granted reality.

On the other hand, for Harumi (39 years old), who had been married for eight years and was a full-time housewife with a six-year-old daughter, the absence of romance and sex was the main concern:

Harumi: I want him to pay attention to the family more. Spend more time, too. Also, we [pause] are no longer a couple. I hate it. We're not a couple, physically and emotionally. I'm lonely and bored. He comes home, eats dinner, and goes to sleep. That's all. I feel, that's not what I expected. I'm really lonely. He has no time [for me]. I have a lot of time. It's disappointing. [watering in eyes] ... We have no conversation. Even when I talk to him, it doesn't become a conversation. He just says, "I see."

Author: How do you spend weekends?

Harumi: We try to go out as a family, but he says he has to work, so he works one day of the two [Saturday or Sunday]. He's facing a computer screen and working. One day is a family service day, and another day is a work day. He does it [family service] for our kid.

Author: Not as a husband?

Harumi: Not as a husband.... I want him to listen to me, but maybe I already gave up on it. It's been years. Sometimes I get really depressed, but he's busy, and he won't change even if I tell him, so recently I think I just have to give up. So, maybe I should change my focus to work or hobbies, something different. Then I could change my pace. I'd start focusing on something else, and could forget about all that unhappiness...

Author: What do you think the disadvantage of marriage is?

Harumi: Monotony (*manneri*). Monotony is the disadvantage. [pause] But young married couples [these days]. They look like friends. I envy them.

Harumi also received little respect from her husband.

Harumi: He always talks down to me. I think he's like he's always right. But he says that's not true. He's giving me advice because I'm so ignorant about the world. I tell him I don't need advice. [soft laugh] I get mad and we start fighting, then he goes, "Okay, *mama* [referring to her] just doesn't listen," and the end of story.... To me, it's not a mutual talk. It's preaching.

Author: So do you feel you're not his equal?

Harumi: I feel that way a lot. He's right about everything. Even interiors of our house [which was remodeled recently]. When I said I wanted to do it this way, he said, "That's wrong. You don't understand. You totally lack a sense of this." And that was it. [soft laugh] So he really makes all the decisions and is stubborn about that. He says this, and it has to be this.... You see that plant over there [pointing to a large potted green plant]? That's what he picked. And that and that [framed photographs on the wall], too. He picked the wall color, too.

Author: How about sharing of housework? Does he do any? Like taking out the garbage?

Harumi: Never. If I'm sleeping, well, I'm usually sleeping when he comes home late [from work]. He wouldn't like to heat up dinner [she made] in the microwave. He hates to do it, so when he guesses I may be asleep, he eats out. He does nothing around the house.

I observed Harumi to be a kind-hearted woman. She went through the trouble of securing two interviewees for me, and even offered her home as the site for all three interviews (including hers). Her house was newly remodeled, quite large compared to the Japanese standard, clean, neatly organized, open and bright. She was petite and baby-faced with big round eyes, like some characters in Japanese comics and animation – the kind of look people would invariably describe as "cute (*kawaii*)" in Japan. In speaking of boredom, she said she thought of taking a part-time job, but her husband opposed that because "he thinks I can't handle it." He was controlling – reminiscent of the head of household from the wartime *ie* ideology – and decisively viewing his wife to be inferior to him.

COHORT CONTRAST IN IMPACTS OF LINKED LIVES

For another married interviewee, Fujiko (38 years old, with two young children), romance was alive but the source of frustration was the absence of her husband and lack of external support that might have allowed her and her husband to spend time as a couple (as well as her to spend time for herself):

Author: Do you have any complaints about your marriage?
Fujiko: Well, of course, I want him [her husband] to come home early and take care of the kids. Please give me time for myself. I also want time for the two of us.
Author: Wouldn't your parents or in-laws watch your kids once in a while [for you two to go out]?
Fujiko: Never. Well, uh, our parents don't understand that kind of thing. Even when my friend's husband passed away and we were going to his funeral, I told them [my parents] I had no choice but to leave the kids with them, and they took them [kids] because it was a funeral, but still said "Why don't you take them with you?" So it just doesn't work. They say they adore the kids to death, but I have to be there, too.

Although this is a personal anecdote, I can relate my experience as a boom cohort woman and wife in an international marriage to Fujiko's story. In Japan, older generations such as the boom cohort's parents typically do not understand that married couples want to spend time as a couple away from children. About a month after our baby daughter was born in the U.S., my (American) father in-law came to visit us from another state and offered to watch her for a couple of hours so that my husband and I could go out for dinner. I still remember the culture shock I experienced at that moment, and how "cool" it was for my father in-law to offer such an amazing thing. In contrast, I once overheard my (Japanese) mother telling her sister in-law about her bewilderment with my brother and his wife, who dropped off their young child at her place so they could have a date. "Looks like these days young people want to do that kind of thing," she said, puzzled. I grew up overhearing my mother, aunts, and their female friends quote, and laugh at, a humorous saying: "the best husband is healthy and out of the home (*teishu genkide rusuga ii*)." For them, husbands were there to provide economically, not to provide emotional support or love, and were often a nuisance or burden to take care of. Thus, wives were happiest when their husbands were not around. Why would one need, let alone want, to spend time with her husband alone? Fujiko was thus frustrated at not being able to secure "time for the two of us," partly because her parents and in-laws did not understand this need and want. On the other hand, Mari seemed to see, or resigned herself to see, marriage in the same manner as older generations of women. At the time of the interview she was settled with her husband's absence – possibly seeing it as a blessing – and done complaining.

Though eight interviewees' accounts are hardly generalizable, their descriptions of married life do match impressions single interviewees had of friends' marriages. Some women were happily married, but good, working marriage models were largely invisible to boom cohort singles.

Recession cohort: visibility of happily married couples

On the other hand, most never-married interviewees of the recession cohort knew someone of their age in a happy marriage. They described their friends' or older siblings' marriages as "very nice," "very happy," etc. Some of my interviewees were "envious" of their friends' or sisters' marriages, and said that was precisely the reason they wanted to marry. For instance, 27-year-old Junko "used to plan to remain single" but because she saw "two people being so happy, I envy them so much," she now wanted to marry one day. For Yayoi (31 years old), her friends' marriages were life transforming because she used to be negative about marriage due to her mother's divorce:

> Yayoi: I used to think it [marriage] isn't a very nice thing, watching my mother. But by watching my friends, I go to visit friends who've been married for some years, and [I realized that] there are many different forms of marriage, different from the impression I had. What they showed me was all positive. Marriage is not a loss, but a gain. I got very good impressions so now I really want to marry.
> *Author: Would you describe what you find positive?*
> Yayoi: Ah, well, the couples are very close. That's one. Also, each of them individually, [for instance] a husband has his own hobby and a wife is going to college. They complement each other's minuses and plusses, getting close yet keeping some space for each other, and create a comfortable, warm space together. This woke me up.
> *Author: Do you see positives among married friends with kids, too?*
> Yayoi: Oh, yes, I do. My friend became very mature. I see her new side as a mother. She had many miscarriages and had a hard time in the past, and she had a baby after going through all that, so everybody is so happy. Her husband used to do whatever he liked to do, but after having their baby, he's being a good father. Well, I was shown very good sides [of marriage] from couples with and without kids, since around last year. There are bad marriages, too, but marriage is not as bad as I used to think.
> *Author: Are there any married ones in your drama club?*
> Yayoi: Yes, one, just recently married. I know her husband well. Yeah. This couple is doing music together, forming a unit, and really nice.

Despite her parents' bad marriage, Yayoi learned from her friends that marital relationships vary and can be "a gain." She saw that her female friends created good marriages by maintaining autonomy from, having fun together with, or getting help from, their husbands.

Notice that Yayoi met her married friends with their husbands and had opportunities to observe these marriages with her own eyes. This was also the case for Shoko (29 years old) and some other single women of this cohort. This visibility of recession cohort marriages contrasted with peer marriages of boom cohort women, and proved important to interviewees' understanding of what marriage could entail:

> *Author: What do you think about your married friends?*
> Shoko: My married friends? Uh, I envy about half and don't like the other half.
> *Author: Would you describe the marriages you envy?*
> Shoko: Oh, they're my ideal. When I go visit them at their home, well, they're like, "Come over!" And their husbands come home, and go, "Why don't you stay overnight?" and their husbands become like my friends. And, they [my friends] stay home, so make everything homemade. They raise their kids well. They [married couples] are close and I've never seen them fight.... And, the bad marriages are, they're always fighting. In front of me, in front of their kids. Fighting over money problems. Why [do they do that]? That's not good for kids [fighting openly]. And towards their husbands, I feel, "Don't you have any pride? Why do you fight in front of your wife's friends?"

Naturally, not all peer marriages were ideal. But Yayoi and Shoko's accounts indicate that married peers' social lives were not as gendered as those described by the boom cohort, nor did these marriages lead to female friends losing touch with each other. Single women stayed in contact with married friends, and were welcomed by their husbands. By observing directly how their friends related to husbands, single women of the recession cohort could evaluate the quality of friends' marriages first hand. This contrasts with boom cohort single women, whose observations were limited to hearing what their married friends said. The visibility of various peer marriages allowed single women of the recession cohort to understand that marriages come in all shapes and sizes. Happiness in marriage, it seemed, was up to each couple/individual; marriage was neither a guarantee of happiness nor a doomed life of misery.

Accounts given by interviewees regarding their interpretation of what marriage entailed revealed other differences by cohort. Recession women saw romance in marriage as normative, as was the case in their parents' generation. Also, recession cohort marriage was sometimes viewed as less confining. For instance, Ryoko (26 years old, cohabiting) originally held an image of marriage as restrictive – just like that held by the boom cohort – but changed this view because of her friend's marriage:

> *Author: What do you think about your friends' marriages?*
> Ryoko: I think my friend who married first is quite free. Before then, I had an image that once you marry, you'd stay home. She became a housewife,... but she calls me, 'Let's get together.' I didn't know we could do that.

Author: Are all of your friends in happy marriages? Are there any marriages you don't like?
Ryoko: They are good, seem happy.
Author: Like, they're close?
Ryoko: Yes, very close. That friend has been with him [her husband] for a long time. They started dating in high school. They've always been close. They're still close.

It is important to point out that some descriptions of peer marriages by the recession cohort reflected the same problems observed in the boom cohort. These included fighting (as mentioned by Shoko, above), issues with in-laws, absence of husbands, loneliness, and loss of love:

Megumi (31 years old, never married): There are some marriages I don't envy. [They make me feel] Ah, that's the reality. [laugh]
Author: Can you describe those marriages?
Megumi: Well, what do I not like about them? Well, hmmmm, well, marriage is not just about two of them, but the family, relatives, uh, ... like hearing about mothers-in-law.... Also, husbands don't come home. Probably busy with work, but they [my friends] say they're lonely. Different from what I imagine as marriage life.... No longer loving, uh, kind of distant. When I see it, I feel, ah, this is the reality.... When I saw them at weddings, I felt envious. But there aren't very many married couples I envy.

Her words indicate that talking positively about one's own marriage violated a norm for this cohort as well. Further:

Mutsumi (32 years old, never married): You know, in Japan, there are more people who'd say they shouldn't have married, aren't there? There aren't many people who'd say they're glad they married, are there? It's embarrassing to say such a thing.
Author: Yeah, others might say, "what are you, newly-weds?"
Mutsumi: Yes, yes, yes, yes, yes! So I rarely hear [good things about marriage], so I hear only negative things, right? Even when I'm not thinking marriage is bad, maybe, unconsciously, I can't make one step towards marriage because of it.

Like Teruko (the boom cohort woman who had lived in Paris, mentioned earlier), Honoka knew couples that involved Westerners and compared Japanese married couples to them:

Honoka (32 years old, never married): Just the other day, I worked with a French top fashion model. She was with her husband and stayed here about a week. They had been married for 13 years or so, but they were so loving

COHORT CONTRAST IN IMPACTS OF LINKED LIVES

to each other. I envy them. After 13 years, they can be so loving to each other, like lovers who just started dating.
Author: Do you normally not see that kind of couple around?
Honoka: No, I don't. Well, the Japanese can't do that, maybe? I don't see any ...
Author: What do you think about your married friends?
Honoka: Well, uh, they don't say good things about each other, you know? My friends who married *gaijin* (a Westerner), or foreign couples, praise each other. Like, "She's a real good cook," "He caught this fish." We don't do that in Japan, do we? We don't respect each other. Saying something like "my stupid wife (*gusai*) is ..." I don't like that. Mostly that kind of marriage [is around me]. They have to say negative things. I feel, then, why did you marry? I really don't like that.
Author: Do you have female friends who married male foreigners?
Honoka: [Nodding] The other way round, too. But they always surprise me by praising each other a lot. Even about tiny little things. [laugh]
Author: Do your Japanese friends who married foreigners praise, too?
Honoka: They praise their partner.... They say to each other, "Wow, how did you do this? Amazing!" I really envy that kind of relationship.

Another similarity to the boom cohort was that some single women of the recession cohort held the image that marriage was restrictive. Based on her observations of friends' marriages, Yuri (32 years old), who was informally engaged at the time of interview, said:

Author: What is the disadvantage of marriage?
Yuri: Well, I'd have less time for myself. I feel that's what'd happen. Also. [short pause] I'd have less freedom (*jiyū*) in many things. Time is one. I wouldn't be able to do anything without getting my husband's permission. I don't know, but I have that kind of image.
Author: Do you feel you'd have to ask your current fiancé for permission?
Yuri: I don't really think so, but by looking at my [married] friends, many can't go out or buy things without getting their husbands' permission.
Author: Are many of your friends married?
Yuri: Most of them are married.
Author: Do they have kids?
Yuri: Yes.
Author: Do you observe them not having much freedom?
Yuri: I haven't gotten together with my friends for a while.

As our conversation continued, she began to point out other negative aspects of her friends' marriages:

Author: Do you have some image about marriage from seeing or hearing about your friends' marriages?

COHORT CONTRAST IN IMPACTS OF LINKED LIVES

Yuri: Well, I hate to say this now that I'm going to marry, but, unfortunately, I have no friends who say, "I'm glad I got married!" It makes me think, what is marriage? Why do we have to marry? Why do they [marriages] turn cold? But, well. [short pause] I don't know what'd happen to me, but I still want to marry. Probably, I think there are probably many things I'd never know unless I do. I don't understand what goes wrong in reality.

Author: Are you saying you have no idea why your friends are unhappy in marriage?

Yuri: Yes. They all married men they loved. Yet one of my friends says she doesn't want him [her husband] around (*uzai*). Another says she doesn't want him to come home. I don't know why. They say love and marriage are two different things, you know?... After all, it's living with a total stranger. It's different from dating. They have to be together all the time. Then you'd start seeing parts that were different from what you saw before, and question what you know about him. Is that what it is?

Author: Hmmm. Do you think their marriages may be restrictive?

Yuri: Yes. Some men have to control, have to know everything about what their wife is doing. I couldn't tell that when I saw them at the weddings.

Some women were affected by boom cohort marriages. For instance, Hitomi, never married, whose parents were divorced, was 36 years old – close to the boom cohort in age. She identified herself as part of the recession ("post-bubble") cohort because she was deprived of good employment opportunities, but her friends were older and belonged to the boom cohort:

Author: What do you think about your friends' marriages?

Hitomi: From my married friends, I hear a lot of stories that their marriages are not going very well. There are many stories that make me wonder what the point of marriage is, staying together that way. My father has four siblings and all their marriages failed. I saw only that kind of case so rather than longing for marriage, I probably thought marriage is trouble ever since I was a kid.... No friends have told me I should marry, or that marriage is nice. ... Most of my married friends don't have kids. So they can get together with me like single women...

Author: Aren't their marriages nice?

Hitomi: Not at all. There's one who had a baby recently that seems happy. She and her husband used to say they didn't like kids, but they totally changed after having a baby. They look really happy. They're building a warm family. When I went to visit them, they looked so happy.... But the rest are, like they have no sexual relationships, they're not interested in each other, and they're having affairs. I feel, since they have no kids, why wouldn't they divorce? But they're doing it [i.e., having affairs] without it [divorce].... They say, marriage is not just about two of them. They involve parents, too, so it's hard [to divorce]. I think that's just an excuse, but it's not my business.

COHORT CONTRAST IN IMPACTS OF LINKED LIVES

Divorces of people they knew also colored recession cohort women's images of marriage. Shizuka (34 years old, never married)'s older sister recently confided to her the possibility of divorce. Kei (35 years old, never married) had several divorced friends and co-workers:

> There are many kinds of women in my company now. There are married women with children, and also *shinguru mazā* ("single mother" literally but referring only to "divorced mothers" in Japan). By hearing their stories, I'm not sure if marriage is hard or nice. When I hear conversations among married women, I feel envious. But when I hear divorced mothers telling about their hard lives, I feel I don't want such a life.... Some of my friends are divorced, too. They say things like, "My husband was stolen and now I'm alone. What am I going to do from now on?" They say it's best not to have a divorce, so I shouldn't get married. It's better to stay away [from marriage] to avoid all the complications.... There are more friends who divorced because of husbands' affairs [*onna mondai*] than because of money problems. They said they had no idea that they [their ex-husbands] were cheating on them. Why would they do that after going through all the trouble to get married?

Emotional distance, infidelity, and lack of freedom – commonly observed in boom cohort marriages – seemed not unusual themes in recession cohort marriages either, at least as related in these accounts. How do these interpretations compare to actual marriages of this cohort? Unfortunately, I interviewed only four married women of the recession cohort, and three of them had been married less than one year (with no children). This being the case, the marriage experiences reported were not as rich as those I heard from the boom cohort. Keeping this limitation in mind, I will convey that these four marriages showed both variety and some commonalities.

It is perhaps not a surprise that the three newlyweds – Akane (34 years old), Kyoko (29 years old) and Kimi (25 years old) – said they were happy in their marriages. Kyoko and Kimi were clearly in love with their husbands, who seemed to treat them with respect. Kimi was enjoying her homemaking role, thinking that she would eventually quit her job in order to focus on this role. Kyoko, on the other hand, expected to continue working as her husband's income was small. Though Akane said she was happy in marriage, she expressed her discontent with her husband's reduced amount of conversation. She felt her husband stopped giving her attention soon after they got married. It sounded like he viewed marriage as a functional unit rather than a romantic involvement.

Rika (29 years old) had a "shotgun wedding" (*dekichatta kekkon*) four years ago, and had one child. Her marriage sounded cold. Her husband spent little time with her, except on weekends when they went out with their four-year-old daughter. She envied her single friends who were active in dating relationships, and focused on parenting as a source of happiness. She wished she had not become pregnant – the only reason she saw for being married already – and was afraid that she and her husband might end up divorced in the near future.

Thus, recession cohort marriages were not uniform. But, though they were distinguishable from those of the boom cohort, comments made by married interviewees indicated that absent husbands and the restrictive nature of marriage may be traits common to both cohorts. Kyoko's husband worked incredibly long hours, as well as on weekends, and she and her husband "hardly spend time together." They were communicating through e-mail and phone calls. Kimi's husband also regularly worked overtime. Akane and Kimi were hesitant about going out with friends in the evenings, even though their husbands never said they had to be home at night. They felt they should not go out because they took the wife's domestic role seriously and did "not want to neglect my duty."

Despite these common, persistent problems in the two cohorts' marriages, overall, positive peer marriages were much more visible to single women of the recession cohort than to those of the boom cohort, and therefore, the recession cohort had a better chance of repairing negative images of marriage painted by parents. On the other hand, the boom cohort, much more likely to grow up with parents in poor quality marriages, had too limited glimpses of peer marriages to change the negative image created by parents.

Chapter summary and discussion

In this chapter, I described the sharp cohort contrast in interviewees' perceptions of parents' and peer marriages, as well as problems commonly observed in both cohorts' marriages. The two cohorts' accounts indicate that the prewar patriarchal family, the *ie* system, left lingering effects on the boom cohort's parents' marriages, whereas the recession cohort's parents were more liberated from the old system.

Could women's views of marriage shaped by their parents and peers have had impacts on their life courses, such as to push their life paths in the direction of singlehood? According to the life course theory, it is highly likely that they did. Individuals are interdependent, and therefore, interactions via *linked lives* affect one's life course. This is not to say that women who grew up viewing their parents' marriages negatively will automatically refuse to marry. People's attitudes do not always predict their behaviors, and individuals change their views according to their circumstances.[25] For instance, in my study, some women (e.g., Eri and Harumi) married even though they thought they never would, specifically because of their parents. Thus, negative views shaped by parents' bad marriages were insufficient in and of themselves to cause permanent singlehood in these cases. Yet the presence and absence of positive marriage models have tremendous influence on women's views, and, in turn, their level of enthusiasm towards marriage. Those who held on to a negative outlook on marriage may not have actively pursued marital partners if they were able to stay economically self-sufficient through employment, had limited chances to encounter romantic partners, etc. I illustrate this with six cases of never-married interviewees.

I mentioned the case of Yayoi (31 years old), who initially considered marriage a "bad thing" due to her parents' divorce, but completely changed her outlook because of her friends' good marriages. Natsumi (43 years old), who did not seriously consider marriage in the past because of her parents' conflict-ridden marriage, also altered her ideas:

> It's a little embarrassing, but it was only recently that I started thinking I really want to marry. [laugh] I began to think it [my parents' marriage] is nice since I got more mature and my parents got more mature and we came to be more thoughtful towards each other. I go visit my parents. We just eat meals together.... My father and mother were not really in a good relationship. But now, it [their marriage]'s still continuing, and ah, that's what family is about. Very close families talk about anything, don't they? We aren't like that. We aren't like that, but we eat meals together happily, and ah, this is what the family is about. I finally began to understand that recently. I feel relieved when I go to my parents' home. It's really nice. We don't do anything special, but it's really relaxing, and I feel, ah, family is good.... Rather than a lover, I want to have a man as a marital partner. I started thinking in this way just recently. I finally understood the meaning of marriage, I think.

She observed a change in the quality of her parents' marriage in recent years and this, together with her own "maturity," changed her view. She was the interviewee who made an observant comment about the invisibility of peer marriages. This insight was probably due to her recent association with a couple who had "married in old age (*bankon*)." The couple socialized with friends together, including Natsumi:

> The relationship of this couple is really nice. They become friends with other married couples.... Then I started thinking, ah, that's how marriage is. Ah, it's fun to live as a single woman, but living with someone else may be fun in different ways. So I started thinking in more positive ways.

Likewise, Izumi (46 years old), who was so appalled by her parents' marriage, in which her mother "worked around her husband's schedule," envied her younger brother's marriage, which she perceived to be very happy:

> His wife is a housewife.... She quit [her job] with her first pregnancy. She's good at cooking. She bakes cakes nicely. I visit them once in a while, and she's a good hostess and enjoys parenting. They look so happy.... Looks

hard, too. Three kids, and all kinds of mess, but.... My brother never liked kids, yet he's being a real good father, and that's so interesting. He takes days off to attend kids' school events and stuff.

If a happy marriage model was available when these interviewees were younger, would their life paths have been different? Yayoi and Natsumi dramatically changed their orientations, going from a pejorative evaluation of marriage to wanting it eagerly. Izumi was more passive in expressing her desire to marry, saying she had little confidence in adjusting her life to another person at her age, and yet she concluded, "Don't get me wrong. I still want to marry." Both Izumi and Natsumi put marriage on the backburner when they were in their twenties, enjoying their stimulating jobs (as discussed in Chapter 2). Their negative sentiments regarding marriage may have contributed to this neglect of relationships, and the same may apply to many other boom cohort women.

I also saw the profound impacts of negative parental models, combined with lack of exposure to good peer marriages, in two recession cohort, never-married women – Hitomi (36 years old) and Kei (35 years old). As quoted earlier, Hitomi's parents went through a bad divorce, and Kei's parents' relationship was filled with conflict and insults. Their mothers' hardships seemed deeply ingrained in these two interviewees' minds. Further, unlike Yayoi or Natsumi, Hitomi and Kei were distressed by terrible peer marriages. Both still expressed that they wished to marry, but rather ambivalently. Hitomi said, "I want to marry one day, but somewhere back in my mind, I feel marriage is the end of the world." Kei said she wanted "to marry while I'm in my thirties ... but I feel marriage is trouble (*mendō*)." These two were close in age to the boom cohort, and their social lives were highly gendered. In other words, peer marriages were invisible to them, just like for many boom cohort women. It is interesting to compare these two women to Shoko (29 years old), who was "envious of" her parents' marriage, calling it her "ideal." She did evaluate half of her friends' marriages as "bad," showing disgust towards them, and yet she was very eager to marry, talking about marriage only in positive terms. (She was, however, working in a female-dominated occupation – elderly care service – and frustrated with the "wishy-washy" men she dated, and thus unable to marry for other reasons.) Perhaps those from backgrounds with positive parental models of marriage were more able to recognize variation in marriage and not allow negative peer models to override their desire to marry.

In the previous two chapters, I showed that the marriage age norm declined, employment opportunities for women changed, opportunities for romantic encounters were limited, and desirable men were scarce, and argued that these factors led many women to remain single. I also observed that many of my single interviewees were passive when it came to searching for potential marital partners. This passivity is likely to do with, at least partially and for some women, negative images of marriage held by women. These life experiences and attitudes apply particularly to boom cohort women, though some recession cohort women like Hitomi and Kei were in the same boat.

If this is indeed the case, it means that the patriarchal ideology and family practices of the era of imperial expansion, officially dismantled in the late 1940s, are still affecting contemporary Japanese society – from individual life circumstances/paths to major demographic shifts (i.e., increased singlehood, declined birth rates, and aging population). Additionally, under this ideology, women were treated as mere "birth-giving machines," and this way of viewing women still persists in in Japan – as reflected in the Tokyo Assembly heckling incident and stigmatizing label placed upon single women (discussed in the first chapter). As I discuss more in Chapter 6, in the recent past some elected officials have derived their prejudice against single women from this view,[26] and the Japanese government's approach to the "population problem" is strikingly similar to that of the era of the Pacific War (1932–1945).[27] Should the government wish to resolve the population issues, eradication of outdated sexist ideology must come first.

I would also like to reiterate the toll of wartime patriarchy on family relationships. We have seen the disheartening, detrimental impact of the *ie* ideology on boom cohort women's relationships with their mothers. Despite the fact that both boom cohort women and their mothers stand as victims of gender injustice, these two generations of women failed to bond together and fight against the common enemy (i.e., patriarchy or patriarchal husbands/fathers). Instead, many daughters felt angry with their mothers and maintained distant relationships. In addition to being sad, this state of affairs shows how complex the impact of gender injustice can be.

I have wondered how the remnant of *ie* practices affected men, especially of the boom cohort. Though some men may feel resentful towards the model of marriage displayed by their parents, others may take male authority for granted or claim it to be proper. My married interviewees' accounts imply both may apply. The existence of the latter type of man must have further contributed to the scarcity of good men available to boom cohort women.

In the present and the two previous chapters, my interviewees' views toward gender roles were mentioned numerous times. The next chapter focuses on these views, describing cohort difference and similarity in detail and discussing the relevance of these to increased singlehood in Japan.

Notes

1 See Elder 1994, 1995.
2 Midori's father died when she was an infant. Her mother never remarried, so she had no memory of her parents' marriage. Saori and Seiko lost their mothers at elementary school age and their fathers did not remarry. Their memories of parents' marriages were too limited for analysis. Honoka's mother was never married. Because questions regarding parents' marriages were originally prepared as a tool to assess interviewees' conceptions of gender roles, these questions were omitted for my second interviewee,

Tsuneko. Her stories and answers to other questions provided enough data on her ideas about gender roles. I also wanted to be sensitive to the fact that she had recently lost her mother, and so avoided asking questions regarding her parents.

3 A typical *kaminari oyaji* (thunder father). White (2002) refers to this type of father, common in prewar Japan.

4 Tomomi was referring to *Terauchi Kantarō ikka* (The Family of Kantaro Terauchi), which was based on Kuniko Mukoda's book of the same title and broadcast on television in 1974. The Terauchi family is a three-generation family residing in *shitamachi* (lit. low city), Tokyo. The program is centered around 50-year-old, stubborn, short-tempered, authoritarian father Kantaro, portrayed by Asei Kobayashi. It is said that Mukoda wrote this book in memory of her own father who died in 1969. The drama was extremely popular, recording high viewing rates.

5 In Hochschild's study (1989) on dual income married couples with children in the U.S., some husbands refused to take up domestic tasks precisely because their wives' earnings were higher than theirs. Hochschild argues that wives' higher earnings threatened masculine identity – though some other men welcomed their wives' higher earnings – and therefore, these men deliberately made their wives take the traditional women's role, and maintained the gender hierarchy within marriage.

6 Divorce rates in Japan in the 1960s and 1970s were low, at fewer than 1.0 divorces per 1,000 women. The rates began to increase in the late 1980s, and the most notable increase was observed starting in the 1990s, and reaching over 2.0 divorces per 1,000 women in the 2000s (MHLW 2009). Still, Japan's divorce rates have been lower than those found among developed nations, and below OECD averages (OECD 2015f).

7 Japan was involved in a series of wars from the late nineteenth century to the end of World War II: the Sino-Japanese War (1894–1895), the Russo-Japanese War (1904–1905), World War I (1914–1918), and the Pacific War (1931–1945).

8 Jansen 2000, S. Kaneko 2011, Molony 2005, Oki 1987.

9 Tokugawa period (1603–1868) refers to the time period when shoguns of the Tokugawa family ruled the country.

10 According to S. Kaneko (2011), letters to the editors in magazines for married women, popularly circulated in the early to mid 1900s, indicate that more and more women wished to marry someone they had feelings for, instead of their marriages being arranged by a third party.

11 The content of letters studied in S. Kaneko (2011) reflect married women's circumstances. Many were unable to divorce and endured problems such as husbands' extramarital affairs, violence, abuse, alcoholism, gambling habits, and poverty due to husbands' selfish expenditures.

12 See, for instance, Uno (2005) for the historical development of *ryōsai kenbo* ideology. Additionally, in the first half of the twentieth century when Japan engaged in many wars, raising boys to be good soldiers was included as part of proper socialization of children (Mason 2011).

13 Koyama 1991; Nagahara 1982; Uno 2005.

14 Tokuhiro 2010; White 2002.

15 Article 14 of the new Constitution of Japan (promulgated in 1947) states "All the people are equal under the law and there shall be no discrimination in political, economic or social relations because of race, creed, sex, social status or family origin."

16 McLelland 2010.

17 Salamon (1975) observed that male dominance (*teishu kanpaku*) was mainstream for marriages in the 1960s.

18 Ochiai 2004/2006.

19 Kurotani (2014) explains that parents of the boom cohort (which she calls the "bubble generation") belong to *yakeato sedai* (the "burnt ruins" generation) that

COHORT CONTRAST IN IMPACTS OF LINKED LIVES

spent their childhoods during or in the aftermath of World War II, which was characterized by loss and poverty. Members of this generation experienced improvement of living standards in their adulthoods as Japan's economy grew.

20 Tokuhiro 2010.

21 Elder 1994, 1995.

22 Lebra 1984.

23 Condon 1984; Lebra 1976; Nakane 1970.

24 Long 1996.

25 Kroska and Elman (2009) found that, in the U.S., married women changed their ideas of gender roles depending on their employment status. For instance, women who once opposed maternal employment changed their views to accept it when their life circumstances did not allow them to stay at home.

26 In 2003, then Prime Minister Yoshihiro Mori opined that single, childless women are unworthy of social security benefits because they do not contribute to society by bearing children (AtWiki 2009; BBC News 2004). In 2007, at a local political meeting in Matsue, Shimane Prefecture, the then Health Minister Hakuo Yanagisawa said "(the government) can only ask for (women) to do their best (to have more babies) since the number of birth-giving machines (*umu kikai*) is fixed" (McCurry 2007, *The Japan Times* 2007).

27 There is a spooky parallel between the government's actions of the 1940s and its current approach. According to K. Kondo (1995), Miyake (1991), and Ogino (2006), Japan's fertility rate peaked in 1920 and started to decline due to delayed marriage and wider use of birth control and abortion. In response, the government established a research center for population problems (*Jinkō mondai kenkyūjo*) in 1938, and, based on its recommendation, issued the outline for establishing population growth policy (*jinkō seisaku kakuritsu yōkō*) in 1942. The main objective of this policy was to increase the total population of Japan to 100 million (from about 70 million in the mid 1930s) by increasing birth rates and decreasing mortality rates. For the former, it stipulated that the age at marriage should be reduced by three years (to 21 for women) and that married couples should have five children on average. The policy recommended eleven means to accomplish these goals, which included establishment of matchmaking facilities, restriction of employment of females over 20 years old, tax breaks for married couples and parents, family allowances, preferential treatment of large families, and a ban on birth control. Additionally, birth control for healthy individuals was prohibited by the National Eugenics Law (*kokumin yūsei hō*) in 1941.

5

WOMEN'S IDEAS ABOUT GENDER ROLES

Persistence of traditional gender ideology

> When I was a kid, my mother was always home, and there were some occasions she wasn't there ... just once or twice a year ... when I was in elementary school.... I felt the house was dark and empty, and felt lonely.... So up until kids grow to be adolescents ... it'd be better to stay home.
>
> (Natsumi, never married, 43 years old, freelance illustrator)

> Looking around, there are many working women. And ... there aren't any [men] of my age who are really wealthy, are there? Then, it's better for women to think of a real career.... But ... women can take care of the home better than men. I think we [men and women] are just born that way. So, [for women] working is just assisting, ... men's jobs are more important.
>
> (Megumi, never married, 31 years old, clerical worker)

Japan went through rapid Westernization and industrialization in the latter half of the nineteenth century, became involved in a series of wars, starting with the Sino-Japanese War (1894–1895), and militarily expanded its territory into the Asian continent until the end of World War II. During this time, along with the *ie* (house) system discussed in the previous chapter, government officials considered a consistent gender policy necessary to modernization and the strengthening of the nation. Heavily influenced by the ideology of the *samurai* (warrior) class of the feudal period, and by the Western gender ideology of the Victorian era, the so-called *ryōsai kenbo* (good wife, wise mother) ideology was made official.

This ideology defined the proper role for women as married, managing the household well, and wisely raising children (i.e., the next generation of citizens).[1] That is, married women were to focus on domestic tasks and not take wage employment.[2] Men, on the other hand, were expected to contribute to the nation as workers and soldiers. In other words, what we call today "traditional gender roles" – in which husbands take the breadwinning role and wives take care of home and children – were made the ideal and associated with social responsibilities. It was not just public education, government policies and laws,

106

and the mass media that instilled this ideology into the public mind. Interestingly, feminists and female private school educators supported the ideology, too, partly because education for girls[3] was deemed important to them becoming "wise" mothers.[4] During this time, many married women were actually working on farms and/or in wage employment.[5] But women's ability to manage the home and raise children came to be equated ideologically with true womanhood in the first half of the twentieth century.

I discussed in the previous chapter how the U.S.-driven reforms of the Occupational Period (1945–1952) included the reform of gender (and family) relations. Gender equality was guaranteed in the new constitution drafted by the U.S. Occupational Force. After the Occupation, however, the Japanese government set economic recovery and growth as the nation's primary goal, and renewed propagation of a gendered division of labor.[6] It was said to be patriotic for women to devote themselves to domestic tasks so that men could focus on employment, i.e., economic production.

Subsequently, in the 1960s and 1970s, Japan's economy grew. Many young people migrated to urban regions (including Tokyo) for employment, married, and settled down in cities and suburbs. Good income and living away from families of origin obliged or allowed many young married couples to pursue the socially idealized gender role allocation. The housewife role was elevated to a "profession," as the popularized term *sengyō shufu* (professional housewife) implied. The profession of housewife symbolized middle-class status, and Japan's baby boomers (born in the late 1940s) stayed home as housewives in greater numbers than in previous cohorts.[7]

As discussed in Chapters 2 and 3, this gender role ideology was embedded in the Japanese employment practice of hiring young, unmarried women for easy-to-replace clerical positions only. Women were expected to resign from work upon marriage and become housewives. In the 1970s, the service industry expanded and the need for part-time workers grew. Many married mothers with school-age or grown children took part-time jobs to earn supplementary income for their households. This reentry into the labor force as part-time workers after rearing preschool children became the normative employment pattern for married women.[8]

As we have seen, however, employment opportunities for young women grew during the economic boom in the 1980s, and many women were encouraged to remain in their jobs. One might imagine that young people living through the era of this booming economy would change their views to accept wives' and mothers' employment. My interview research, somewhat contrary to this expectation, indicates that this change in views was ongoing but very slow. The boom cohort held onto the traditional ideology, and, while the recession cohort's views suggest some change, this cohort, too, was still largely traditional. This chapter presents the two cohorts' ideas of gender roles and discusses how this persistence of *ryōsai kenbo*-like gender ideology relates to the phenomenon of increased singlehood.

Questions I asked to measure women's ideas and beliefs

Because ideas and beliefs held by individuals are often taken for granted, people are not necessarily conscious of their own conceptions regarding proper roles of women and men. In order to extract such taken-for-granted ideas and beliefs, I prepared and asked various questions that might lead my interviewees to reveal their ideas and beliefs, rather than asking directly what they think are proper roles for men and women. Two of the several questions that yielded the most about women's conceptions of gender roles were "What type of life course do you think, or did you think in the past, is ideal?" and "What life course do you expect to have in your real life?"

I formulated the questions regarding ideal and expected life courses using survey questions from the National Fertility Surveys (NFS)[9] as a template. I categorized possible life courses into nine: (1) housewife, (2) *saishūshoku* (returning to work after staying home for a while), (3) *ryōritsu* (literally "doing both," meaning having it all – employment, marriage, and family), (4) DINKS ("Double Income No Kids," or *ryōritsu* without children), (5) singlehood, (6) breadwinning with a househusband, (7) unwed motherhood, (8) lifetime cohabitation, and (9) others.[10] I made a small card for each of these life courses, and explained to my interviewees each as I showed these cards. I asked interviewees to choose which was closest to the ideal they held currently, and to the ideal they had held in the past. For single women, I also asked which they thought would be their most likely life course. I asked about reasons for choices, as well as for reasons they did *not* choose other courses.

In addition to the above questions, I asked several more questions with regard to their conceptions of gender roles: Was your mother employed when you were growing up? What did/do you think of her employment status? What do/did you think of your parents' marriage (if they are/were married)? What do you think of your friends' marriages or your own marriage?[11] For each answer, I asked follow-up questions to elicit elaboration (e.g., Why do you think so? How do you feel about it?). I also encouraged my interviewees to bring up any subject they wanted to discuss.

In general, members of the boom cohort held very similar and traditional ideas regardless of background, such as marital status, education, and mother's employment status, whereas the recession cohort was more diverse. Below, I first present views held by boom cohort interviewees, and then those of the recession cohort.

Boom cohort

Housewife as a normative life course

As young women, a majority of never-married interviewees of the boom cohort expected to take the normative female life course: to quit jobs upon marriage

WOMEN'S IDEAS ABOUT GENDER ROLES

(or a few years after marriage), become housewives, and either continue to stay home or return to work as part-time workers. Some attributed this expectation to their mothers' homemaker status (e.g., "Probably because I grew up watching my mother being a housewife"), but interviewees who had employed mothers, such as Rumi (45 years old, never married), also expected to become housewives. Despite her mother's employment, Rumi:

> assumed that I'd marry around 25, and then [become] a housewife.... So, back then, I thought I'd be a housewife primarily, perhaps working part-time occasionally at most.... I just assumed that [becoming a housewife] is the life for women who graduated from two-year college [like me] and wanted to marry.

Rumi, now a vice president of a small company, was one of the interviewees who come across as career-oriented. But in her young days, she "just assumed" she would become a housewife. In conformity to the marriage age norm discussed in Chapter 2, women of the boom cohort took it for granted that they would follow the "normal" life path expected of women.

Such an expectation may have been particularly strong for the boom cohort, considering that these women were born between 1962 and 1972, and thus most of their childhoods was spent during the time when women's "professional housewife (*sengyō shufu*)" role came to be normalized and idealized most intensely. According to Japanese family sociologist Emiko Ochiai,[12] during this time "housewife" was a synonym for womanhood. Most mothers of the interviewees were indeed housewives, and interviewees "didn't think much of" their mother's stay-at-home status, but reported it "was just a very normal thing back then." Employed mothers were invisible to some. As Natsumi (43 years old, never married) put it, "Were there working mothers at all in our time?" On the other hand, for several interviewees (Eri, Chie, Rumi, Harumi, and Mari) who grew up with an employed mother, their mothers' employment was *not* something they took for granted. These women's views toward their mothers' employment varied from "I didn't think much of it" to "I hated that my mother worked," but during their childhoods all were aware that a stay-home mother was mainstream or "normal."

This normalcy of the homemaker role, however, did not necessarily connect with strong desires among interviewees to become housewives. For many, it was only a "vaguely" held expectation or assumption. For instance, Seiko (43 years old, never married) said, "I just had this vague expectation. It was just the way things were." Interestingly, about half of never-married interviewees grew skeptical towards the supposed happy life of housewives after they entered the labor market and/or experienced a slice of life as housewives. Rumi's story illustrates such a shift in views towards this role. As we saw in Chapter 2, Rumi first worked as an OL at an insurance company but "changed" after she obtained a more stimulating job at a small advertising company. Her mother was employed for most of Rumi's childhood, but in spite of this financial standing never considered a divorce from her husband, about whom she complained frequently (as discussed in Chapter 4).

> Rumi: When I was totally intending to marry [in my early twenties], the only model of marriage was my [ten years older] sister. She was the model I could use to see what would happen once I married. My sister also used to work for an insurance company [as an OL], married her co-worker, around 25, then became a housewife and did nothing. I thought that's what marriage was about. An easy life. [laugh] ...
>
> Once, my sister's husband got a disease called malignant lymphoma. ... That was when I was working freelance [before taking a job at the advertising company], and her kids were still little – one first grader and two in preschool – and her husband got hospitalized. So I stayed in their house for about three months, dropping off and picking up kids and cooking. At that time, well, I sent out kids, right? Then, watched *waido shō* (daytime TV shows), read newspapers, had tea, and I thought, 'What's this? This is the life of a housewife? Wow, it's easy. I love it!' [laugh]
>
> But that didn't last even a month. I got so bored. Ugh, I can't stand this! I started looking for part-time work when I was still helping them. I found some jobs like archaeological excavation [laugh], and begged my sister, "You have to let me do this just a few days a week!" At that time, I started thinking I wouldn't be able to be a housewife. It was fun for a month or so. It was easy. I could read books. But then I couldn't stand it. Got so bored. Because all I did was pick up kids, cook, watch TV. It was a very unproductive life with no goal.
>
> *Author: How about perfecting housework to a professional level?*
> Rumi: No one will recognize it. No earnings, either.

At the interview, as presented in Chapter 2, Rumi first reasoned that her job changed her view and led to a break-up with the man with whom she had considered marriage concretely. When she told me this story, she had a lot to explain, which gave me the impression that she had prepared her answers in advance to the anticipated interview question, "Why are you single?" (which I never asked in my research). Questions about preferred life courses were not something she expected. By sharing her views and experiences, she revealed that her skepticism toward the life of housewife was developing before she took her life-changing job. While Rumi had a specific experience that changed her views towards the lives of housewives, other single interviewees did not recall such an event, even though they likewise described the lives of housewives as "boring," "unrewarding," and "living in a small world."

Among my married interviewees, on the other hand, all but one took the role of full-time housewife. Tamami (45 years old) was the exception, and continued to work after marriage and childbearing. Some of these housewife interviewees later worked part-time, but none returned to full-time work. Five out of seven of the married, stay-at-home interviewees were content with their lives as housewives. They preferred to live "dependent on my husband's earnings" and enjoyed doing work around the house. Some of them had no interest in jobs and career and viewed the position of housewife as a privilege because "I can make a living without earning" income. Others worked part-time, or planned to return to part-time work, after they judged their children to be old enough.

Two other housewife interviewees Eri and Fujiko were not happy with the role of housewife. Eri (46 years old) was married for 21 years, had three children (in high school and college), and spent most of her married life as a housewife. At the time of the interview, she was working for her mother's law office part-time and studying to be a certified accountant. She was a graduate of a prestigious four-year college but worked full-time for only two years before marriage. When I asked how she felt about being a housewife, she answered:

> Eri: It was booooring (*tsumannaaaai*)! I'd do laundry, then clean the house, then wait until my husband came home.... Looking back, I could have thrown myself into cooking, but that's not really my thing. [laugh] ...
> I had no idea how restrictive marriage was going to be. So restrictive.
> *Author: What restricted you?*
> Eri: Well, because I have kids. So, I couldn't do anything.
> *Author: Then, that's kids that restricted you, not marriage, isn't it?*
> Eri: If I didn't have kids, I would have had a divorce. [laugh] No way!
> [laugh] I can't imagine being married without kids!

Fujiko, 38 years old, was a full-time housewife with two young children (two and six years old). Whereas Eri's story implies her marital relationship was not very good, Fujiko had a good relationship with her husband (as mentioned in Chapter 4). She was, however, discontented with her lack of personhood and the smallness of her social circle:

> Fujiko: I have a self, only as a mother and a wife. I don't have my individuality. There's no one who knows me as the me that is not a mother or wife.... I think I'm living in a very small world...
> *Author: How many friends do you hang out with regularly?*
> Fujiko: How many friends? Well, I can probably list them all immediately. It's that small a world. [laugh with a tone of self-pity]

The stories of Eri, Fujiko, and Rumi – and descriptions of the housewife role by some of the single interviewees – are reminiscent of the (white, middle-class) housewives in suburban America depicted by Betty Friedan in *The Feminine Mystique*.[13] Whereas some women are happy with the homemaker role, others are not content with a life focusing on domestic tasks and suffering from social isolation and a lack of sense of personhood. Yet among these discontented women I did not observe any sign of critical views that might challenge existing, traditional gender ideology – the seeds of a collective feminist movement. Eri and Fujiko merely waited for different opportunities to come. Eri was studying to become an accountant, which she saw as an opportunity to be economically independent. She waited to do this until her last child entered high school. Fujiko was waiting for her children to grow older and hoping that her life would shift. Even single interviewees, who held doubts about the appeal of the housewife role, were not critical of the traditional gender ideology (as I discuss in the following section).

The only interviewee who, as a young woman, consciously resisted the traditional norm was Tamami, a 45-year-old married woman. She had worked as a social worker throughout her 20 years of marriage, raising two children (6 and 19 years old). When she was young and unmarried, she thought employment was a means of "self-actualization (*jiko jitsugen*)," and felt she "wanted to have a lot of 'drawers.' Even when I raise my kids, I wanted to have other drawers than ones for kids. I didn't want to be the kind of mother who can talk only about my kids." By "drawers" Tamami meant multiple dimensions or depth in her life, persona, skills, and so forth. In other words, she did not want to possess a "self, only as a wife and a mother" as Fujiko put it. But the "having it all (*ryōritsu*)" lifestyle Tamami pursued, or the maternal employment, did not win approval among most interviewees of this cohort, as I discuss next.

Resistance to ryōritsu *(having-it-all): impossible, too hard, or bad for children*

As discussed in Chapter 2, this cohort of unmarried women enjoyed new opportunities due to the economic boom. Having given consideration to these newly gained employment opportunities, which allowed more fulfilling jobs and income to spend on luxuries and leisure, some single women were unsure about the role of housewife. One would expect that these women might have changed their views and advocated maternal employment and egalitarian gender roles. Yet among women of this cohort, maternal employment – the lifestyle of *ryōritsu*, or having-it-all – was viewed almost unvaryingly in a negative or disapproving light. Many women thought maternal employment was "bad for children," attributing this opinion to their experiences growing up with stay-at-home mothers. For instance, below is the conversation I had with Natsumi, a 43-year-old, successful freelance illustrator, who was never married:

Author: What was your ideal life course when you were younger?
Natsumi: You mean when I was in my twenties?
Author: [nodding]
Natsumi: Well, I thought I'd marry, and I thought I'd marry and work. Ah, after having babies, I'd take some break, and then go back to work, something like that.

112

Author: Like taking a parental leave for a year?
Natsumi: Hmmm, no, like two or three years. I think when kids are little, they're adorable. So one year is, uh, I'm not very *kiyō* [meaning "skilled," in this case implying the skill to balance the demands of many tasks], so, well, maybe I need to spend more time [at home]. Ah, but when I was a kid, my mother was always home, and there were some occasions she wasn't there, you know? It was just once or twice a year. But when I was in elementary school, [when she wasn't home when I came home] I felt the house was dark and empty, and felt lonely, so I think kids would feel that way. I thought that wouldn't be good for kids (*kawaisō*). So up until kids grow to be adolescents, when they feel annoyed about mom staying home, it'd be better to stay home. I knew someone of my generation who kept working. I didn't want that. I thought doing housewife would be interesting.

Some women derived the idea of "bad for children" from their experiences with an employed mother as well. Chie, 45 years old, married with two children, had a mother who worked for life because "my father's earnings were too small, I think" and she was very sorry for her mother (as discussed in Chapter 4). As an elementary-school-aged child, Chie never told her mother how lonely she felt about her mother's absence, but she was "so envious of other kids" who had stay-at-home mothers. She recalled the days she stood at a bus stop in the evenings, waiting for her mother's return. Chie was "thankful for my husband's income" that allowed her to stay home for her two children when they were young. For her, mothers should work *only* when the family has financial need:

Chie: I didn't want to work when my kids were small. Even now, when I see [other] mothers putting kids in daycare, looking so unhappy, I wish they didn't need to put kids [in daycare]. They might want to take care of kids by themselves until they enter elementary school.
Author: What do you mean by "they didn't need to put kids?" When do they need to do so? Is it when they need money?
Chie: Yes, yes. Only for financial reasons. I don't see any other reason [for mothers] to work, leaving young kids behind. If women want careers, ah, ... [they should remain single]. To me, no matter what, kids can't be replaced with jobs.

Thus, for Chie, children need their mothers, and motherhood is incompatible with a career. When she was young, her dream was to become a school teacher – a dream left unfulfilled because she failed the entrance examination for a public college with a strong education program. Chie ended up taking a job at a corporation as an OL at age 18 and married her senior worker at age 24 (as explained in Chapter 3). But back when she dreamed about a teaching career, she "just expected to stay single."

Another married woman who grew up with an employed mother, Mari (38 years old), also expressed resentment towards employed mothers:

> Rather than working, leaving preschoolers and second-graders behind, I think these people shouldn't make two, three kids. Shouldn't they work without having kids? I can't help thinking so.

Mari was a nurse before she married at age 27, and her hospital had an environment that welcomed nurses to continue working after marriage and childbearing. She said she could easily return to work if she chose to do so, but had no such intention until her children grew up.

Thus Mari, along with several other boom cohort women, fell into a category of women who firmly believed maternal employment to be detrimental to children. Employment due to financial need was tolerated as a sorry situation, but mothers working for the sake of wanting to work were viewed as selfish or irresponsible.

Other women did not see maternal employment as bad for children, but neither did they judge the "having it all" life course as ideal, perceiving the task of balancing motherhood and employment to be "too hard" or "impossible":

> Hmmmm, probably, vaguely, I wanted to return to work [after child-rearing]. [But] I thought this [pointing to a card for "*ryōritsu* (having it all)"] is hard.... I knew some people doing it, but I'd have no energy to do that.
>
> (Izumi, 46 years old, never married)

> I probably wanted to have it all. But I believed that was impossible. Raising kids is, watching my older sister and others, I thought it's impossible to work and to take care of kids.... I thought I'd have kids one day, and once a kid is born, I thought I couldn't do both.
>
> (Rumi, 45 years old, never married)

> Ah, for me, [uncomfortable laugh], for me, it's impossible to work when my kids are little. [uncomfortable laugh] Well, others, ah, there are women who work, leaving kids in daycare, but, for me, kids, ah, it's impossible to raise little kids and work and do housework. It's too much, and I knew it was impossible for me.
>
> (Nozomi, 40 years old, married with one child)

> Fujiko (38 years old, married with two children): Well, of course, it'd be the best if I ... can be married, keep working, and raise kids. But ... I doubt I could do it without getting stressed. So it [having-it-all] is my ideal, but realistically, ah, how can I explain?!
> *Author: What part do you feel you can't do?*

WOMEN'S IDEAS ABOUT GENDER ROLES

Fujiko: What is it, well, ah, you know, I can't be laid back. I'd have to be disciplined, making schedules. If I don't plan things well, it'd be impossible – that's what I think. And then, would I be able to live every day, smiling [if I do it all]? I have no confidence. Hurry, hurry!, you know? Ah, I couldn't do that.

Author: Now that you have kids, do you still feel that way?

Fujiko: I do.

Author: But did you think so before you had kids?

Fujiko: Yes.

Clearly, these women assumed that the "having-it-all" lifestyle meant that wives/mothers would take full responsibility for housework and child rearing, on top of the employment responsibilities. They seemed not only to expect the nonparticipation of men in domestic tasks, but to view the roles of good wife and mother as demanding on their own. In their view, mothers were responsible not only for raising their children, but were ideally:

> supposed to get up earlier than anybody else in the morning, cook breakfast, always smiling, pay careful attention to nutrition, too, perfect housework, maintain good relationships with others in the community, and more.
>
> (Fujiko, 38 years old, married)

In her study of Japanese women's nurturing role, Long[14] observed the following three social expectations to be distinct to Japan (in comparison to what she is accustomed to as an American): (1) to be physically there to provide care and comfort for family members, (2) to mediate and maintain peace in the household by avoiding confrontation, not complaining, and repressing negative emotions, and (3) to prioritize the nurturing role over all other activities (such as employment and leisure). Long and other scholars[15] also pointed out that women's self-sacrifice for family members is not only expected as proper, but characterized as fulfilling for women. As the term *sengyō shufu* (professional housewife) implies, housewife is akin to a professional occupation that requires expert knowledge and skills. The role is also analogous to that of the salaryman (i.e., the hegemonic masculinity), expected to devote time and energy to his occupation to an extent that could be described as self-sacrificial. If women believe that this is the role they must fulfill, it is no mystery that they find balancing it with employment to be "hard" or "impossible." It is interesting (and disappointing to me) that none of these women expressed the opinion that such demands on women might be unfair, or insisted that husbands needed to share household tasks. Their words reflected the ubiquity of a culturally prescribed "good woman's role" among this cohort.

Most interviewees of this cohort did not know employed mothers personally, and they seemed to be assessing the impossibility and undesirability of mothers' employment based on the demanding nature of women's role in marriage. Some, however, witnessed the hardship of the having-it-all lifestyle hands on. As mentioned in Chapter 4, Eri's mother was a lawyer, earning more than her father. Growing up, her mother constantly preached to her about the importance of women's economic independence in marriage. Yet Eri's observations of her mother strongly deterred her from maternal employment. As a sort of compromise, when she was younger, Eri planned to become economically independent, but remain single. As it turned out, she married her boyfriend from college and conceived their first child in the first year of marriage. She chose to become a housewife. To my question of why she did not follow the path her mother encouraged, she answered:

> Because she had a real hard life! I saw her having such hardships. Growing up, I always had to be conscious of not causing any trouble to my mother. She had to take care of her husband and ... kids.... She did all the housework.... My father never helped around the house.... No way [I'd have such a life]!

For single women of this cohort, who had some personal contact with employed mothers, this limited glimpse seemed only to help shape negative perceptions:

> Most of my married friends became housewives. There are only a few who have both career and marriage. Really a few. And, those friends are, how shall I put it, they talk about their husband and money and, well, I don't really understand what they're talking about. Really stressed and I don't get along with them. On the other hand, my housewife friends have a totally different life, but ah, it's still interesting [to talk with them]. Ah, now kids' schools are that way, ah, things have changed, like that. Hearing their stories, I learn some new things. But those who are working [and married] are so edgy.... I hate to get together with them.
>
> (Tsuneko, 43 years old, never married)

The unique circumstance of Tamami (45 years old), the only "having-it-all" interviewee, is informative here. As with the cases just discussed, her story indicated a lack of social acceptance. Although Tamami was raised by a stay-at-home mother, she never liked to have her mother around the house when she was growing up. She married at age 25, had her first child at 26, and had another child 13 years later, at age 39. She had worked as a social worker, putting both of her children in daycare. When she worked while her first baby was in daycare in the late 1980s and early 1990s, Tamami faced difficulties and criticism:

> *Author: So, what did people say about you putting your child in daycare?*

Tamami: It was mostly a bit older women (who said things). You know, what's that called? You have to raise kids at home until they turn three.[16] I was told that constantly.
Author: From a bit older women only?
Tamami: Yes.
Author: How about women of the same age group?
Tamami: Same age group ... back then, they probably didn't say anything. [trying to recall her memories]
Author: I remember my friend [who also had it all in the same era] complained that people assumed her husband didn't earn enough.
Tamami: Ah, ah, ah, yes! They said that kind of thing. "Problem with money?" "So sorry (*kawaisō*) for your kid." I was told this kind of thing very often.
Author: How did you feel about it?
Tamami: Well, whatever! [laugh] It's none of your business!... I think I was seen as an outlaw (*autorō*) by both housewives and unmarried women.
Author: One single interviewee said she can't get along with her ryōritsu friends because they're so edgy.
Tamami: [Bursts into laughter] We probably are!
Author: How was the daycare? I heard that many places didn't keep children past 5 o'clock back then.
Tamami: Yes, that was the case. It was called double daycare (*nijū hoiku*). When kids were very young, daycare didn't keep them until late. So my child went to a home with someone called a "daycare mom" (*hoiku mama san*). She kept him for a while, and I went to pick him up there. So it was hard, yeah.... The quality [of the daycare] was also not so good. Just keeping kids. And it had high turnover rates. Daycare workers were young and changing constantly.

Tamami said she had forgotten about these negative experiences for a long time. She had another child in daycare at the time of the interview and said she realized how much she took it for granted that daycare quality had improved and that "maternal employment became more common." She reacted with amusement to her memories of those bad old days. Her unique circumstance of having a young child in the 1980s and 1990s, and another in the 2000s, provided an interesting illustration of the changing of social climates surrounding employed mothers.

As expressed in Tamami's words, employed mothers were often viewed pejoratively by boom cohort women, who saw them as neglecting maternal duties, or pitied them for being in desperate financial need. The latter view is reflected in Sumire (45 years old, never married)'s comment:

Well, I think, really smart, really smart women are not working. That may be because they married rich men, but in any case, they're not working. The smarter they are, the less likely that they work. Maybe because they were smart, so they found good husbands. And women, who are ... not as smart, I don't know if their husbands should be blamed, but they don't have money, so they're working. It's a rude thing to say about working mothers, and maybe it's just women I see at my workplace, but ... I think the reason [married] women work is just for money.

Seiko (43 years old, never married) worked for an American firm as a certified public accountant (CPA), but was critical of the company's progressive policy that encouraged married women's employment:

Seiko: My company is saying "diversity" and trying to promote women. But I think they shouldn't do anything special for women.
Author: Are you saying that you're critical because your company promotes women who don't deserve to be promoted?
Seiko: No, that's not it. Women, uh, quit when they have a baby or that kind of thing. My company gives training [for women] to encourage them to stay. It's trying to help women.

Seiko was firmly against women continuing work after having a baby. Likewise, many women of this cohort, including those (like Seiko) in professional occupations, believed that good women should dedicate themselves to domestic tasks once they marry, and that the only valid reason for them to work is financial need. For this reason, Rumi (45 years old, never married), as a vice president, discouraged her able female subordinates from marrying:

I don't want good [female] employees to marry. I'm telling [employee X] not to marry but stay working. For other women, who don't have any special talents, I think they'd be happy if they married and quit and became housewives.

I asked if she said the same thing to talented male employees. She said she never even thought of it, and that she need not worry about it, since men have wives to take care of their homes. It was shocking to me that such conformity to traditional gender roles was so firmly assumed or taken for granted by exceptionally successful, professional women such as Rumi, Seiko, and others.[17]

Contradictory ideas

The findings presented above may portray these women as strong advocates of traditional gender ideology. However, views toward women's roles held by single women were not coherent; there were some ambiguous and contradictory elements. Take Rumi as an example. She originally had the traditional expectation to marry during *tekireiki* (the appropriate age of marriage for women) and become a housewife. But then she grew skeptical of the housewife role from

WOMEN'S IDEAS ABOUT GENDER ROLES

glimpsing life in her sister's home, and felt resentful of her boyfriend's expectation that she take the domestic role in their future marriage (mentioned in Chapter 2). She attributed the breakup to his traditional expectation. She resented this expectation, yet took it for granted, as reflected in her own use of discriminatory employment practices, discussed above; she even felt it proper. Additionally, she was repulsed by her parents' patriarchal marriage and disrespected her mother for lacking independence. Rumi's account, below, demonstrates this incoherent view towards roles of men and women:

> Rumi: [Growing up,] I really hated to be told things like, "You've got to do this because you're a girl," "Because you're a girl, you have to do the housework." I think that was because of my mother. I have an older brother. And when she needed help preparing dinner and stuff, she said, "Rumi, you're a girl, so you do it." And my brother didn't need to. We both had homework, you know? Why do I have to do it because I am a girl? I resisted it, and I never stood with her in our kitchen. [laugh] If she didn't say, "because you're a girl," but said, "let's make dinner," I'd probably have done it. But I felt I'd never do it. I felt "Why do you treat me differently from my brother?" ... I think men and women are the same.... When I visit my mother and eat with my sister and brother and their spouses, my brother just sits and eats. I help cleaning up. I work longer hours than he does. That's just wrong. I think that's wrong, but if my brother washes dishes with us, I may feel sorry (*kawaisō*) for him. When I hear men doing things around the house a lot, they do laundry every day, I feel sorry for them.
> *Author: Sorry? Or nasakenai (a feeling that the person is pathetic, in this context because he is not masculine)?*
> Rumi: Not *nasakenai*. Sorry. What is that, really? I can't explain, but if I hear that my brother is doing laundry at home, I'd feel sorry.

She felt it was wrong that her brother did not do house chores while she was expected to, and yet also felt it would be wrong for her brother to do them. Implicitly, she felt it was his wife's role to do dishes, laundry, and other house chores, and felt sorry for him when imagining this hypothetical loss of male privilege – even if it meant more work for women like herself.

Similar resentment was expressed by other single interviewees. They "hated it" when someone (such as their mother and men) "told me to help [around the house] because I'm a girl" or "girls should pretend to be stupid." But interestingly, such resentment was not necessarily a rejection of the traditional female (and male) role, as implied in Rumi's account as well as Sumire's (45 years old, never married):

> Sumire: Once I had a *miai* [a mediated meeting with a possible marital partner], and ... he [the man she met at the *miai*] said that kind of thing.

Author: What kind of thing?
Sumire: Something like, "If we get married, I'd want you to stay home." I was offended.
Author: Why were you offended?
Sumire: I think I felt I was told to stay still or something.

She was offended by the question he asked so she did not meet this man again. I asked if this meant that she wanted to continue working after marriage. She answered:

Sumire: Well, uh, maybe I'm contradicting myself, but, well, it's contradicting. I said I got offended when he told me to stay home ... but if some guy tells me I don't need to work [after we marry], I may just quit.
Author: So why did you get offended before?
Sumire: I don't know. Maybe because he said it first thing at our meeting? [laugh]

In fact, Sumire's ideal life course was to marry and become a housewife, working part-time, at most, after children grew up. As mentioned earlier, she held the prejudice that working mothers were not very smart. However, she had recently entertained the thought of the having-it-all lifestyle after witnessing her much younger co-worker continue to work after having a baby. The co-worker took advantage of newly established on-site daycare at the hospital where she worked as a pharmacist:

I saw my [much younger] co-worker had a baby and continued to work. That made me feel maybe I could do it, too, if I try. In the past, I thought it was absolutely impossible to do such a thing! In my hospital, she's still young, 25, she had a baby last year and returned to work recently. Leaving a one-year-old child in [daycare]. Our hospital built a daycare center last year. If she can do it, [I should be/have been able to do]. [laugh]

Similarly, Teruko (41 years old, never married), after studying in Paris in her thirties, changed her view:

In Japan, one works and the other raises kids. But when I went to Paris, women were working and raising kids. I was really shocked first, but then I thought that's so great.

Teruko and Sumire initially believed that maternal employment was impossible and bad for children, but came to see it as doable. In this manner, several single boom cohort interviewees went back and forth between rejection and acceptance of the traditional women's role, and held incoherent, contradictory ideas.

Men's role in marriage: traditional

When it came to men's roles, on the other hand, unmarried women of this cohort held expectations that were more solid and traditional. Boom cohort single interviewees expected their future husbands to have careers and take the breadwinning role. Stable employment in white-collar occupations – expected in the "hegemonic masculinity" of Japan (discussed in Chapter 3) – was important for most single interviewees. Some came to the view that "in recent years" farmers were acceptable as potential partners as long as they were independent and not poor. Blue-collar workers and men with casual work (*furītā*) were utterly rejected by single interviewees.

Men taking a full-time domestic role (i.e., househusband) were "out of the question" for *all* unmarried interviewees of this cohort, as well as for most married ones. It was not simply because they planned to depend on husbands economically; employment was the central component of their image of masculinity. Men who wished to stay home were thus considered "*nasakenai* (pathetic)" and/or "*otoko-rashikunai* (not masculine)" by boom cohort interviewees, regardless of marital status. For instance, Rumi and Seiko had careers with high earnings – enough to support a family, even in the expensive city of Tokyo. Rumi, in particular, loved her job at a small company, in which she was a vice president, and did not want to give up her job for marriage. I suggested that the solution for her situation could be to marry a man who is willing to stay at home. She looked surprised, agreed that it would solve her problem, but immediately rejected it because "I can't accept such a man." I asked why, and she first answered that she did "not have much respect for people who don't work." In response to this, I asked more questions:

> *Author: So do you mean you don't have much respect for housewives?*
> Rumi: Oh, no, that's fine for them. If they're happy with that, then I'm happy for them.
> *Author: How about men who would be happy with the househusband's role?*
> Rumi: When it comes to men, I'd feel, "What's wrong with you? You're a man! Where's your spine?"
> *Author: Even when a married couple is happy with that arrangement?*
> Rumi: Even when it's fine for them. I'd feel, "Are you sure that's okay with you?" Strange, I admit. But I'd think so, even when those people are happy with it.

In answering my question, she realized her own bias or double standard by gender. She looked very amused by her own prejudice, but admitted that she would not be able to change her view. "Men are not real men if they don't want to work," she said.

Two women were exceptions. They did not adhere strongly to a traditional conception of the male role. One was Tamami, the only having-it-all interviewee. She clearly stated that "there is no difference between men's and women's roles" and believed husbands and wives should share provider and domestic responsibilities. In reality, however, she was frustrated with her husband's smaller contribution to domestic chores. The other was Eri, whose mother was a lawyer. She was striving to achieve economic independence by becoming an accountant, and her husband wanted to stay home once she attained a breadwinning income. Her intentions were unclear, however. When I asked her what she thought of her husband's wants, Eri answered "I don't care what he does" with a grin, and, with a laugh, refused to elaborate further. She later insinuated the possibility of divorce. Thus, she did not clearly communicate to me her views towards men who wish to become househusbands. As described earlier, she was bored with the housewife role and did not like to cook. It seemed that married women who did not embrace homemaking role of a wife may have, due to their own experiences, been receptive to the idea of a househusband, while unmarried women maintained a more idealistic or theoretical take on role allocation in marriage.

Recession cohort

How do ideas about gender roles held by the recession cohort compare to those held by the boom cohort? Although certain aspects of traditional gender ideology linger among many women of the boom cohort, my recession cohort interviewees' ideas were more diverse, and women showed more flexibility in their views.

"Return to work after childrearing": the most chosen life course

Many women of the recession cohort chose "return to work (*saishūshoku*)" as an ideal/preferred life course. Like most boom cohort women, these women believed that it is better for mothers to stay home while they raise young children because:

> It's better for kids to be with their mothers when they are little.... I don't want to leave them [my kids] to other people when I'm at work.
>> (Ran, 29 years old, never married, medical researcher)

> I'd like to be with them [my kids] when they're little.... When I saw newborn babies left in daycare [referring to the daycare where she once worked as a nutritionist], I felt sad and painful (*setsunai*). [quiet laugh] Personally, I wish mothers stayed with them [kids] a bit longer.
>> (Ryoko, 26 years old, cohabiting, between jobs)

> I think it's better that one [her or her lesbian partner] stays home [for kids], because I grew up that way.
>> (Maya, 26 years old, cohabiting, between jobs)

WOMEN'S IDEAS ABOUT GENDER ROLES

I definitely want to raise my kids at home when they're little. I want to stay home until they finish preschool.... There's a coworker in my department who has a preschooler. She works full-time but she takes days off for her kid. That causes trouble to our company.... Another co-worker has a son going to middle school. She tried to work before, but up until the boy was a first or second grader, he ran a fever due just to a small change in environment. So she couldn't work full-time, she said. She started working after her kid was a third or fourth grader.

(Yoko, 36 years old, never married, section manager)

I don't think I can do both [family and work] because I'd worry about my kids during work and I'd think about work when I took care of my kids.

(Mutsumi, 32 years old, never married, temp worker)

Although they emphasized the importance of mothers' stay-at-home role during the time children are young, these women had *no* intention of living as housewives for life. They "would not marry a man who would demand I become a housewife." Yoko said, "It's probably impossible for me [to become a housewife]. I'm not the type to stay at home forever. I would be stressed." Although most of my recession cohort interviewees did not particularly enjoy their jobs, employment was considered important to these women for various reasons. For Yoko and Mutsumi mentioned above, and Yuri (32 years old, engaged), jobs were a means to be connected with the outside world (*shakai*) and/or earn some income. They had no preference in terms of the types of jobs they would take after childrearing. Yoko, a section manager of a mid sized hotel managing company, "would be happy to work as a grocery store cashier part-time" and Yuri preferred part-time work (of any type) to full-time employment. Mutsumi, on the other hand, wanted a full-time job, and Ran (29 years old, never married), who had a medical degree and had started a research position just a few months before the interview, hoped to return to the field of medicine after her childrearing years.

In contrast, Ryoko, a cohabiting 26 year old, saw the choice of part-time work after childrearing as a compromise:

Author: Do you want to return to work part-time or full-time?
Ryoko: Hmmm. Which is better? Part-time is better, maybe? But, well, I guess it's fine as long as I have an interesting part-time job.
Author: So, it depends on the kind of job?
Ryoko: I think so.
Author: Do you prefer part-time because you can have time with children?
Ryoko: It's easy to make time [for them]. Yes. Well, also because I'm not sure if I can do both [full-time work and childrearing]. [laugh] When I was working at the daycare, I was amazed by those mothers [who were doing both].

All of these women were in relationships, and were hoping to marry or had discussed marriage with their current partners.

Kyoko, an energetic, 29-year-old married woman, had been married for less than a year and was working full-time at the time of the interview. Like other women discussed here, her ideal was to return to work after childrearing because she wanted "to raise my kids on my own." But because her husband's income was small and she was good at her job, she thought of employment after childbearing flexibly:

> Kyoko: The ideal is this [pointing to a card for "return to work" (*saishūshoku*)]. I wish I could leave my job once [I have a child]. But our financial condition and also my position at work. I'm in a position to organize and lead others so I feel I shouldn't let them [company] down, so I want to do it all [work, marriage, and childrearing] if possible. I want to raise my kids on my own, but financially, our [combined] incomes are equivalent to one person's income, so it'd be hard to live unless we both work.
> *Author: Does your workplace allow you to return to work after a while?*
> Kyoko: Yes, they do. But I wonder who could fill the hole I'd leave. I think my company would be in trouble if I leave. I know it.
> *Author: Do you wish to stay in your job because you feel responsible, or for the sake of your own career? Or both?*
> Kyoko: Hmmmm, maybe both.
> *Author: But you can leave your company once [you have a child] and return, correct?*
> Kyoko: I think it's possible.
> *Author: Do you think you can return to that leadership position?*
> Kyoko: It's possible.
> *Author: So, you'd be worried about the company during the time you're gone?*
> Kyoko: Yes, that's right.
> *Author: What if there was no problem with your husband's income?*
> Kyoko: Then, return to work.
> *Author: What do you think of a life as a housewife?*
> Kyoko: I don't want it.
> *Author: Didn't you say your mother [who was a housewife] is your role model?*
> Kyoko: She's my role model, but the job is a hobby for me. So I want to keep my job. ... I feel I'd waste my time by staying at home. Right now, it's not hard to do both housework and work, so I don't need to change this balance.

Two women – Rika (29 years old, married with one child) and Megumi (31 years old, never married) – used to think that the housewife role was ideal when they were younger, but changed their views later in life. Rika married as a result

WOMEN'S IDEAS ABOUT GENDER ROLES

of premarital pregnancy (as discussed in the previous chapter) and began to work part-time (three days a week) after her daughter turned two:

> Rika: I wanted to put her [in daycare] one year earlier, but I drew a losing number [referring to drawing for daycare].... So I put up with it [staying home with her child] for about a year.
> *Author: What was your ideal life course before you married?*
> Rika: Before I married, I thought housewife would be nice....
> *Author: How come you don't think it's nice any more?*
> Rika: Of course, uh, financially, it's better that I work. Also, housewives spend a lot of time at home, so it's stressful. I was a housewife until she turned two, you know? I felt depressed a lot, and didn't go out much, so it's better to work, then you'd have no time to feel that way and you'd have a world with others, not just home.... So I thought it's better to work, and I started working.
> *Author: Are you happier now that you're working?*
> Rika: Yes, I am.
> *Author: What if you didn't need to earn for the family? Would you like to be a housewife?*
> Rika: ... I'd like to cut hours [of work], like to twice a week or so.
> *Author: Do you want more time for home and your child?*
> Rika: Ah, home, too, but I want to have time just for myself.... Just a little more. I work only three days a week, but from 9:30 to 5. It's just a part-time job, but it's demanding. I get exhausted from it, so when I get home, I'm really exhausted. But I have to give a bath to my child. I get tired. I want more time.
> *Author: What do you think of women who are housewives?*
> Rika: I wonder if they're bored. Well, if they're really rich and have a lot of money, maybe they can do a lot of things. Otherwise, hmmmm.

A never-married woman, Megumi, realized the problem of women's economic dependence after she broke up with the boyfriend she wanted to marry. She broke up with him because he quit college and she could not accept such a move by a man. But, as discussed in Chapter 3, she had little luck meeting a potential partner afterwards and deeply regretted letting him go.

> Megumi: I don't hate working. I'm probably the kind of woman who hates to be inactive, staying at home. But I don't prefer to work after I get pregnant. Once I have kids, I'd like to stay home for seven years or so until they enter elementary school.... It's my ideal that I return to work after kids start their schooling.
> *Author: Was it always your ideal?*
> Megumi: I used to think housewife was an ideal. Up until I graduated from college and started my first job, I wanted to become a housewife.

125

Author: Why did you change your mind?

Megumi: Hmmm. I think, up until then, I observed my [stay-at-home] mother and thought housewife was good, well, rather than good, it was just normal.... So I had no intention of working for life, and didn't do the job search seriously [when I was finishing college]....Why did I not stay with my boyfriend? That's because I was thinking in that way, well, I was expecting him to support me, and I think that's why we broke up. If I was [economically] independent ... we may have stayed together. When I thought of it, I realized that dependence is bad. In the future, how, well, there may be a path to be a housewife, but, I think, you know, I couldn't hold my head high if I live depending on someone.... Up until then, until when I was graduating from college, watching my parents, I thought it [to be housewives for women] was normal. But now looking around, there are many working women. And men, those men who work for top companies may be earning good income, but there aren't any [men] of my age who are really wealthy, are there? Then, it's better for women to think of a real career. What if I get a divorce and I have nothing because I married and became a housewife? I'd have nothing, wouldn't I? I want to work and keep working now, so, because of that, I came to think becoming a housewife isn't good. But besides that, women shouldn't live dependently, should be able to live on their own. Well, we could have a time like this [referring to the current recession], you know? Lay-off, lay-off. If they [wives] are dependent, the burden goes to husbands. I think I'd complain to him [my future husband], "You aren't working!" even though I wouldn't be working, either. [laugh] Rather than that, I came to think it's better for women to be independent and work. I should acquire some skills so I can return to work after I quit ... I once asked my mother. "How did you become a housewife? Didn't you feel any remorse about depending completely on your husband?" [She said] That was the way it was. When wives worked, people thought husbands were incompetent, and that was the way it was.

The want and need for employment among women of the recession cohort clearly reflects the economic context they were in – precarious, poorer economic conditions for young men (and women) of this cohort. This contrasts with the boom cohort women, some of whom mentioned the "return to work" as an ideal and/or expected life course, but did not connect it to the possibility of a future husband's lay-off or insufficient income. Megumi, like Kyoko, felt that having-it-all is "definitely possible" even "though that's not what I wish."

Housewife: still ideal for some but viewed as unrealistic

Three never-married interviewees – Shizuka (34 years old), Momoe (30 years old), and Shoko (29 years old) – strongly wished to become housewives and

WOMEN'S IDEAS ABOUT GENDER ROLES

preferred not to work (outside home) at all after they married. They wanted "to spend time on cooking ... and scrapbooking, and making kids' clothes," "to do everything for him [her husband]," even taking off his socks, and/or "to watch every moment" of their children's growth. Yet for them, "the ideal is a house-wife, but the realistic course is to return to work after childrearing." As Momoe put it:

> You never know, right? He [her future husband] could get laid off after we marry.... I may have to work. If we live close to my parents, I'd leave them [kids] to them. Or if there are places we can feel safe about leaving them, well, there's no choice but work. I'm not like, things have to be this way! or I'd divorce otherwise!

The position of housewife, taken for granted as normative by boom cohort interviewees, was viewed by recession cohort women as a sort of privileged posi-tion that could well be out of reach for those who desired that life course. These women were flexible in their expectations, unlike boom cohort women. The three never-married interviewees were raised by stay-at-home mothers, but the life course of their mothers was no longer taken for granted, indicating another strong impact of the shrinking economy.

Daughters of employed mothers: acceptance of maternal employment

For recession cohort women, the impact of their mothers' employment differed from that of the boom cohort. Many of them advocated maternal employment and did not think mothers needed to stay home for children. However, whereas all employed mothers of boom cohort women were married, mothers of reces-sion cohort women were more diverse in marital status. The mothers of Hitomi and Yayoi were divorced, Midori's was widowed, Honoka's was never married, and Kei and Akane's were married. Of the latter two, Kei's mother owned her own pharmacy next to her husband's fish store, and the family lived on the second floor of these shops. Akane's mother worked for the government, which rarely required overtime work. Kei's father scarcely helped with house chores, whereas Akane's father, who was also a government employee, shared a substan-tial amount of the housework (as mentioned in Chapter 4). Of these six women, Akane was the only married interviewee.

Whereas Hitomi (36 years old) and Akane (34 years old) believed in mothers' stay-at-home role, Midori (36 years old), Kei (35 years old), Honoka (32 years old), and Yayoi (31 years old) felt there was no problem working full-time while raising children. Honoka thought:

> Whichever [a father or a mother] who has time should raise kids. Or, I hope we [my future husband and I]'ll have enough earnings to put the kids in daycare or preschool. [When I was a kid] I stayed half a day at daycare

and spent the rest with my grandmother. I think it's good for kids to get used to the outside air early, from my own experience. I don't like clinging relationships [between a mother and children].

Midori and Honoka – daughters of employed, unmarried mothers – "always wanted to do it all." Kei, whose mother was a pharmacist, said that she "can't imagine being a housewife, growing up watching my mother work."

Yayoi used to want to become a housewife. I asked her if she wanted to stay home for childrearing and she responded, "I'm not sure. My mother didn't take a break for that. But I grew up just fine. So I don't need to. It's up to how things are going at that time." The reason she wanted to become a housewife was that she had little confidence in holding on to a full-time job. However, she said she had gained confidence with her current job, and passionately told me that she was even willing to be a breadwinner if her future income permitted.

Shifting ideals through different life stages

As we saw above, women's choice of life course came to be more contingent upon other conditions, particularly husbands' economic situation. Women's ideas also changed as they went through different life stages. We saw that Megumi and Rika changed their views to value wives' employment. Additionally, Akane (34 years old, married) used to want to return to work but now was content with her housewife role, and wished to stay home for life. These shifting ideas regarding ideal life course were most pronounced in the accounts of two young women – Junko (27 years old, never married) and Kimi (25 years old, newlywed):

Author: What is your ideal life course?
Junko: Recently, I've been going to a lot of weddings of my friends and seeing them being so happy, and I don't like my job, so I felt I want to marry and stay home, but everybody says I'd be bored in three months. [laugh] So, if possible, this [pointing to the card for "returning to work"]. It's my ideal that I work part-time once I have kids. I work until I have kids, and then when I have kids, I take a break, and when they get old enough, I work part-time.
Author: What do you mean by "when they get old enough?"
Junko: Probably, I'd change my mind once I'm there, but probably when they're in elementary school.
Author: So, do you mean you plan to work when they're in school?
Junko: Right.
Author: So that means that you want to stay home longer than three months [referring to her friends' comment that she would be bored in three months], right?
Junko: That's right. [laugh] Ideal, isn't that my ideal? It's my wish. If I can marry, that's what I want to do.

Author: Did you want to become a housewife in the past?
Junko: No, in the past, I wanted this [pointing to the card for "single-hood"]. I wanted to live a life with a career. But recently, I saw my friends getting married, and I felt tired of working for a living. I'm changing as I get older.

The above account shows that Junko used to think the "singlehood with career" life course was her ideal, but recently changed her mind to favor the "return to work" life course. However, the subsequent conversation revealed her contradictory views:

Author: Do you not want to have it all?
Junko: I don't think I could do it. Probably, well, I'm a kind of person who gets stressed with too much work. I'd like to do both, but I'd get stressed because I'd like to do both perfectly.
Author: Do you mean that you want to do housework and childrearing all by yourself?
Junko: Ah, you're right. I should ask him [my husband] to help. I assumed I can't do so, so there goes my answer. [laugh]
Author: What if you marry a man who's willing to share?
Junko: Well, but, overtime work (*zangyō*). If I work full-time, that'd require overtime work, so probably not. I could work after I marry, but not after I give birth.
Author: So are you saying that you wouldn't work because your work conditions wouldn't allow you time to raise kids?
Junko: Right.
Author: What if you can go home without overtime?
Junko: Ah, then, I'd keep working. But that wouldn't happen in reality.

So, it seems that her true wish was the "having-it-all" life course, if conditions allowed. In the earlier part of the interview (mentioned in Chapter 2), Junko said she was planning to go back to school and become a teacher. Yet her view towards a lifetime career became unclear or contradictory as we continued our conversation:

Author: There aren't many part-time career jobs. You may have to take a job like cashier at a grocery store. What do you think of it?
Junko: That's not a problem at all. I worked at McDonalds for about seven years. There were many married women and it was fun, so I could work there. [laugh] ... I'd like to work. When I lived alone, I realized it's bad to be alone at home. I need to get out, or I'd go crazy.
Author: So, is work an opportunity to get out?
Junko: Yes.
Author: Not a career?

Junko: No.
Author: But you said you want to become a teacher and go back to school for it.
Junko: Yes, I do want to do that.
Author: So what if you become a teacher and want to marry?
Junko: Oh, yeah. [laugh] If I become a teacher, I'd probably take this path [pointing to the card for "singlehood"]. I'd do teaching for about three years, and marry. While I'm a teacher, I wouldn't think about marriage.
Author: So, it's not like you'd stay single for life.
Junko: No.
Author: You just want to stay unmarried when you're a teacher.
Junko: Yeah.

Similarly, for a newlywed interviewee Kimi, her ideal changed from "having-it-all" to "return to work" yet remained ambiguous:

Author: How long do you want to continue your current job?
Kimi: Well, because I'm married now, so once I get pregnant, I'm sort of thinking I would quit once. Also, if others, if I can get help from others, uh, I don't know. If I have an environment where I can keep working after having kids, I'd like to keep working.
Author: What is your ideal life course?
Kimi: Hmmmm. Honestly, I wish I could have this [pointing to the card for "having-it-all"], but if I think realistically, it's probably this [pointing to the card for "returning to work"].
Author: What do you mean by thinking realistically?
Kimi: After having a child, well, I'd like to raise my kids on my own until they're okay to let them go. Then, it's impossible to keep working with the current conditions. So, realistically, this.
Author: Why is it impossible? Is time an issue?
Kimi: Time, yes, time is an issue.
Author: Didn't you say your bank has programs for women to balance family and work?
Kimi: Yes, it does. But do I want to use them? Well, at the headquarters, women use these programs, but in small branches [like mine], I'd have to worry about other people, and other people also would worry about me. Could I say, "good bye," [when others are working overtime]? I think others would forgive me, they'd understand since that's the policy, but I can't imagine myself leaving work behind and saying good-bye. Rather than that, I'd just quit, and then return to work after my kids get older.

Like Junko, Kimi changed her view because she began to think about what is possible "realistically," not just ideally. She later restated that her "real ideal is, I think having-it-all. But, realistically, return to work." As the following exchange

130

shows, it seems that she began to change her sentiments about her "real ideal" life course after she married:

Author: Do you think you could have it all if your husband didn't have to be transferred?
Kimi: Yes, but. There's a [married] female worker in my office, age 34 or 35. She doesn't have kids. She told me she always buys prepared meals, and I feel, well, that raises a question for me. She doesn't cook for her husband and dinners are always prepared meals she buys. When I imagine that kind of life, I ask myself if I really want to continue working doing such a thing, I'd feel, why, then, did I marry? I feel responsibility for that part [referring to cooking and other housework]. Now that I'm married, I'd like to do what I should do for him [my husband]. So, recently, I'm thinking I should choose family [over career].... When I walk by a daycare, I hear babies crying. Sounds like they were only a few days old. I feel, what is the point of working, leaving such little babies in daycare? It's okay to let kids go from my arms once they're old enough. But I thought I may not be able to go [to work leaving my babies].

Both Junko and Kimi came across as intelligent women who had career ambitions at some point in their lives. But what life course did they envision at the time of the interview? Both came to realize that full-time jobs require overtime work which collides with homemaking and childcare. This "reality" does not allow both partners of a married couple to have full-time jobs, they said.

Shaping this reality are inequalities of power: corporate exploitation of labor in a capitalist economy and the demanding domestic tasks expected of women. Kimi's words clearly reflected her belief in mothers' physical presence for children ("let kids go from *my arms* once they're old enough"). Her thoughts on "pointless" marriages, in which wives would not prepare home-cooked meals for their husbands, indicated that she believed it proper for wives to dedicate their energy and time to homemaking.[18] But she was married for only one year, and a growing number of studies[19] show that a significant proportion of married women in Japan are not happy with the demands of these expected domestic tasks. If everyone in full-time jobs worked only within some reasonable (perhaps legally established) limit of weekly hours, would these women (and others) consider retaining their careers upon marriage? It seems a distinct possibility! Sadly, these interviewees took for granted, and were not critical of, the common employment requirement of excessive overtime work; they adjusted their own ideas to match this reality instead of challenging the norm. With some irony we may note that Kimi's company had a generous, family-friendly policy allowing women to stay employed and yet, apparently, that policy by itself was not sufficient to allow women (and men) to balance work and family.[20] The Japanese government has been encouraging married women to take employment,[21] but most married mothers with young children still choose to stay home.[22]

Corporate demand for long work hours, combined with highly intensive domestic tasks expected of women, shape women's opportunities in yet another way that can affect the life path.

No specific vision

None of the categories from the prepared list had ever been considered by one never-married interviewee, Hitomi (36 years old):

> *Author: Which life course do you envision yourself taking five or ten years from now?*
> Hitomi: [long pause] Hmmm, the closest among these is [pause] probably DINKS. Hmmmm. I don't mean I want to be doing this. Just vaguely, I don't know if I'll marry, well, if possible I'd like to meet my lifetime partner and marry. In terms of children,... I don't feel I've got to have kids, honestly. Honestly, I don't want to work for life, either. I'm lazy. Once I marry, why don't I stay home? I feel that way, too. [laugh] I don't think I could have career and children, so I'd like to choose either or. Even if I do DINKS, rather than having a career job, rather than working hard, it'd be easier to work just enough to get connected to the outside world.
> *Author: Do you mean that housewife could be your ideal life course, too?*
> Hitomi: Yes, that's right. That's definitely an option. I'm telling my boss that my ultimate dream is to become a housewife, quitting my job, receiving a flower bouquet [from him]. My friends tell me I'd get bored soon, but I feel becoming a housewife is just fine. If you do everything seriously, it [housework] couldn't be underestimated. I think I can make use of my time even if I don't work [outside home]. For example, I can take lessons and do volunteer work, too. I think it's wrong to take a job just because someone is bored of housework.
> *Author: What was your ideal life course in the past?*
> Hitomi: Ideal? Huh, ideal? [pause] Hmmmmm. [pause] Honestly, I've probably never thought of it.
> *Author: Were you always uninterested in having kids?*
> Hitomi: No, not necessarily. I'm just thinking, what'd happen if I give birth. Once I give birth, I'd like to focus on childrearing. Well, not that I want to focus, but I'd have to focus, I guess.... I'm not sure if I could.

I observed this absence of clear visions for the future among many of my never-married interviewees across both cohorts. They were more likely to halfheartedly (*nantonaku, bakuzento*) expect to take the course of life presented to them, putting little of their own thoughts into the matter. Quite a number of them, including Hitomi, were in career positions – the type people would often assume must have chosen career over marriage. Yet, surprisingly, these interviewees were not goal-oriented but passive drifters, leading me to conclude that "drift" (not "agency") better captures the character of increased singlehood in Japan.

Men's role in marriage and gender ideology: diversity but lingering traditional ideas

Answers to the question regarding ideal and expected life courses revealed that most women of the recession cohort either wanted or expected to return to work after childrearing. Some women also preferred or anticipated working full-time, continuously after childbearing. Many were aware of poorer economic prospects for male peers. What role did they expect men to take? In contrast to the boom cohort women, who were almost uniformly traditional, women of the recession cohort were diverse in their ideas about men's role in marriage.

Nine out of twenty-one women of this cohort were traditional, expecting their husbands to "support the family economically" (i.e., to take the breadwinning role) and perceiving women's domestic role as "natural" or "normal." Earning for the family was seen as the man's role, and men were expected to "work for life." Men must "have a stable job and income in order to marry," and male ability to work and/or confidence and pride in work were viewed as important aspects of manhood. Gender hierarchy (i.e., male superiority and female submission) was also expected, as reflected in the account of Hitomi, a 36-year-old, never-married, marketing consultant:

> I think I'm expecting men to be stronger, superior to me. In terms of ability and. [pause] What is it? How shall I put? Not quite that I want men to protect me, but, for men. [pause] I think, compared to men, women have more weaknesses. Men can complement women's weaknesses so that probably means that men have more abilities than me...
>
> I don't like men who aren't competent at their jobs. I prefer a man who chooses work over women.... I wouldn't be able to see a man as the opposite sex [if he is not good at work]. No matter how handsome he is, no matter how our values match.... If I have to choose between a handsome man who doesn't work and an ugly man who is good at work, I'd choose the latter. I don't mean that I like workaholics who'd neglect the family, but I like men who have confidence and pride in their jobs.

As we have seen, some of these women expressed desires or expectations to return to work after childrearing. I asked if reentry into the labor force meant they would share breadwinning tasks equally. It turned out that these women considered their earnings to be only supplementary to the household income, or for spending on their own leisure. Even Megumi, who discussed at length the importance of a wife's economic independence (presented above), expected her future husband to be the primary earner. Her husband's competence at work would be necessary, she said, if she was going to respect him and feel inspired about pursuing a career. For these women, wives should not be completely economically dependent because the economy is precarious, but men should be independent as traditionally expected. Despite rhetoric about the importance of wives' employment, these interviewees' expectations, fundamentally, were very traditional.

Though some recession cohort women expected their husbands to take part in childrearing, all of them wanted "to do all the housework" or "wouldn't mind at all" if their husband did not help around the house. Interestingly, homemaking, rather than childrearing, was viewed as married women's central role. All these interviewees were raised by stay-at-home mothers, except for Hitomi whose mother was divorced. Observing a gendered division of labor in which their mothers devoted themselves to the care of family and household, recession cohort women perceived traditional gender roles as *natural* and *normal*:

> *Author: So, do you think breadwinning is a man's job and women should take care of households?*
> Megumi (31 years old, never married): Hmmmm, Hmmmm. There is this kind of couple [pointing to the card for breadwinning with a house-husband]. But I think women's and men's roles are, well, our society now has a lot of working women but fundamentally, instinctively, I think women make home and men work. Women can take care of the home better than men. I think we [men and women] are just born that way. So, [for women] working is just assisting, well, I don't mean to work half-heartedly, but relatively, men's jobs are more important.

> *Author: You said the wife's job is homemaking. Is this what you want to do, or what you feel you'd have to do?*
> Kimi (25 years old, married): Well, I don't think that's what I'd have to do, but that's what I'd like to do for him [my husband]. Well, how shall I put it? It's not like that's my mission, but, well, I grew up watching my mother doing everything for my father. He doesn't do anything [around the house], so my mother did everything for him. So I feel it's normal for me to do things for him [my husband].... I think women are better at that kind of thing, so I'd like to do that personally. I don't want to sacrifice, well, I feel it's a sacrifice, if I don't do it [housework] because of my job [at her bank]. So, I want to keep my job, but I don't want to work if I have to sacrifice all that.

These interviewees' image of the ideal wife was thus similar to that of boom cohort women. Mutsumi described this ideal as a wife who "can do things around the house perfectly, comfort her husband, and support him discreetly."

This is almost identical to the image described by Fujiko, one of the boom cohort women.

Other qualities of men were thought to be important for good husbands and fathers. Decisiveness was expected of men, and some women thought important decisions should be made by their husbands. Men were also expected to be dignified, strong, protective, and possess abilities superior to their wives. "I want my husband to be *daikoku bashira* (the central pillar of a house)." In their eyes, mothers are often "ineffective in disciplining children" because they "nag and scold about small everyday things." Fathers should be a presence that is more dignified so that "children will respect and listen," or someone who "comforts children after mothers scold them too much." These women found male superiority legitimate, and endorsed power inequality by gender within marriage.

On the other hand, five recession cohort women were willing to share the breadwinning role, yet wanted their husbands to stay away from housework. Earning a living "should be split into half," "is the role for whoever can do it," or "may be shared half and half if a husband cannot earn enough." With the exception of Ran (29 years old, never married), all these women were aware of the unreliability of men's earnings based on personal observations. They were either raised by an employed mother who supported the family primarily, or were in a relationship or marriage with a man whose earnings were small. These women were sympathetic to men's economic hardship under the long-lasting economic recession and did not perceive the low income of men as a sign of deficient masculinity. They did not expect men to shoulder the provider role alone. Even so, these women felt household chores to be their job, thinking of it as *natural* or *normal*, just like the traditional women discussed above. For instance:

Watching my own mother, I'd like to do all the work around the house. Cleaning, laundry, all of it. She does it all because my father never did. And it's not a problem to me. I just think that's the way it is. I get pissed off if someone says "that's a women's job," though. [laugh]

(Kyoko, 29 years old, married, cook)

In Ran's case, her boyfriend, to whom she was informally engaged, was a physician and his income was (and expected to remain) high. Ran who met her boyfriend in a medical school was a medical researcher. She did not want to give up on her career because "what I do is quite amazing. I have an extraordinary career most people can't have." But she completely took it for granted that wives take care of the home:

Author: Do you have any ideas about what you should do as a wife?
Ran: As a wife? Well, I'd like to take care of home well.
Author: Home means housework?
Ran: Yes.

Author: Is it like you'd take care of all the housework so your husband can focus on his job?
Ran: Yes, sort of. My boyfriend has no ability to do housework, so I don't think I'd ask him to do it. If he has something he can do, that'd be great. But it'd be easier if I do it.
Author: Earlier, you said you want to stay home for childrearing. Do you feel it has to be the mother who quits her job to raise kids?
Ran: Well, either one could do it, it's about which does what, but, personally, I think it [childrearing] is a women's job. Fathers, how shall I put it? Children need their mothers when they are little, I think. It's the same for animals, right? There aren't many cases where fathers raise kids.

Interestingly, for Kei (35 years old, never married) and Yayoi (31 years old, never married), having employed mothers caused them to feel they should take the homemaking role while being employed full-time. When she was growing up, Kei's father did no housework, and she thought wives:

> should do all the housework. Even when they work, they have to take care of the home properly. I don't think wives should do things just for their own wants. Wives should take care of their husbands. That's how women should be.

Yayoi's mother was a divorced single mother who, she perceived, did "not do a very good job taking care of the household." For this reason, Yayoi wanted "to do housework perfectly," and did not expect her husband to do half the housework even if she took on half the task of providing.

Though they were amenable to flexibility in men's roles, they were almost stubborn about retaining housework as their job. This reflects how persistently the role of homemaking – more so than childrearing – is attached to womanhood and how normative activities for one's sex construct gender identity. These women took pride in their (potential) ability to do perfect housework. Giving up housework in favor of employment was seen as giving up on being a woman. It was as if they refused to relinquish the homemaking role in order to remain feminine. However, most of these women were not married, and those who were married had no children, and therefore, they lacked a realistic assessment of what it would mean to shoulder all the housework while juggling that with employment and childrearing. It would appear we are witnessing the dawn of the era of the *second shift*[23] – the unfair burden of domestic tasks taken by employed mothers – in Japan.

On the other hand, five other interviewees of the recession cohort – all never married – held more egalitarian expectations. Midori (36 years old), Junko (27 years old) and Yuki (26 years old) did not think earning was a man's role exclusively, and wanted their partners to share work around the house equally. Honoka (32 years old) and Ryoko (26 years old) felt that, rather than allocation by gender, "who is good at it should take the tasks" they are good at. Thirty-six-year-old Midori lost her father when she was little and was raised by an employed mother and grandparents in a rural farm village in Northern Japan. Her rural upbringing may have an impact on her view. She felt that her egalitarian expectation was rather unusual among women of her age group in Tokyo:

> Probably because I grew up with one parent and my mother was doing all the men's work, and ... I also grew up taking care of myself, so ... I went to college [in Tokyo] and my friends talked about their fathers who were the bosses of the house (*teishu kanpaku*). [Because of this upbringing] They [my friends] would feel sorry for men if they are pouring tea on their own. And so, they'd offer to help. I was shocked.

Midori, Ryoko, and Yuki were cohabiting at the time of the interview. Yuki's 40-year-old boyfriend – a divorced man with ill, elderly parents – did grocery shopping and cooking, and took the garbage out. She did cleaning and dishes and felt they shared housework about 50/50. Ryoko was doing most of the chores because she was "between jobs at this moment, and my boyfriend works long hours." She was wondering whether he would share half once she got a job. Midori was frustrated with her partner's unequal sharing of housework:

> Midori: Compared to my friends' husbands or boyfriends, I think my partner does a lot more. Still, when I come home in the morning after working the whole night and see the garbage not taken out, I get irritated and feel why in the world I have to take out the garbage after all night at work.... Compared to other men, I think he does quite a bit. But still inequality is inequality. I know he does more than the average Japanese man. But no matter how busy I am, he wouldn't do cleaning and laundry.... I do laundry once a week, but he won't do it until he runs out of underpants. He'd never say I should do laundry, but he seems to be able to put up with dirty clothes longer than me. So, I don't feel he's making me do it, but I end up doing it.
> *Author: Why don't you tell him to do the laundry?*
> Midori: Well, that's because, what if I'm in his shoes? If he tells me to do it when I'm busy, I'd get pissed. Why do I have to do it when I can wait longer? That's how I see it.... So I get irritated, but I don't feel right about arguing about this with him.

This is a common experience for wives with egalitarian minds, as observed in *The Second Shift* by Arlie Hochschild[24] and other, related literature.

Interestingly, although these women expected equal sharing in terms of providing and domestic responsibilities, they expected their husbands to be superior to them in other dimensions. For example:

I think it's fine for men to be authoritarian.... Women should be submissive. [laugh] ... Women are too strong these days. Women used to be submissive. I admire women in those good old days, though I don't think I could be one. [laugh] ... Like my grandmother, she was respectful to her husband. Well, she wasn't really respecting him, she said later, but she acted that way. I admire it. [Now] there're no rules. There's too much we have to figure out. That's confusing. Things are getting more and more confusing.... Equality is tiring (*tsukareru*). [laugh] ... Let men make decisions.

(Honoka, 32 years old, never married, marketing consultant)

Author: Do you have ideas about how your husband should be?
Ryoko (26 years old, cohabiting, between jobs): Ah. Well, my father was the boss (*teishu kanpaku*), so I want my husband to make important decisions. I want him to be decisive.
Author: How should a wife be?
Ryoko: [short pause] Well, she should respect her husband and support him. Sounds a bit old-fashioned, but I think so.
Author: Like your mother?
Ryoko: Yes. Ah, yes, really. I guess that's what it is.

Author: Is it correct to say that you don't like a man who'd say men should be this way and women should be that way?
Midori (36 years old, cohabiting, copy writer): Well, it's correct, but there's another self [laugh] and that self tells me I should pay due respect (*tateru*) to a man [my husband] and be submissive (*hikaeme*). So I'm contradicting myself. When I see men who want that kind [of women], I go, "whatever!" But when I meet that kind of woman, I admire them – women who pay due respect to men, are submissive, but actually have good control over men in a discreet way.
Author: What about the sharing of housework? Is 50/50 your ideal?
Midori: Yes, 50/50.... Equality is my ideal, but my admiration for that kind of woman is another story.

In each of the above cases, the traditional image of a "good" Japanese wife who stands in the shadow of her husband persists. By rejecting the notion of equal power in marriage, these women were not quite egalitarian, but only *near* egalitarian.

Two other women were a little different from those discussed above. One was Yuri (32 years old), who was informally engaged to her co-worker. Though her plan was to have a "return to work" life course, and she expected her husband to be the breadwinner, when it came to housework and childrearing, "I may sound selfish, but I want him to do everything together with me. He'd work full-time, but after he comes home, I want him to take care of our kids....

a cooperative husband is my ideal." Another was Maya (26 years old), who was cohabiting with her female partner. She had only recently begun to think about the possibility of marriage because her European partner influenced her views on equal rights for same-sex couples. She had no clear vision regarding role allocation. After she gave thought to my question for several seconds, she answered, "Whatever is fine." This absence of ideas on role allocation reflects how powerful gender is in determining who should do what in romantic relationships.

When it came to men's househusband role, women of the recession cohort were generally quite receptive. This contrasted sharply with boom cohort women, who viewed househusbands as pathetic or non-masculine; some could not even accept the role when it pertained to someone else's marriage. Four women (Yoko, Kyoko, Honoka, and Yayoi) said they would happily take a breadwinning role and have their husband stay home if they could earn enough. Other women, however, thought it was a "totally acceptable" lifestyle only for others and would "not think of these men as non-masculine or pathetic," but would not consider it for their own lives. Still, a majority of recession cohort women thought some men "are suited for that kind of role.... Some men love to raise kids. They may want to spend time with little kids and return to work later. Some men are better at cooking and things like that."

In the late 1990s, the Japanese government ran a massive campaign to promote paternal involvement in childrearing, and highlighted a popular celebrity couple who took on "reversed" gender roles.[25] Recession cohort women's acceptance of this new vision of fatherhood may have been affected by media portrayal of this popular man in the househusband role. It is interesting that the boom cohort women were not impressed by the new image. The recession cohort's receptive, flexible views may be a result of the campaign, which ran during their young adulthood, and of experiencing economic recession at that time, during which many young men (and women) suffered from lay-offs and un-(or under-)employment.

Chapter summary and discussion

In her groundbreaking work, *The Second Shift*, Arlie Hochschild categorized gender ideology into three types: *traditional, transitional,* and *egalitarian*.[26] *Traditional* ideology refers to the idea that wives are identified with domestic activities and husbands are to base their activities at work and hold more power, even when wives (plan to) work. *Egalitarian* ideology holds that wives and husbands equally share power in marriage, as well as work outside and inside the home. *Transitional* ideology is that wives are identified with both paid work and home, but husbands are to focus on work outside home.

In this light, boom cohort interviewees' conceptions of gender roles can be summarized overall as "mostly traditional." Despite expanded employment and leisure opportunities (as discussed in Chapter 2), mothers' employment was disapproved of or regarded as impossible or too hard by most of the interviewees. This view reflects the deeply internalized belief in homemaking as the mark of true womanhood: Married women should dedicate their lives to housework and children, or they are not truly women. The majority of boom cohort women endorsed the housewife role as proper, even though some were skeptical about taking this role personally. Women were solid in their acceptance of the traditional men's role. Employment, particularly in the white-collar sector, signified masculinity, and breadwinning was expected from men regardless of women's present earning power.

I say "mostly traditional" because not all the women were uniformly happy with traditional role expectations, and some contradictory views were observed. Some women felt resentful when others told them to conform to the traditional female role. One married woman, Tamami, spoke of egalitarian gender ideology but was taking on most of the domestic chores. This reminded me of many women categorized by Hochschild in her study to be in transitional marriages. Though some women like Tamami chose the having-it-all lifestyle, by putting children in daycare, they faced disapproval from other women of the same cohort because they defied the idea of true womanhood. Such working mothers were considered deviant (or "outlaws," to use Tamami's word). Juggling home, children, and paid work was indeed hard and stressful for women at that time, and many single women's exposure to this only helped solidify their negativity towards the having-it-all (*ryōritsu*) life course.

Recession cohort women were more diverse in their visions and conceptions, and varied from *traditional* to *near egalitarian*. The life of housewife, taken for granted as "normal" by the boom cohort, was regarded as either undesirable or out of reach by the recession cohort. Though most of them preferred that mothers stay home to raise young children, the "having-it-all" lifestyle was accepted or understood as a necessity, and some anticipated it as their potential life course. Unlike the boom cohort, recession cohort women who were raised by an employed mother either found no problem with maternal employment, or preferred that mothers work. Still, *ryōsai kenbo*-like gender ideology was strong in the minds of these women. A belief equating domestic responsibilities, particularly housework, with womanhood persisted firmly, and power inequality in marriage – the notion that men make important decisions and women submit – was embraced.[27]

Why do many women in Japan cling to, or even embrace, the beliefs and practices associated with gender hierarchy and gendered division of labor? We could consider this as not necessarily confined to women of Japan. Continuous or intensified dedication to motherhood by employed women has been observed, for instance, in the works of American sociologists such as Sharon Hays,[28] Annette Lareau,[29] and Mary Blair-Loy,[30] in addition to the already-mentioned Arlie Hochschild. Hays describes this phenomenon as "cultural contradiction," as one would expect a reduction in mothering activities, instead of intensification, during a time of increased maternal labor force participation.[31]

But many scholars have pointed out that women (and men) in Japan tend to hold more traditional gender ideology[32] than their Western – as well as some of their Asian[33] – counterparts. People in Japan also work longer hours than those in other developed nations. According to the OECD reports on "Gender Equity," men in Japan, on average, spend more hours on paid work than men of any other OECD countries.[34] In terms of unpaid work, women in Japan spend the longest hours,[35] and the gender gap here is second only to India.[36] Based solely on these statistics, we cannot infer whether women in Japan do more (and men do less) because of their gender beliefs, or because of men's absence from home due to long hours of work.[37] In any case, the vicious cycle of beliefs in, and practices of, gendered division of labor will not be broken so long as excessively long work hours remain normative and required.

How does the persistently strong belief in *ryōsai kenbo*-like ideology relate to increased singlehood? During the economic boom, boom cohort women landed interesting jobs and/or enjoyed the leisure opportunities their employment permitted. Firmly believing the domestic role of married women to be proper, and lacking viable marriage models demonstrating balanced employment and mothering, many women considered the simultaneous maintenance of employment and marriage to be out of question. When we add this to their skepticism towards happy marriage, shaped by parents, how can we think it strange that these women put off thinking about and planning marriage during their twenties? My interviewees, some repeatedly, claimed that they did not mean to remain single for life. They felt it was acceptable to focus on present pleasures in a particular social context – one in which many young women stayed single and flourished in the labor force. Unfortunately, by not considering marriage seriously when the time was right, they "missed the boat" that would take them to marriage.

This is not to say that they necessarily would have been better off by marrying, as a good number of these women did not want to become housewives, or "have it all." However, at the time of interviews, most women still wished to marry, and as I discuss in the next chapter, many were very concerned about their futures, should they remain unmarried. As I have shown in this book, increased singlehood is a complex phenomenon involving multiple causal factors. The persistent belief in traditional gender ideology must be added to the list. My contention is that these women lacked the cultural tools that might have allowed them to keep employment and balance it with marriage and family, and because of the absence of these tools, they ended up drifting into singlehood.

The same argument applies to men of the recession cohort. As we have seen, women of the recession cohort were more flexible, accepting maternal employment and male inability to take the sole provider role. But observations made by my interviewees indicate that men were not so flexible in accepting their future wives' employment, sharing domestic tasks, or relinquishing male privilege and power within marriage. Just like women of the boom cohort, recession cohort

WOMEN'S IDEAS ABOUT GENDER ROLES

men held onto an outdated cultural tool which did not allow them to marry in the precarious economy. With men clinging to the traditional gender ideology, women's willingness to share the provision role had no effect. Here, we see another sense in which women of the recession cohort are victims of the *ryōsai kenbo*-like gender ideology.

In these ways, gender ideology powerfully affected the life paths of the two cohorts of women (and men). Increased singlehood (in Japan) is indeed a *gendered* phenomenon.

Notes

1 There is ample literature on the *ryōsai kenbo* ideology. For literature in the Japanese language see, for instance, Kauchi 1984; K. Kondo 1995; Koyama 1991; and Oki 2004. For English language literature see, for instance, Garon 1997; Holloway 2010; Lock 1996; Miyake 1991; Nolte and Hastings 1991; Ohinata 1995; Shinotsuka 1994; Ueno 1994; Uno 1991, 2005; and White 2002.
2 Young, unmarried women were mobilized to take wage employment in the rapidly industrializing Japan, especially in the textile industry. They were, however, expected to eventually marry and leave the labor force (Faison 2007).
3 Higher education for girls was, however, limited mainly to moral education and domestic science. Subjects such as mathematics and sciences, needed for middle-class occupations, were not part of the core curriculum of such schools (Uno 2005).
4 This was due in part to the influence of feminist thought, popular in Sweden at the time, which emphasized the role of mothers. For more detail on the feminist movement, the ideology of motherhood, and debate over feminism among feminists, see for instance S. Kaneko 2011; Molony 2005; Tomida 2004; and Uno 2005.
5 Most married women in rural regions had to work on farms (Ochiai 2004/2006). Wars caused casualties and the deaths of young men, and many wives and widows had no choice but to take wage employment (Uno 2005).
6 Ochiai 2004/2006.
7 Ochiai (2004/2006) discusses that "housewifization" of women in Japan occurred during this period of high economic growth, and provides more detail on this phenomenon.
8 Yu 2002.
9 The National Fertility Surveys have been conducted by the National Institute of Population and Social Security Research (NIPSSR) on nationally representative samples of single men and women in Japan since 1982, and included the questions on ideal and expected life course since the 1992 survey.
10 I modified the categories used in the NFS. For more detail, please see Appendix A.
11 As already discussed in Chapter 4, the last two questions revealed important cohort differences in the marriages that surrounded the two cohorts of women.
12 Ochiai 2004/2006.
13 Friedan 1963.
14 Long 1996.
15 Holloway 2010; Imamura 1987; Jolivet 1997; Ohinata 1995; Sasagawa 2006.
16 Tamami was referring to the common saying, *mitsugo no tamashii hyaku made*, which literally means that the soul of a three-year-old (will last) until (one is) 100 years old. It is similar to the English saying, "what is learned in the cradle is carried to the grave."
17 This sort of strong resistance against the "having-it-all" lifestyle was also observed among female executives in the U.S., who were born around World War II, in Blair-Loy's study (2003). These women were the first wave of women who entered and

142

WOMEN'S IDEAS ABOUT GENDER ROLES

succeeded in the traditionally men's world, graduating from college in between the late 1950s and late 1960s. These women remained either unmarried or childless, and did not approve of women who wanted both.

18 Sasagawa (2006) shows how mothers are expected to prepare homemade things for their preschool children, and that such dedication is considered a sign of being a good mother. Kimi's words reflect the same kind of expectation placed on wives.

19 Holloway 2010; Long 1996; Sasagawa 2006.

20 Creighton (1996) observed the same among women who worked at department stores in the 1980s.

21 See, for instance, Sekiguchi 2014.

22 According to the White Paper on Gender Equality (Gender Equity Bureau Cabinet Office, 2016), labor force participation rates remain significantly lower among married women in comparison to unmarried women in Japan, and in 2009, approximately 60 percent of employed women who gave birth left the labor force.

23 See Hochschild 1989.

24 Hochschild 1989.

25 In the late 1990s, the Ministry of Health and Welfare campaigned for fathers to take parental leave, using the husband of a popular singer, Namie Amuro, in TV ads and posters (Roberts 2002). The public reactions were mixed, however. See Nakatani (2006) for a good analysis of discourses on nurturing fathers.

26 Hochschild 1989.

27 Charlebois (2010) observed varying views toward femininities among 20 women in Japan he interviewed, and concluded that some change is under way.

28 Hays 1996.

29 Lareau's study (2011) suggests intensive parenting, which she labels "concerted cultivation," is more likely among the middle-class than working- and lower-classes.

30 Blair-Loy (2003) studied female executives of three cohorts and found that many of them were caught between two competing cultural expectations of devotion: work and family devotion schemes.

31 Hays 1996.

32 For instance, Creighton 1996; Hertog 2009; Holloway 2010; Kamano 2005; Kelsky 2001; Lee, Tufiş, and Alwin 2010; Nemoto 2008; North 2009; Retherford, Ogawa, and Matsukura 2001; Sasagawa 2006; Shirahase 2005; Tokuhiro 2010.

33 Ochiai and Molony 2008.

34 OECD 2015c, 2015d.

35 According to OECD (2015c), in 2011, women spent 26 minutes per day (on average) on care of household members, while men spent only seven minutes per day. For routine housework, women spent 199 minutes per day whereas men spent 24 minutes.

36 Among 29 countries compared in OECD (2015c).

37 According to Lee and Ono (2008), in Japan, couples who divide labor by gender are happier than those who do not, while this pattern is not as clear for the case of the U.S.

6

WHY AREN'T JAPANESE WOMEN GETTING MARRIED?

Conclusion and implications

Work!!?? [We are single because we] Wanted to work?!?! [long pause] ... No, not that. [It's to do with] What was happening in the society.
(Tsuneko, 43 years old, never married, marketing consultant)

It's just that I can't help thinking all the time.... It may be endless if I start talking about my concerns [about the future].
(Kazuko, 45 years old, never married, artist/art instructor)

I want to have two children before I turn 40. So I'm in a big hurry.
(Yoko, 36 years old, never married, section manager)

I always wanted to marry.... I could have married even at age 20.... I love children.... I wanted to have babies sooner.... What'll happen to me!?
(Shoko, 29 years old, never married, elderly care worker)

The never-married single population has surged in Japan, and many have attributed this to women's *choice* to remain unmarried. The popular media and some social scientists in Japan assumed that women stayed single because they prioritized career over marriage, selfishly pursued materialistic luxury, or resisted succumbing to patriarchy. With this assumption and the association of singlehood with population problems, women's single status has been an open target of criticism and ridicule – or falsely celebrated as a sign of advancement in women's social position.

However, my research findings, presented in the previous four chapters, show that *choice was not the driving force of this phenomenon* and that *women are far from equal to men in Japan.* Many factors were involved in the process of the single population's increase: Two major shifts in the economy (first the boom and then the recession) were pivotal; Single women's life circumstances differed between the two cohorts, and this led to cohort differences in reasons women stayed unmarried; Enforcement of the traditional marriage age norm rapidly weakened, but traditional gender ideology persisted while showing some sign of change among the younger cohort; Parents' and peers' marriages influenced women's views of marriage, but differently by cohort; Multiple factors mutually affected each other and caused many women to *drift into singlehood*. The answer to the question "Why aren't Japanese women getting married?" is complex. In this concluding chapter, I first summarize how a large number of women from each cohort ended up single – sorting out this seeming jumble of too many factors – and then point out key explanatory variables.

As I mentioned in the first chapter, the single population increased and is increasing significantly in a great many countries, yet this global social phenomenon has been relatively understudied – and definitely undertheorized in sociology. But, in the context of Japan, this subject has been well studied by social scientists, primarily because of its association with demographic problems (i.e., declined birth rates, aging population, and population decline). Most studies on Japan, however, were limited in scope and only tested the applicability of existing theories. Moreover, though many of these studies failed to support current sociological theories built mostly on observations of (a limited number of) Western countries,[1] they did not contribute to the improvement of theory.[2] Most of them also assumed women's "choice" to remain unmarried.[3] The government and popular media in Japan also took interests in increased singlehood, particularly among women (due to its association with the demographic problem), and the Japanese government implemented various social policies and programs aimed at increasing fertility (within marriage, and thus indirectly at increasing marriage). Yet, the single population continued to rise and fertility rates hardly changed. These policies and programs have been largely ineffective in solving this "problem."

My study delved into the life stories of two cohorts of women – both of which saw a surge in the number of never-married singles – and identifies previously overlooked causal factors and an intricate process behind the increase in single population. Within these factors and this process, the persistence of gender inequality was salient. Thus, this study has implications for the sociological theory of singlehood, social policies, and the empowerment of women in Japan (and perhaps elsewhere). I discuss my study's implications after giving a summary of the research findings.

Summary: why women of the two cohorts had a high likelihood of remaining unmarried

Process of drift for each cohort

Boom cohort

For most Japanese women who grew up in the 1960s and 1970s – the era of economic growth and cultural idealization of the professional housewife role – the norm of appropriate marriage age (*tekireiki*) and beliefs about traditional gender roles (i.e., female-homemaker and male-breadwinner roles) were internalized in childhood. Many had stay-at-home mothers, but even when they did not, this cohort of women perceived the mother's homemaking role as the norm. They also took marriage for granted as the normal life path. When the older boom cohort women finished school and began working, employment practice was still aligned with the marriage-age norm. Women were hired into dead-end clerical positions and pressured to resign from work during *tekireiki*, which was the early twenties or by age 25. Some of these women witnessed the negative treatment of their senior female workers for being "Christmas cake" or unmarried past *tekireiki*. They themselves treated or viewed these women negatively as well, and some experienced pressure to resign from work when they were in *tekireiki*. Marriage during *tekireiki* was still the norm during much of the 1980s.

However, from the late 1980s to the early 1990s (when boom cohort women were in their early to mid twenties), Japan's economy grew at an unprecedented rate. The boom led to a serious labor shortage, and many employers turned to previously undesired segments of the population for labor needs, which included unmarried women in their late twenties and/or with higher education. Single women were suddenly in high demand in the labor market. Even clerical workers were encouraged to stay employed past *tekireiki*, and many women were hired into career positions that were formerly reserved exclusively for men. This change, along with the strong Japanese yen, allowed single women to enjoy luxurious leisure activities and consumption, as well as stimulating jobs (for some). Because devotion to work was the norm of corporate workers in career-track positions, women who were placed in such positions spent excessively long hours at work (just as many men did). During this era of economic boom, labor force participation among (unmarried) women in their late twenties soared, and career women in business suits became visible and even glorified in the popular media. Optimism that accompanied the ascending economy, and positive images of career women – along with the sheer number of single women in the work force – made many unmarried women of this cohort feel comfortable with staying single past the traditional *tekireiki*.

Despite this change in women's employment opportunities, most women of the boom cohort held on to traditional beliefs when it came to gender roles within marriage. Though some women felt somewhat resentful of such social expectations, they nevertheless believed strongly that is was most proper for married women to focus on homemaking and childrearing. They perceived the having-it-all lifestyle to be bad for children, impossible, or too hard. Marriage and paid work were thus seen as incompatible. Women of this cohort lacked the cultural tools needed to reconcile two competing desires – one for earnings/leisure/jobs and the other for marriage and family. Only a small number of women of this cohort chose the having-it-all life course. Most women either married and resigned from work or stayed employed and postponed marriage.

146

WHY AREN'T JAPANESE WOMEN GETTING MARRIED?

Women of this cohort were also typically deprived of positive images of marriage. Their parents grew up in wartime, when the patriarchal *ie* (house) ideology ruled marriage and family, and many of these parents' marriages were characterized by husbands' dominance, emotional distance, and conflict. Peer marriages were largely invisible to single women, and the limited glimpses they had of married peers only reinforced negative images of marriage: restrictive, unhappy, and loveless were typical descriptive terms. The absence of positive marriage models hindered many women who might otherwise have thought concretely of marriage.

The direct cause of singlehood, however, was that structural and cultural conditions left women with very limited opportunities for finding marital partners or developing relationships. First, many single women were segregated from single men at work vertically, spatially, and horizontally. Company-sponsored social events still allowed singles to intermingle once in a while, but supervisors refrained from the previously common practice of matchmaking their female subordinates because they were needed in their workplaces (and female workers were expected to resign upon marriage or pregnancy). Second, men as well as career women were expected to demonstrate their devotion to work through long hours of labor and, by complying with this expectation, they had little time, energy, or opportunity to meet dating partners and develop romantic relationships. Third, career women were not pursued by men due to sexist prejudice that associated job competence with an absence of femininity and interest in marriage. Fourth, desirable men were scarce. Many single men in white-collar occupations lacked cultural fluency and communication skills, making them unappealing to many women who were culturally sophisticated. Intimate relationships were also plagued by infidelity, abuse, control, and other problems and many women viewed relationships (and marriage) as obstacles to the enjoyment of leisure and work. Women also held gendered prejudice. Many preferred men to be "superior" to themselves – e.g., culturally savvier, earning higher incomes, occupying higher status white-collar occupations, taking the lead within relationships, etc. They rejected men who were socially awkward, low income, in blue-collar occupations, and in casual employment. This belief in gender hierarchy by women further limited the pool of candidates for marriage.

In 2009 when I conducted the interviews, my boom cohort interviewees were aged between 38 and 46. In 2010, 17.4 percent of women (i.e., more than one out of six women) in the age group 40–44 and 12.6 percent of those (i.e., about one out of eight women) 45–49 had never married. These were the highest never-married rates ever recorded in Japan for women of these age groups. The corresponding figures for 2000 were 8.6 and 6.3 percent respectively. Thus, the boom cohort women were twice as likely to remain unmarried in their forties compared to the cohort before them. At the time of interviews, all but one of the never-married interviewees wished or hoped to marry – some expressed their desires eagerly while others did so rather ambivalently. Some of them, in their late thirties and early forties, were hoping to have their *own* children (i.e., not by adoption). Others expressed regret, sadness, and concern over not having had children. Still others either had no interest in motherhood or tried to focus on the positives of childfree lives. Whereas some women were hopeful and had a positive outlook on life, many others were deeply concerned about their future (as I will discuss later in this chapter).

Recession cohort

The recession cohort was born in the 1970s or first half of the 1980s. By the time women of this cohort reached their twenties, singlehood among women of that age was common and the average age of marriage for women had risen to the late twenties. The once-strong marriage-age (*tekireiki*) norm was apparently no longer in effect; indeed, it was not even known among women of this cohort. No longer dictated by a societal norm, the timing of marriage instead depended on each individual's beliefs and circumstances. Still, most women of this cohort took the marriage life path for granted – just like boom cohort women – and wished to marry and have children. Therefore, the perceived age limit for childbearing typically shaped their ideas about timing of marriage: most wanted to marry around age 30. These women knew at least one single woman in their late thirties or forties. Exposure to such women, however, did not move them to embrace singlehood or consider lifetime singlehood as a viable lifestyle option. Instead, the presence of older single women presented a cautionary tale.

In contrast to boom cohort women, many women of the recession cohort grew up with happily married parents and held a positive outlook on marriage. In cases where parents painted a negative picture, recession cohort women had better chances (than the boom cohort) to observe peers who were married happily, and thus to revitalize positive assessments. Positive images, however, were not shaped by egalitarianism within marriage. Parents' marriages were characterized by traditional gender roles and male authority. But, unlike the boom cohort, the recession cohort parents were observed to be harmonious – emotionally close, openly expressing affection, and avoiding harsh conflict (at least in front of children).

Another contrast with the boom cohort was that recession cohort women were more diverse in their gender role conceptions (from traditional to near-egalitarian), and receptive of maternal employment. Living through severe economic recession during their younger years, many women of this cohort thought that rigid division of labor by gender (male breadwinning; female homemaking) may not be possible. These women also engaged in more modest leisure activities (than the boom cohort) and viewed jobs as necessary rather than enjoyable. Thus, unlike the boom cohort, women of the recession cohort did not view leisure and jobs to be incompatible with romantic relationships and marriage. But most women still equated womanhood with domesticity and planned to take the primary role in homemaking. Their emphasis on maternal employment was for earning supplementary household income and/or self-development.

Their positive outlook on marriage and flexible ideas about role allocation in marriage should have given this cohort of women better chances of marriage than the boom cohort women, who could not reconcile two competing desires. But the recession cohort faced many other obstacles. One was the declined marriage-age norm. Receiving little social pressure to marry by a certain deadline, each individual had to figure out her own timing. Another was the same as that faced by the boom cohort: limited opportunities for romantic encounters. Gender segregation at work, long work hours by men and some women, and prejudice against career women reduced the chance of romance. For this cohort, however, gender segregation was more severe. Following the economic recession many companies slashed budgets, hiring fewer new graduates and sponsoring fewer social events. Further, corporate hiring freezes caused many more women to take jobs in female-dominated occupations such as elderly care, segregating them from men spatially and horizontally.

Another obstacle was male reluctance to marry. National surveys indicate that the great majority of single men of this cohort wished to marry, but my interviewees' stories and other studies indicate that many men hesitated possibly because: (a) their un-/under-employment made men feel like inadequate candidates; (b) long work hours demotivated them, since marriage would take away already limited personal time; (c) they preferred their (future) wives to take sole responsibility for domestic tasks; and (d) they found career women unappealing. These sentiments suggest the strong impact of traditional gender ideology, deteriorated economic prospects among the cohort, and persistent workplace practices requiring long work hours, on men's thoughts about marriage. There is a striking similarity between recession cohort men and boom cohort women. Both lacked the cultural tools needed to reconcile two competing devotions – one to jobs and the other to family. It is possible that many men of this cohort, similarly to boom cohort women, put marriage on the backburner, viewing the having-it-all lifestyle as too hard or undesirable.

Although women of the recession cohort were receptive of men's non-traditional role, most still rejected "indecisive" men – seeing decisiveness as a desired "masculine" trait – and wished men to lead within relationships. Thus, traditional gender ideology largely persists and reinforces the gender hierarchy.[4] It is quite ironic that both men and women of this cohort seemed to believe in the same ideology, yet men assumed its incompatibility with, for instance, career women.[5]

At the time of interviews in 2009, my recession cohort interviewees were aged between 25 and 36. All the unmarried interviewees wished to marry, most of them eagerly, and almost all wanted to marry before they passed perceived age limits for childbearing or childrearing ("by 30" or "by 35 at the latest"). In 2010, the percentages of never-married women of the age groups 25–29, 30–34, and 35–39 were 60.3 (i.e., three out of five), 34.5 (i.e., more than one out of three), and 23.1 percent (almost one out of four), respectively. These were record high figures for Japanese women of each age group. In other words, recession cohort women were more likely to remain single in their twenties and thirties than the boom cohort, even though they despised singlehood among the boom cohort. My interviewees did not accept the idea of unwed motherhood or adoption of babies and children, all of which remain rare in Japan. Women have little control over gender segregation in employment and men's hesitance to marry. Unless drastic measures are taken to alter these circumstances, Japan is highly likely to see a record-high number of women foregoing motherhood in the near future – despite the fact that most wish and hope to marry and have children!

Key factors in summary

Table 6.1 summarizes the key causal factors identified in my research for the two cohorts. Singlehood increased because: (a) the marriage-age norm weakened; (b) opportunities of romantic encounters and development of intimate relationships were limited due to gender segregation at work, long work hours, gender prejudice, and scarcity of desirable men; (c) women were unsure of happiness in marriage because of negative images shaped and reinforced by parents and peers; and (d) women held gender role conceptions that matched neither real-life situations nor men's preferences. In the last row, I tentatively put the likely gender role conceptions held by men of each cohort, implied in my research but indicated in other literature. These are likely to explain why good men were scarce: for the boom cohort, many men were patriarchal and thus unappealing to women, promiscuous, unfaithful, abusive, controlling, prejudiced against career women, etc; for the recession cohort, many men were traditional and thus hesitated to consider marriage that might require sharing of domestic tasks or sole breadwinning, and rejected career women.

Three factors – gender segregation, long work hours, and men's prejudice against career women – were common to both cohorts, but the rest differed between the two. Marriage age norms were weaker and gender segregation was more severe for the recession cohort than for the boom cohort, but the negative impact of parents' and peers' marriages was much more pronounced among the boom cohort. The nature of men and gender role conceptions differed, too, though both cohorts were still largely traditional.

Implications of this study for sociological theory of singlehood

My research findings suggest that sociological theory of singlehood will benefit from shifting its focus to gender and other forms of power and social inequality and incorporating the concepts of *anomie* (by Emile Durkheim), *drift* (from my research), and *cohort effects* and *linked lives* (from life course theory). I discuss the implication of my research for sociological theory below.

Shifting the focus to gender and inequality

Notice that *gender* – socially constructed ideas regarding what is expected of males and females – has relevance to every single cell in Table 6.1. The marriage age norm, employment patterns, work hours, prejudice, nature of and expectations from potential partners, parents' and peer marriages, and ideas about role allocations were all patterned by gender. Inequality based on gender is clear and straightforward in some instances, and subtle in others. For example, patriarchal marriage and the gender-based employment system (that placed women only in clerical positions) systematically assigned women to weaker positions; that this is unfair and discriminatory is apparent. On the other hand, prejudice against career women, who are seen as masculine, is subtle. These women were in a better economic position in comparison to women in clerical positions and most women of the past. This appears, and is mistakenly regarded by many, to be a sign of women's advancement. But these women were effectively "barred" from relationships and marriage through stigma and prejudice. Why? Because they crossed the gender line. Economic power was supposed to belong to men, and, therefore, women who entered men's domain were penalized. Men viewed them as "masculine," and by defining them as "uninterested in marriage," disallowed their entry into women's domain (i.e., marriage). It is interesting that many *married* men pursued employed, single women. Apparently, these men deemed such women attractive enough to pursue sexually.

It was not just men who upheld the belief in women's traditional role; at a glance, it appears that women actually preferred it. Recall, however, that not all women were entirely happy about this social expectation – especially if it had to be met in addition to career employment that required long work hours. Contradictory sentiments towards and preference for women's homemaker role were, therefore, shaped by structural constraints and internalization of culture (i.e., values, norms, beliefs, ideology, etc.) through socialization.

These observations demonstrate how pervasively and sometimes subtly gender is entrenched in, and permeated into, social systems and culture. As Judith Lorber succinctly stated in *Paradoxes of Gender*, gender is part of the social stratification system, is a social institution and social process, and is embedded in social structure.[6] Gender is inseparable from formations of intimate relationships, marriage, and family, as it has been an integral part of these social institutions throughout human history and societies. Thus, gender and gender inequality must be primary foci in studies and theories of singlehood.

Yet current sociological theories of singlehood either completely neglect the impact of gender or treat it too lightly. One of the most influential theories of singlehood is economic (or rational choice) theory by Gary Becker.[7] This theory predicts that singlehood increases as women gain economic independence. According to this theory, the benefits of marriage are lower for women who can earn their own living, and therefore such women have a high likelihood of choosing to remain single (or divorce). Other economic theorists, such as

Table 6.1 Summary: causes of singlehood for the boom and recession cohorts

		Boom cohort	*Recession cohort*
Weakened marriage-age (*Tekireiki*) norm		Internalized and followed, but its enforcement at workplaces weakened due to a labor shortage caused by booming economy	Norm absent: Timing of marriage was up to individual (i.e., *anomie*)
Limited chances of romantic encounters/ development of intimate relationships	**Gender segregation at work**	Vertical, spatial, and horizontal gender segregation	
		Spatial segregation somewhat mitigated as company-sponsored social events were still common; matchmaking by supervisors was lessened	Severe spatial and horizontal, due to corporate hiring freezes and budget slashes on company-sponsored social events
	Long work hours	Excessively long work hours by men and career women	
	Gender prejudice	Men's prejudice against career women as unfeminine and uninterested in marriage	
		Women's prejudice against non-hegemonic and one-dimensional men as non-masculine	Women's prejudice against indecisive men as feminine
	Scarcity of desirable men	Corporate hegemonic men were one-dimensional and unappealing; married men had affairs with single women; men were unfaithful, abusive, etc.	Men who were reluctant to marry (due to adherence to traditional gender ideology?)

Negative images of marriage	**Impacts of parents' marriage**	Patriarchal, emotionally distant, conflict-ridden marriages shaped negative images of marriage	Most grew up with parents in emotionally close marriages, which shaped positive image of marriage; some held negative views due to parents in cold marriages or bad parental divorces
	Impacts of peer marriage	Mostly invisible and this reinforced negative images of marriage (restrictive, troublesome, unhappy, loveless, etc.)	Positive models were visible for many to inspire single women to wish to marry and renew positive images
Gender role conceptions that did not match reality/desires/men's wants	**Women's role in marriage**	Almost uniformly traditional (Domestic role as proper; having-it-all as bad for children, impossible, or too hard); some were resentful but did not challenge the idea; = they lacked the cultural tools to have it all	More diverse and flexible (Domestic role as proper and natural but receptive to maternal employment)
	Men's role in marriage	Almost uniformly traditional (Breadwinning role as proper; men should make decisions, lead, and do better economically than their partners)	More diverse and flexible (Receptive to men's inability to provide solely); still expected men to be decision-makers
	Ideas held by men	*Very traditional/patriarchal?*	*Mostly traditional? = Their expectation did not match women's.*

Valerie Oppenheimer, however, have shown that empirical evidence from the U.S. did not support Becker's theory, and instead argue that it is deterioration of men's economic prospects that causes the increase of singlehood.[8] These two theories do take gender into consideration, but in very limited ways – only as it relates to economic prospects or conditions. As mentioned earlier, numerous empirical studies from Japan rejected or only partially supported these theories (please see note 33 of Chapter 1 for more detail).

The other standard theoretical camp focuses on the impact of cultural changes. The most prominent theory is the second demographic transition theory.[9] This theory forecasts that the development of society leads to increases in cohabitation, unwed motherhood, divorce, and postponement of or retreat from marriage. According to this theory, individuals need not worry about sustenance in the developed world, and can therefore afford to focus on self-fulfillment, seeking alternative ways to form intimate relationships instead of conforming to tradition (i.e., marriage). Proponents of this theory, such as Ron Lesthaeghe, thus interpret the increase of non-marriage as a sign of increased personal freedom. This line of theories[10] generally disregards issues of gender (and other social) inequality. Several empirical studies from Japan strongly dispute this theory (please see note 33 for this as well).

These theories have some merit, but downplay the impact of gender and other forms of social inequality, and overrate individuals' agency – the ability to direct and choose life paths. A basic tenet of the sociological perspective, however, asserts that individuals' "choices" are patterned and restricted by social structure and culture, and gender scholarship points out that gender is embedded in social structure and culture. Those in disadvantageous positions/groups tend to have little power in deciding their life paths. Gender is also complex. (In)equality based on gender cannot be measured simply in terms of women's and men's economic conditions or prospects.

It is imperative to appreciate the importance, in my analysis, of inequality that was not based on gender: other forms of power and social inequality played major roles in the increase of singlehood in Japan. Exploitative use of workers' labor (particularly that of men), coupled with precarious employment conditions (among young men and women) since the economic recession, had the most detrimental impact on other factors related to singlehood. Yet current sociological theories of singlehood tend to focus on the impacts of individuals' liberation – such as women's gained economic independence and greater personal freedom – as causes of singlehood. While one may argue that Japan, where work devotion through long work hours is socially expected and gender inequality is severe, is an exception to the rule/theories, I doubt this is the case for two reasons.

First, in addition to Japan, never-married rates are high in Southern Europe (e.g., Italy, Greece, and Portugal)[11] and Asian countries (e.g., South Korea, Taiwan, Singapore, and the Philippines),[12] and in these countries, cohabitation and unwed childbearing – alternative relationship formations according to the second demographic transition theory – remain rare.[13] We can safely assume that these countries are rather conservative in terms of gender compared to other developed nations, such as the Nordic countries. Second, in the case of the U.S. – which we may consider relatively egalitarian in gender beliefs – cohabitation and unwed motherhood are more likely among poorer groups,[14] and never-married rates are the highest among African American women, including those in middle-class occupations.[15] Qualitative interview research conducted by Kathryn Edin and Maria Kefalas on young, poor, unwed mothers,[16] and that of Ralph Richard Banks on highly educated African American women,[17] suggest that most unmarried women in these groups adhere to the marriage institution, and strongly wish to marry, but cannot marry due largely to structural and cultural barriers. Further, in the U.S., divorce rates have increased among lower-educated women but decreased among the higher educated in the last three decades.[18] These realities indicate that Japan is not the only country in which power and social inequality contributed to increased singlehood.

I feel that the neglect of gender (and other forms of power and social inequality) in sociological theories of singlehood is perhaps related to the fact that this subject has been studied first and more extensively by demographers and other quantitative-oriented researchers, predominantly white and/or male, who had very limited knowledge of gender/feminist scholarship (and gender's intersection with race, ethnicity, etc.). This state of affairs has been detrimental to theory development. Again, gender is inseparable from (lack of) marriage and family formation, and we need to shift our focus to gender – and power and social inequality in general – to study singlehood and understand it theoretically.

The issue of methodology connects to problems with theory. My research, which employed a life story interview research method, generated extraordinarily rich data. From women's lived experiences, I could reconstruct the social context they lived through and identify several causal factors and the process of increased singlehood. Feminist methodology encourages putting women's (and other disadvantaged groups') subjective experiences in the center of research (and also empowering them in the processes of research by, for instance, giving them voice). This method certainly has many advantages in comparison to data collected from survey questionnaires and vital statistics. Unfortunately, however, some quantitative researchers remain skeptical of qualitative (or feminist) research methodology and reject it as invalid, or rank it as second class. Perhaps some quality work done by feminist scholars on singlehood in Japan[19] was not taken seriously enough to effect revision of existing theories. If so, this reflects gender inequality within the disciplines of sociology and demography. We need to achieve equal status for feminist methodology, which I believe significantly improves our understanding of the subject and theorization efforts.

Incorporating the four concepts: anomie, drift, cohort effects, and linked lives

Though gender (inequality) was fundamental in understanding increased single-hood, gender inequality obviously existed before the single population surged. The catalysts of the demographic change were two major shifts in the Japanese economy – the boom in the late 1980s and the recession of the 1990s. They tipped the balance of social systems and culture.

To make sense out of this, it is helpful to apply Emile Durkheim's theory of *anomie*.[20] Prior to the economic boom, social systems – such as the gendered employment system, matchmaking practices in the workplace, and the *miai* mate selection system – were aligned with cultural expectations that everyone should marry during *tekireiki*, and that within marriage individuals should take the role assigned to them based on their sex. This alignment began to distort, first because the booming economy kept women in the labor force past *tekireiki*. This resulted in the (gendered) traditional marriage-age norm weakening, and ultimately disappearing. Next, the economic recession deteriorated young men's economic prospects. In the meantime, however, traditional gender ideology persisted, and contradicted the changing employment opportunities of young women during the boom (i.e., better ones than their predecessors) and young men during the recession (i.e., worse ones than their predecessors). In the midst of this cultural contradiction and weakening marriage-age norm, many women and men were unable to figure out the right life path to take, and ended up remaining single.

Their society was rapidly changing – becoming increasingly contradictory, inconsistent, and confusing. This is *anomie*: due to rapid social change, social norms no longer, or only weakly, guide individuals' behaviors and life paths. Theoretically speaking, if a society was completely anomic, individuals would have to navigate their lives with total independence from society's guidance. No real society is in such a state – but this concept helps us understand why many women *drifted* into singlehood.

To borrow my interviewees' words, people in Japan used to marry "automatically" by a certain age. If one had no marriage prospects, other people got involved and helped – or even forced – one to marry. Though it is certainly nice that most people in Japan today need not be forced to marry, this should not be confused with freedom. As I have shown, there were numerous obstacles to marriage, many of which were unavoidable or impossible to overcome at an individual level. These were structural or cultural barriers. Some women had fewer obstacles than others, and they could marry. Others consciously navigated through obstacles to make marriage happen. But others – a significantly large number of women – simply waited. It was like letting the social current direct their lives – which most of their predecessors did. The current, however, was changing dramatically and unclearly (i.e., anomic). Without intent, many women (and men) reached the destination they did not desire to reach: singlehood. In other words, rather than strategic, rational choices, agency, or self-directedness by women, I contend that increased singlehood in Japan (and perhaps elsewhere) can be captured and understood better by Durkheim's concept of *anomie* as well as my concept of *drift*. Indeed, as mentioned in previous chapters, other qualitative researchers also observed little agency among single women in Japan.

Lastly, life course theory provides a useful theoretical framework for studying increased singlehood. As I have shown, the pathways to singlehood differed between the two cohorts, and women's views of marriage were influenced strongly by their parents and peers – people whom they were closely linked with. Life course theory informs us that individuals' life courses are shaped by four principles: time and location, timing of lives, linked lives, and individual agency.[21] In short, this theory predicts that macro-level social events (e.g., economic boom and recession) experienced especially at young ages (i.e., childhood, adolescence, and young adulthood) and micro-level connections (e.g., parents and other people to whom one is closely connected) have tremendous impacts on individuals' life courses. The principle of individual agency – which I am wary to apply, as the concept is problematic and loaded – adds that individuals direct their own life courses within limits placed by the three other principles.

The first two principles (i.e., time and location; timing of lives) suggest *cohort effects*. When society is changing rapidly, cohort membership has significant effects on one's life course and shapes it differently from those of other cohorts. In other words, those who experienced the same historical event(s) at a similar stage in their lives – such as the cohort of women who experienced the booming economy in young adulthood – tend to take a similar life course (e.g., singlehood), which differs significantly from other cohorts (e.g., the cohort before them that married at high rates).[22] I believe the utility of this concept for understanding increased singlehood is clear.

Another apparently useful concept from life course theory is the principle of *linked lives*. However, I only accidentally, or inductively, found profound contrasts (between the two cohorts) in parents' and peers' marriages – and their impacts on women's views of marriage – from the data I collected. The concept of linked lives is not part of theories of singlehood, and further research needs to examine more systematically (than was done in my research) the impacts of micro-level, interpersonal connections on singlehood.

In sum, we should be able to improve the theory of singlehood by shifting the focus to gender and power and social inequality, by employing and respecting data yielded via feminist methodology, and by incorporating the concepts of anomie, drift, cohort effects, and linked lives.

Implications of this study for women's empowerment and government policies

When I gave a talk on my research at a university in Japan in 2011, one of the attendees, an intelligent (unmarried) female graduate student in her mid twenties, approached me after the talk. My presentation was on the research findings discussed in Chapters 2 and 3 of this book. She told me that every single factor I pointed out about the recession cohort applied to her, saying, "It was like the story of my life." She then added, "This is depressing. This means I can't do anything about it, you know?" referring to my conclusion that *structural* barriers kept women from marrying.

Her comment was shocking to me, as I intended that my research *empower* women. My thinking was that identifying the structural causes should free single women from unreasonable stigma and blame, and, I hoped, move society to remove such barriers. What can be done to help more women in Japan materialize such basic desires as intimate partners and children? Below I discuss my suggestions, as well as possible issues that need to be resolved.

Promotion of work–life balance and gender equality

One obvious evil is the incredibly long hours spent on work by Japanese workers, especially by men but also by women. Though labor statistics indicate declining work hours by Japanese employees, they still spend more hours on work than workers of most other developed nations, and we have good reason to suspect that many Japanese are putting more hours into work and work-related obligations than official statistics show.[23] As we have seen, long work hours inhibited young women and men from pursuing romantic encounters, dating, and developing romantic relationships. Recently, Prime Minister Shinzo Abe's government began the funding of matchmaking services for single people.[24] Putting aside questions about the effectiveness and desirability of such services, we must ask how exactly young people will use them to find marital partners when long hours of employment have left them with no time or energy to date. As discussed in Chapter 3, numerous studies have shown the detrimental impact of long work hours on Japanese workers. Japan's Labor Standard Act limits official overtime work hours,[25] but apparently the law on its own has not been sufficient to reduce actual work hours.

One of my acquaintances from Japan, a married woman in her early thirties, read an earlier version of Chapter 3 and shared her observations with me. At a company for which she used to work, her boss told his subordinates not to work overtime, or else they would not be able to marry. She and I discussed how such bosses are still rare in Japan, and how more supervisors need to be like him. It is important that both employees and employers become aware of the detriment of long work hours to individuals' lives (and also worker productivity!). Those in positions of power (i.e., employers and supervisors) especially need to make conscious efforts to alter a workplace culture that accepts or demands overtime work, because subordinates are in too vulnerable a position to defy the long tradition of devotion to work. This is particularly the case in a precarious economy. Perhaps we need a system that rewards corporations and supervisors for encouraging employees to work within set limits of hours.

The issue of employment relates to work–life balance and gender equality. To these ends, the Japanese government has implemented various policies, programs, and systems since the mid 1980s. These included the Equal Employment Opportunity Law (first enacted in 1987 and later revised in 1997 and 2014), the Plan for Gender Equality (in 1996), the Basic Law for a Gender-Equal Society (in 1999), Childcare Leave Law (in 1991, later extended to Childcare and Family Care Leave Law in 1999, and revised in 2009), and the Angel Plans (i.e., the plans to provide support for childrearing, in 1994 and 1999).[26] To encourage fathers' involvement in childcare, the government ran two major campaigns: one in the late 1990s and the other since 2010.[27] In recent years, Prime Minister Abe, calling his agenda "Womenomics," declared that Japan would increase women's representation in positions of power and actively utilize women's labor for the improvement of the country's economy.[28]

Much of these work–life balance policies and programs were adopted from European models.[29] They have had little impact in Japan. Most married women do not return to the labor force after childbirth, most workers who take advantage of parental leave are mothers,[30] men who take or try to take parental leave face resistance at work and from others including relatives,[31] the never-married population continues to rise, birth rates only slightly increased,[32] women's representation in positions of power remains pathetically low, women in full-time regular employment earn only about 70 percent of what their male counterparts earn on average, and more women are un- and underemployed than men.[33]

One reason for the ineffectiveness of these policies and programs is the motivation of the Japanese government. Promotion of gender equality is driven primarily by external pressure, such as the demand for improvement made by the United Nations.[34] The true purpose of work–life balance programs and policies was to increase fertility and improve the Japanese economy.[35] Prime Minister Abe's plan to increase female representation by affirmative action clearly indicates a superficial level of understanding of gender inequality by him and his cabinet members. Further, work–life balance programs and policies are pronatalist, strikingly resembling the policies of wartime during which the Japanese government treated women as mere birth-giving machines.[36] Policies that carry over such sexist ideas are clearly not implemented to promote gender equality.

In any case, increasing birth rates at this point will not sufficiently address Japan's aging population. Members of Japan's largest age cohort – *dankai no sedai* or "baby boomer" equivalent – were born between 1947 and 1949 and therefore, are already in their late sixties. Increasing birth rates now will only worsen the dependency ratio – the number of working-age persons in the population per those who are dependent (i.e., aged under 15 and 65+). The government seems to be concerned about Japan's economic productivity in the future, but there is a large pool of potential workers, such as un-/underemployed women and men, those who wish to work past the mandatory retirement age (mid sixties), and foreign nationals who would love to live and work in Japan.

Although personally I have mixed feelings about encouraging fertility on an overpopulated planet, it can be argued that having children is a basic human right. In this sense, work–life balance programs and policies, implemented by the government, are welcome. But the ineffectiveness of those offered thus far clearly indicates that the relevant problems lie elsewhere – and I have pointed out many. Generally speaking, I think that the state should shift focus from solving "the demographic crisis" to improving individual wellbeing. As the King of Bhutan Jigme Singye Wangchuck declared in 1972, "Gross National Happiness (GNH)" should be prioritized over Gross National Product (GNP).[37] In Japan's case, this would involve a serious tackling of problems related to work hours, gender equality, work–life balance, etc. Common enough is the criticism that profit-driven policies exploit a large segment of the population, but, as we have seen in Japan's case, an unforeseen consequence of this is that people have actually lost the opportunity to reproduce.

Preventing repercussions of increased singlehood on work–life balance and gender equality

Ironically, it may be that singles themselves are inhibiting the realization of the work–life balance, and gender equality, they desperately need to achieve goals of marriage and family. This is another reason why society needs to focus on happiness for *all*, rather than creating policies and programs that target certain segments of the population. The following personal anecdote – regarding an event that provided insight on yet another potential repercussion of increased single population – should serve to clarify.

A few years ago, I had a long, interesting conversation with a man seated next to me on the lengthy flight from the U.S. to Tokyo (Narita Airport). He was a Japanese national, married, and in his mid thirties. He had been recently relocated to his Japanese company's small branch office in the U.S., and was on his way to spend time in Japan with his first child and his wife, who was about to give birth to their second child. He was also going to help his whole family move to the U.S. after the birth. He happened to have majored in sociology in college, and upon finding out my occupation, urged me to talk about my research. I explained my findings on limited chances for romance due to gender segregation at work. He affirmed it to be a very likely explanation and shared his personal experience. His company hired mostly men, and in the department he was first placed in, there was only one unmarried, young female worker – who later became his wife. She was a clerical worker and, half-jokingly, he said he pursued her vigorously because otherwise he thought he may not be able to marry. He said most of his (male) co-workers and supervisors were still unmarried.

I told him that it was nice that he could take time off to help with his wife's childbirth and visit his family, and asked if his company had a family-friendly work environment. In response to this he frowned, telling me that the contrary was the case. He explained he could take time off only because he was practically his own boss at the small U.S. office, and also had bargaining power due to possessing a scarce skill – fluency in English. Then he added an interesting observation. He said some supervisors he worked under in his company were unmarried and childless, and that these men were worse (than married supervisors) when it came to accommodating subordinates' needs and wants for family time. With an expression of repulsion, he further criticized single supervisors as "selfish" and "immature," attributing such qualities to their never-married, childless status – indicators of their absence of experience providing care to family members.

This intelligent, inquisitive man's insight made me connect some dots. A similar lack of understanding (of family needs) was exhibited by two of my never-married interviewees, Rumi and Sachiko, who earned exceptionally high incomes. As a vice president of a company, Rumi expected her male subordinates, regardless of their marital status, to work single-mindedly and for many hours. She held a double standard for women, acknowledging the needs of married women to be home, and hence hoped that her able female workers would never marry. Sachiko, a CPA accountant who worked for an American firm, criticized her company for promoting programs aimed to help female employees balance jobs and family. She thought such special treatment was unnecessary. These two women's views suggest that unmarried supervisors (with no children) may require their subordinates to work harder, oblivious of needs and wants associated with family life.

The same pattern was observed in Mary Blair-Loy's study on three cohorts of female executives in the U.S.[38] Women of the oldest cohort, that of the World War II era, forewent either marriage or childbearing, viewing marriage/motherhood and employment to be incompatible (sounds familiar?). These women were the least accepting of the idea of work–life balance, and did not show understanding towards younger female executives who wanted or had both career and family. This potential repercussion of increased singlehood on work–life balance and gender equality – effectively a self-perpetuating cycle – should be taken seriously.

Need for policies and programs that help alleviate problems faced by single women (and men)

Never-married individuals, especially women, are the victims of structural and cultural constraints. My research subjects made it clear that they wished to marry but could not. Single women, particularly from the older age group, expressed concerns over their future. Financial, psychological, and emotional insecurities were mentioned most. Below, I share the words of two never-married women – Kazuko (45 years old) and Tsuneko (43 years old)[39] – who spoke of their concerns at length. These accounts are good representations of concerns and sentiments shared by many never-married interviewees:

Kazuko: What is it, really? It's just that I can't help thinking all the time, though sort of vaguely. What is it? [pause] It may be endless if I start talking about my concerns. For instance, financial. [pause] It's okay now because I have my parents but. [pause] How shall I put it? If you're married, you'd take care of each other. [pause] Ummm, how shall I put it? [pause] It's like being embraced, you know? It's your husband, sort of like parents. My worry is that I'd lose that completely because my parents are getting old. [pause] If I had a partner or a husband, unless we don't get sick, you know, it's like being protected, I'd be in good hands, I'd feel safe, that kind of feeling.
Author: You can't get it from your friends?
Kazuko: No. Yeah, that kind of feeling. When I become old, well, for now, too, I'd feel safe [if I were married]. So, it's about the mental state. [pause] If I start talking about physical stuff, it'd be endless. What should I do if I get sick? [pause] What'd happen when I die? Well, these go to everyone, but, okay, [let's focus on the time] before I die. [pause] Like I feel lonely on days off. You know? Yeah. Even if I still have my parents. [pause] Umm, well. [pause] When I had a boyfriend, that warm feeling, [in contrast to] not having a boyfriend so I have to figure out what fun things I can do alone. That sort of thing. And I worry if this will continue forever.
Author: Do you think this is a bigger concern than financial insecurity?
Kazuko: What? No! I can't compare. About the same. If I start talking about finance, money, it'd be endless. I can't help thinking, it's better to be two than one (*hitori yori futari*).... It's not that I want someone I can share my feelings with when I'm having a hard time.... When I'm being happy, when I had something good [to share, I want] someone who'd be happy for me and with me. [pause] It's sad not having someone like that, you know?

Tsuneko: Disadvantage of singlehood? Well, many things. Well, I have to manage all the finances on my own, I have to pay for rent and everything on my own. Also, not trusted by society ... I recently came to realize.
Author: When did you feel so?
Tsuneko: Well, I live alone, right? And I'm renting an apartment. But recently, I thought of moving to a new place, so I was looking around. I ran into one I kind of liked, so asked if I can look at the place.... I was given an application form but I had to give names of guarantors (*rentai*

hoshōnin). My father is already retired, you know? And I realized. Wait a minute. Whom can I ask? Who can sign? Also, I had to write my annual salary. I realized this is to be not trusted by society.... It's different for men who have a certain level of status. If you want to buy a condo, it's a totally different story for men working for large well-known corporations. [It's hard] for single women to borrow money. You see what I mean?

Author: Are you saying that single women are in a disadvantageous position when getting loans?

Tsuneko: I believe so. It may be different if women have the same kind of jobs as those men.

Author: Do you have any thoughts on your future?

Tsuneko: Future? I think of the time when I am old. [laugh]

Author: Such as?

Tsuneko: I wonder if it's okay to keep living alone, unmarried like this. Money, too. But recently my mother passed away, and I can't help thinking what'd happen when I die. I never thought of such a thing before but now that I passed 40, I think of the time I will get old.

Author: Any other concerns over your future?

Tsuneko: Of course there are. You know, my job? I'd never know if I could keep working with the same income. I hope I'll stay healthy and can work, but in this era [of precarious economy] you'd never know what'd happen. If I'm not married, I could count only on myself. Is this okay? Can I keep going? If I own a house, it'd be nice. Yeah, I won't have a place to live. It's a harsh reality.

Compared to men, women earn significantly less, on average, and are more likely to be un-/underemployed. But they also face ageism in employment[40] and gender discrimination in the housing market.[41] Beyond such financial concerns, these two women's words reflect a longing for lifetime partnership, and worries about health and death.

This is one of the main reasons I argue passionately against the portrayal – by the popular media[42] and social scientists[43] – of single women as strong, independent, and carefree, with the capability to direct their lives however they wish. No doubt such women exist in Japan. But consider Tsuneko, a marketing consultant, who came across as one such independent, single career woman. She spent over four hours in interview, and for some time maintained her bearing – both physically and mentally – as a strong, rational woman. Any emotional weakness she might have felt was kept contained. But by the mid point of the interview, Tsuneko began to reveal her worries at length (recounted above, in part).

I find the popular portrayal of single women as "strong and independent" to be dangerous because, in the face of this expectation, such women may find themselves unable to share their worries with others, instead holding negative thoughts and feelings inside. Many of my single interviewees thanked me, saying they felt like they had received counseling or therapy. Further, the widespread image of single women enjoying luxurious, carefree lifestyles could marginalize (and probably has marginalized) single women who have little economic independence. In contrast to this image, many single women live with their parents because they cannot afford to live on their own.

The belief that single women are doing well financially, or living selfishly, justifies the already-unsympathetic treatment of them by the public and government. A prime minister of the past once expressed the opinion that single women did not deserve governmental assistance since they selfishly forewent childbearing. The heckling incident in the Tokyo Assembly (mentioned in the first chapter) lends support to the conclusion that such sentiments remain strong among elected representatives. As an aside, we should point out that it is unfair to characterize childless women as removed from a nurturing role, as many single women are either taking care of, or expected to take care of, aging parents.[44]

Conservatives demonize single women, liberals glorify them; both kinds of rhetoric harm them. This will continue until the public gives glib oratory the skepticism it deserves and pays attention to what is happening to real women in the real world. Current governmental programs motivated by fertility increase and economic productivity fail to solve problems faced by such real women, especially those who have passed reproductive age. Their issues are genuine and urgent: that is why the wellbeing of people living *now* must be prioritized over the fantasy of returning Japan to the population pyramid it had in the early twentieth century!

Better understanding of common issues observed within marriage

This book focused on singlehood among women – I interviewed married interviewees for the purpose of comparison. But as you have seen, stories shared by my married interviewees reveal common problems faced by married women in Japan. Within sociology, I am not aware of many scholarly studies on the quality of marriage in Japan,[45] whereas housework division of labor seems to have gotten a lot of attention. Qualitative research on marriage (as it relates to gender) in Japan has increased but remains scarce, particularly by scholars living in Japan. This understudied area needs to be better explored.

Hearing unhappy stories, and observing unhappily married interviewees, I was honestly unsure about whether my single interviewees would have been better off if they married as desired. Many single interviewees had richer life experiences than many of my married interviewees.[46] I wish I could have interviewed more married women, or presented more of the stories shared by those I did interview. These data were, however, beyond the scope of my project. I should note at this point that, though this book has sought to answer the question of why many women were *unable* to marry, this question became pertinent simply because most women in Japan wish to marry. I do not mean to suggest that every woman should marry, or that marriage is necessarily the route to happiness for all women.

Wartime patriarchy and aging Japan

As mentioned in the first chapter, Japanese society is aging fast, meaning that the elderly share of the population is growing exponentially. It is projected that, by 2035, close to one out of three residents will be aged 65 or older, and that every two workers will have to support one elderly person. The Japanese government implemented the long-term care insurance system in 2000 and provided other policies for elderly care.[47] Yet, currently, much of the burden of elder care is falling onto family members, especially women. Many wives, daughters, and daughters-in-law are daily providing physical and emotional care for Japan's elderly population.[48] Additionally, elder care workers and nurses, most of whom are women, provide various forms of service for the elderly who need assistance and/or are ill. The aging population is, therefore, another gendered phenomenon.

The wartime patriarchal ideology has had serious consequences for aging Japan. As I discussed in Chapter 4, many marriages of boom cohort parents – the wartime generation – were especially patriarchal. This people of this generation are currently in their seventies or older. Many of them hold onto patriarchal beliefs which manifest in their expectations, thinking, attitudes, behaviors, and so forth. This creates a very tough situation for many caretakers, and causes tension and conflict within spousal, parent–child, sibling, extended-kin, and patient–care worker relationships. Note that such tension and conflict occurs in already stressful situations in which people are dealing with illness, dying, and death. The damage done to relationships under such conditions may be permanent.

In taking care of my dying mother, including after her death, I experienced and observed the detrimental impacts of wartime patriarchal ideology first hand.[49] This experience moves me to voice loudly that the issue of aging in Japan (and perhaps elsewhere) is not just one of quantity – e.g., a shortage of care facilities and workers (not to downplay this problem at all) – but one of quality: human relations. The wartime ideology was supposedly abolished, officially and legally, in the 1940s. Yet it continues to affect countless individuals. As a society, Japan must recognize the damage still being done by this relic of imperialism, militarism, nationalism, and callous patriarchy – and make efforts to relegate it to the same historical dust heap.

Need for women to stand up for their own rights

Throughout the book, I mentioned that I (and some other researchers[50]) observed that single women were passive and held little interest in promotion of gender equality. Such passivity was also indicated in the comment made by the graduate student after my talk. Although I have concluded that increased single-hood was caused largely by structural barriers, the idea is not to let women off the hook! Feminism in Japan is too weak.[51] If Japanese women do not believe in gender equality, who will?

Although Japan has a history of feminist movements,[52] most equal rights for women were handed down from the top. For instance, women's suffrage was granted soon after the end of World War II in the process of U.S.-led reform. The laws and policies related to gender equality were implemented by a govern-ment trying to solve demographic and/or economic problems, or in response to external pressures (as discussed above). Although there are Japanese feminists who fought in the past, and some who are currently fighting, throughout Japa-nese history women have almost never won their rights through arduous struggle. I wonder if this is one reason that women in Japan are, in comparison to other societies, relatively uninterested in feminism.

The bad news is that the Japanese government is unlikely to budge when it comes to assisting single women, which should lead us to the conclusion that Japanese women will have to stand up for their own rights! I apologize, good reader, if you found my book depressing, but I refuse to draw a rosy picture that does not exist. Understanding the drift into singlehood should not lead to acceptance of a dismal fate fueled by powerful social forces, but to a wake-up call for single women. It should be part of a larger effort to learn more about gender (inequality) from other sources, to think, to discuss, and to take actions – however small – towards the improvement of the status and lives of women.

Conclusion

Increased singlehood is a *gendered* phenomenon. Gender inequality embedded in social structure and culture, interacting with changing economic contexts to create contradictions and absence of culture, left many women in Japan drifting towards singlehood. Other forms of power and social inequality played signi-ficant roles in keeping women unmarried against their wishes. This conclusion differs from what existing theories of singlehood predict. It also criticizes current social policies and calls for true empowerment of women in Japan.

The single population is on the rise across the globe. I hope that this phe-nomenon can be better understood by shifting our focus, from individual agency to power and social inequality, taking changing social contexts into account. The feminist perspective that conceptualizes gender as social structure, Durkheim's concept of anomie as well as my concept of drift, and cohort effects and linked lives are useful theoretical tools in the analysis of this phenomenon. My study also attests the advantage of feminist methodology.

My research explored the lived experiences of two cohorts of women who resided in the Greater Tokyo Area in 2009. My sample included only one sexual minority, one member of an ethnic minority,[53] and no one with physical disabil-ities. Some interviewees were originally from rural regions, but most grew up in the Tokyo Area. They were diverse in terms of socioeconomic background (measured by their levels of education and parents' occupations), and I did not find discernable differences by social class, but there may be class-specific issues I have missed. Additionally, one of my interviewees implied potential impacts of gendered schooling – she went to an all-girl high school and two-year vocational school, the students of which were mostly female. Schools in Japan are highly gender segregated, and this may have had important impacts on singlehood as well.

I hope subsequent research will investigate never-married singlehood in different countries and among people of various social locations (e.g., by gender, class, race, ethnicity, sexual orientation, age, (dis)ability, migrant status, etc.)[54] The single population is expected to grow globally and the economy can be volatile. I conclude this book with hope for a better understanding and theorizing of singlehood which leads to better lives and social policies in all societies.

Notes

1 See note 34 of Chapter 1 for more detail.
2 Nemoto (2008) argued that increased singlehood among women in Japan was due to gender inequality, and Nemoto, Fuwa, and Ishiguro (2012) attributed the cause of increased singlehood among men to the decline of the marriage-age norm and to men's beliefs regarding gender roles in marriage. Though not all chapters conform to the theme, the book, *Kekkon no kabe* (*Obstacles to Marriage*), edited by Sato, Nagai, and Miwa (2010) argues that the fundamental cause of increased singlehood in Japan is changes in social structure instead of those of individuals. Despite such arguments, economic theories (represented in Becker's women's independence hypothesis) and cultural theories (that attribute the cause of increased singlehood/declined marriage to ideational or attitudinal change) appear to remain dominant in sociology (Raymo *et al.* 2015). In the Japanese context, Japanese sociologist Masahiro Yamada (1999) theorized that parents of the cohort of increased singlehood were affluent and could afford to allow their grown children to reside with them, and many young adults preferred co-residence with parents to marriage because they could enjoy free time and use their own income for leisure. Empirical studies from Japan (Genda 2005; Honda 2002/2005; Kukimoto 2005; Oishi 2004; Raymo 2003b; Shirahase 2005; Tanaka 2003), however, do not support his "parasite singles" theory.
3 Recent works that framed women's single status as their "choice" or agency (e.g., resistance) are Nagase 2006; L. Nakano 2010; Rosenberger 2013; Tashiro 2015; Tokuhiro 2010; and Tsuya, Mason, and Bumpass 2004.
4 By saying indecisive men were "feminine," recession cohort women were *doing gender* – in West and Zimmerman's terms (1987). This doing of gender reinforces and perpetuates gender stereotypes and inequality.
5 Ehara (2005) indeed observed in her focus group interviews of single women and men that gender role expectations were similar for the two sexes, yet men and women viewed the opposite sex's attitudes as incompatible. In this study, men accepted their future wife's employment and expected to share some domestic responsibilities with her, yet expressed a strong aversion to women who are assertive about equal sharing of the domestic role. Women, on the other hand, showed a strong negative view towards men who refused to discuss such sharing, but they did not expect their future husbands to take an equal share of domestic work, instead accepting that they would

do more of it than men. Ehara concluded that this was due to interviewees' inability to communicate effectively, caused by anomie – individualistic foci and a lack of cultural scripts.

6 Lorber 1994.

7 Becker 1981/1991/1993.

8 Oppenheimer 1988, 1994, 1997, 2000; Oppenheimer, Blossfeld, and Wackerow 1995; Oppenheimer, Kalmijn, and Lim 1997; Oppenheimer and Lew 1995.

9 Lesthaeghe 2010; Lesthaeghe and Neidert 2006; van de Kaa 1987.

10 Other similar theories include those by Beck and Beck-Gernsheim (2005) and Giddens (1991).

11 Lesthaeghe 2010.

12 Jones and Yeung 2014.

13 For instance, for Southern Europe, see Kiernan 2000, 2004; Lesthaeghe 2010; and Rossi 1997. For Asia, see Raymo *et al.* 2015. Also see OECD 2015a, 2015b for rates of cohabitation and unwed motherhood.

14 Smock, Manning, and Porter 2005.

15 Banks 2011.

16 Edin and Kefalas 2005 and Edin and Reed 2005.

17 Banks 2011.

18 S. Martin 2006.

19 For example, Nemoto 2008.

20 Durkheim 1951/1979.

21 Elder 1994, 1995; Elder, Johnson, and Crosnoe 2003; Elder and Pallerin 1998; Settersten 2003.

22 Glen H. Elder, Jr. (1999), American sociologist and the major proponent of life course theory, demonstrates this point in his study of the cohort of the Great Depression: those who spent their childhood during this time exhibited similar traits, such as frugality.

23 Kitanaka 2012; Sugimoto 2010.

24 Ujikane and Shimodoi 2014.

25 MHLW 2012.

26 See Boling 2008; Gelb 2003; MHLW 2010; Molony 1995; Rebick 2006; Roberts 2002, 2005; and Takeda 2011 for more detail.

27 The Ministry of Health and Welfare carried out a campaign in 1999 to encourage paternal involvement in childcare using "Sam," a celebrity and then-husband of popular singer Amuro Namie. Sam stayed at home to raise their child. For a description and reactions to this campaign, see Nakatani (2006) and Roberts (2002). More recently, the Ministry of Health, Labor, and Welfare (MHLW) began a new campaign called the "*Ikumen* project," which promotes and rewards involved fathers, claiming paternal involvement is not only important but also enjoyable. For details of this campaign, see Mizukoshi, Kohlbacher, and Schimkowsky (2015) and the MHLW website on the project (2016).

28 Macnaughtan 2015.

29 Boling 2008; Gelb 2003; Roberts 2002.

30 MHLW 2013b.

31 Matsuda 2011.

32 MHLW 2014b.

33 MHLW 2014a.

34 Molony 1995.

35 Makita 2010; Roberts 2005; Takeda 2011.

36 According to Miyake (1991), Ogino (2006), and Shioda (2000) in observing the declining fertility rates since 1920, the government formed a group to study population problems (called *Jinkō mondai kenkyūkai*) in 1933, and established the Institute

of Population Research (*Jinkō mondai kenkyūsho*) in 1938. Now called the National Institute of Population and Social Security Research (NIPSSR or *Kokuritsu shakai hoshō jinkō mondai kenkyūsho*), the latter continues to be the major governmental apparatus for studying fertility trends. In this book, I cited findings from the National Fertility Surveys conducted by the NIPSSR. In 1942, the Institute of Population Research issued a recommendation, the main objective of which was to increase the total population of Japan by increasing birth rates and decreasing mortality rates. In order to increase birth rates, it stipulated that marriage age should be reduced and married couples should have five children on average. The government implemented 11 means to accomplish these goals, including establishment of matchmaking facilities, tax breaks for married couples and parents, family allowances, preferential treatment of large families, restriction of employment, banning use of birth control, shorter work hours for employed mothers, and protection of female bodies (e.g., women were not to work in environments that made their lower backs and legs get too cold – considered harmful to women's fertility in those days). At the same time, as discussed in Chapter 5, the government was propagating the good wife, wise mother (*ryōsai kenbo*) ideology and defined devotion to childrearing and home as women's social role. Sasagawa (2006) points out that, since the government defined the birth rate decline as Japan's social problem in the 1990s, it began to fund local governments' educational programs for prenatal care and childcare. In the childcare education programs she observed in a suburb of Tokyo, though many mothers were happy to have venues allowing connection to other mothers, the programs demanded that mothers focus too intensively on childcare.

37 GNH Centre Bhutan 2016. According to the Sustainable Development Solutions Network 2013, Japan is one of the least happy countries in the developed region.
38 Blair-Loy 2003.
39 In 2016, Kazuko had been married to a man in his sixties for about two years. Tsuneko remained unmarried.
40 Tachibanaki 2006. Single women interviewed in L. Nakano's study (2014) expressed their concerns over future employment opportunities, believing that their value in the employment market (and marriage market) would decline with age.
41 Ronald and Hirayama 2009; Ronald and L. Nakano 2013.
42 For instance, Dales (2015) studied two TV shows (*dorama*) in which single women in their thirties were the main characters. In both shows, the female leads were economically independent, in professional occupations, and healthy.
43 For instance, L. Nakano (2014), L. Nakano and Wagatsuma (2004), and Rosenberger (2013) interpreted singlehood among women as a type of resistance to marriage/ traditional culture, Iwashita (2001) and Ueno (2009) depicted single, middle-age women to be independent (though their focus was once-married singles, not never-married single women).
44 Lee 2010; Long 2008; Makita 2010; L. Nakano and Wagatsuma 2004.
45 Gordon Mathews (2014) interviewed men and women from 1989–1990 and revisited some of them in 2011. He observed that 20 years later many of them were unhappily married or divorced. He argued that meanings attached to marriage changed significantly in those two decades, with more importance placed on emotional connection and communication between spouses (instead of on performing the proscribed social roles of men and women). His sample in the second phase of interviews is extremely small, though very informative. More studies are needed on this subject.
46 Though women on average earn less than men, according to Tashiro (2015), single female workers earn better than their married counterparts.
47 Izuhara 2006.
48 Lee 2010; Long 2008; Makita 2010.
49 I am currently working on an autoethnographic paper on this subject.

50 Kurotani (2014) observed that the boom cohort (which she labeled the "bubble generation") lacked agency. Kelsky (2001), Nemoto (2008), and Tokuhiro (2010) discussed how the single women they interviewed were uninterested in improvement of women's status.
51 See Ochiai 2004/2006; Tokuhiro 2010; Wakakuwa and Fujimura-Fanselow 2011 for more detail.
52 See, for instance, Fujieda 2011; S. Kaneko 2011; and Tokuhiro 2010 for feminist movements in the late 1800s and early 1900s. For the women's liberation movement of the 1970s, see Ochiai 2004/2006.
53 See Appendix A for limitations of my study.
54 Examination of social locations should not be done separately but in combinations – see Collins 1998 on the idea of *intersectionality*.

APPENDIX A
Research method

My research was approved by the Institutional Review Board at the University of Oklahoma in April 2009, prior to the data collection I conducted in the summer of that year. The details of my research method are described below.

Sampling method

I conducted in-depth interviews with 40 Japanese never-married and married women in the Greater Tokyo Area between May and July 2009. Because there was no systematic list of never-married and married women from which to draw a probability sample, I used purposive, convenience, and snowball sampling methods. Several months before the field research, I began to contact several acquaintances I had in Japan via email, and asked whether they could introduce me to potential research participants. I explained what my research was about, attached a copy of the "information sheet for consent" (in Japanese), and requested referrals to women who were either never married or married, and aged between 25 and 50.

I spent the first 28 years of my life in Japan, and maintained a personal network with a range of individuals I had met through school, work, social organizations, and academic activities. Additionally, just about a year before I launched this research project, I happened to become reconnected with my cohort of elementary school graduates through an internet social networking site. This allowed me access to individuals from diverse backgrounds. I was thus able to diversify my network of acquaintances, in terms of educational and occupational background, in the hopes of gaining referrals to women with different levels of education.

I asked each of my acquaintances to forward or hand the information sheet, which included my e-mail address and other contact information, to potential interviewees. I requested that acquaintances ask potential interviewees to send me an e-mail message or provide me with e-mail addresses and/or phone numbers I could use to contact them. I secured 13 volunteers and scheduled interviews with them before landing in Japan.

After arriving, I continued to recruit research participants by asking interviewees and other acquaintances for referrals. Many interviewees enjoyed the interviews and were willing to give me referrals to their friends, co-workers, etc. Because I wanted to have approximately equal proportions of interviewees in three age groups (twenties, thirties, and forties) and a larger sample of never-married women than married women, I sometimes made specific requests for referrals (e.g., "Can you introduce me to an unmarried woman who is in her late twenties?").

Sample size

I interviewed 40 women in total, but had no pre-determined number for the sampling size. Qualitative researchers recommend that sample size be determined in the course of research.[1] Data collection should end when findings reach a saturation point in which no new themes appear to be emerging from additional interviews. Interviews with women in their forties reached a saturation point after six or so interviews. There were remarkable similarities in their accounts, regardless of marital status, in terms both of my hypothesized themes and others that emerged. There was more diversity in patterns of accounts among women in their thirties and twenties, and thus larger samples were required for them. In order to have an approximately equal proportion of interviewees in each age group, I continued interviewing women in their forties despite saturation. In other words, the total sample size of 40 was more than I needed. I turned down a few volunteers for this reason.

Characteristics of the sample

Among the 40 interviewees, 28 women had never married and 12 were married at the time of the interviews. There were 15 women in their forties (10 never-married and 5 married), 16 in their thirties (12 never-married and 4 married), and 9 in their twenties (6 never-married and 3 married). Because I was not certain about what age would be a reasonable divide point between the boom and recession cohorts, I tried to even out the ages of study participants so that I would have an approximately equal number of interviewees in two cohorts.

The age of interviewees ranged from 25 to 46 (i.e., born between 1962 and 1984). The upper age limit for participant recruitment was 50, but I had no volunteers aged 47 and over. The number of participants in their twenties was smaller because they represented ages 25 to 29, a shorter range. I excluded women younger than 25 because the mean age at first marriage for Japanese women was 28.5 in 2008, and a great majority of women below 25 had never been married.[2] Since being single in one's early twenties is normative in Japan today, and my purpose was to discover causes of non-marriage, it was not meaningful to interview that younger group.

Interviewees were diverse in terms of their levels of education, though women with high school only were relatively underrepresented. There were 4 interviewees who had graduate degrees, 18 with college degrees, 15 with

APPENDICES

two-year college or vocational schooling, and 3 with high school education. Interviewees were also diverse in terms of occupation and income and, in the cases of single women, in terms of patterns of residence and current relationships. More detailed information on the study participants is provided in Appendix C. All interviewees were living in the Greater Tokyo Area at the time of the interview, but some of them were originally from other areas, including rural regions.

Interview questions

I conducted in-depth, semi-structured, open-ended, face-to-face interviews in Japanese. I am a native of Japan and speak Japanese as a first language. With interviewees' consent, all interviews were digitally recorded and transcribed by me. I followed the prepared interview guide, which was a revised version of an initial set of questions pretested with four volunteers in November, 2008. The interview guide is provided in Appendix B, in its English translation.

I began most interviews with background questions, such as those asking for age, level of education, year of graduation, and residence pattern. This is recommended by some qualitative researchers[3] as an effective way to establish rapport with the researched. As discussed below, the technique bore fruit for my research as well. Subsequently questions covered job history, parents' marriage, past and current relationships, ideal life course, marriage, singlehood, ideal marital partners, gender roles, leisure time, friends and social life, future plans, etc. I asked follow-up questions to clarify or elaborate upon answers and comments, and also encouraged interviewees to talk freely if they felt like doing so.

Because the never-married status is stigmatized in Japan, I never asked women direct questions about why they remained single, because that could have made unmarried interviewees feel uncomfortable or defensive. Instead, I asked various questions on life circumstances, views, etc. (see Appendix B). Typically, interviewees' intention to marry was revealed or stated in the process of the interviews, but in cases where this remained unclear, the direct question (i.e., "So, do you (not) want to marry?") was asked, only towards the end of the interview. In the information sheet initially provided to interviewees, the purpose of my research was explained as an attempt to understand what marriage means to Japanese women. At the end of the interview, I debriefed interviewees by informing them that the intent of this research was to understand the causes of increased singlehood. I encouraged my interviewees to discuss anything they wanted in reference to this phenomenon.

Some questions from the interview guide were dropped, as I found them uninformative after running several interviews. Detailed questions on ideal division of household labor are examples of such cases. The order of questions in the interview guide was not always followed, depending on the flow of conversations.

173

The questions on life courses were based upon the National Fertility Survey (NFS) by NIPSSR, which asked respondents to choose their ideal and expected life courses out of five set life courses: housewife, *saishūshoku* (returning to work after staying home for a while), *ryōritsu* (literally "doing both," meaning having it all – employment, marriage, and family), DINKS ("Double Income No Kids," or *ryōritsu* without children), and singlehood. In the 1992 survey, among single women aged 18 to 34, "housewife" was the most frequently chosen ideal life course. But in the 1997 and 2002 surveys, "return to work" was the most popular, followed by "having it all" and "housewife."[4]

I used a question similar to the NFS life course question for a few reasons. First, this categorization of women's life courses is reasonable, considering that Japanese women (and men) are socially expected to move through life stages almost uniformly according to age intervals.[5] Second, I would have the opportunity to compare my interview results with survey findings that show a shift in women's perceptions, and explore why women's views differ by cohort – as well as what the shift means to women. Third, I wanted to test the validity of this survey question because I felt women may not necessarily be able to choose one life course over another, which the survey requires them to do.

Because these five life courses are not exhaustive, I added three other life courses to my interview question: "breadwinning with a househusband," "unwed motherhood," and "lifetime cohabitation." I also added complexity to the "singlehood" and "return to work" categories, separating them into "singlehood living alone," "singlehood living with someone – parents, siblings, friends, and/or others," "return to work full-time," and "return to work part-time." Further, I added "others" so that interviewees would not feel compelled to choose from preconceived life courses.

I used small cards, each stating one of the life courses, simply because I thought they would make it easier for interviewees to compare and choose from the 11 life courses I had prepared. The use of cards turned out to be a good tool for facilitating interviews. Many of my interviewees were initially concerned that they might not be able to contribute to my research because they were very "normal (*futsū*)" and had nothing special to tell. Some were also not completely comfortable facing a researcher and telling their stories. In retrospect, the use of cards seems to have helped create a game-like atmosphere (as one of my interviewees commented, "Oh, it's like playing a game – how fun!"), which relaxed nervous interviewees and helped many express ideas and opinions. The existence of the cards allowed interviewees to gaze at them and talk, which probably provided a nice break from the discomfort of staring me in the face.

Notes on fieldnote taking

Though some qualitative researchers recommend that interviewers take notes during interviews, I purposely chose not to because I felt the gesture of taking notes might make interviewees nervous and self-conscious about what they said.

APPENDICES

Culturally, the Japanese are expected to be attentive to other people's reactions.[6] Seeing me take notes might have prompted interviewees to interpret my motives, perhaps leading them to think that what they said was inappropriate, unusual, strange, etc. I wanted to minimize the risk of interviewees censoring themselves. As it turns out, after the interviews, two of my interviewees mentioned that they anticipated I was going to take notes, but were glad that I did not because it would have made them nervous and self-conscious. Thus, I believe the decision to refrain from note taking was more sensitive to Japanese culture and communication patterns. Additionally, I believe it allowed me to pay closer attention to interviewees' words, facial expressions, and body language, as well as to the flow of conversation. I took mental notes on important non-verbal cues (e.g., tone of voice, facial expressions, body language) that might indicate respondents' perceptions and feelings, and on other important visual information (e.g., manner of dress, attractiveness), and recorded these as field notes as soon as I parted with interviewees.

Length of interviews

The length of interviews ranged from 40 minutes to four 4 and 33 minutes, with an average of 2 hours and 13 minutes. The portion of the interview that went along with my interview guide was usually completed in 50 to 90 minutes. Interviews with older women, especially single women, typically took longer because most of them had longer work histories and more romantic relationships. One interview, lasting only 40 minutes, was an unusual case. The interviewee worked in the same office as another interviewee who referred her to me, and had only one job and one brief romantic relationship to discuss.

At the end of each interview, I asked interviewees whether they had anything to add, any issues they wished to discuss with me, or any questions they wanted to ask me. All but one interviewee asked me at least one question, and with some women I spent one or more hours on this portion of the interview. My interviewees asked me a great many interesting questions, ranging from whether I was happy in my marriage, to whether American TV dramas accurately portray dating/courting patterns of Americans. It turned out that the questions and conversations I had after the guided interviews provided great insights for my research.

Interview locations

Interviews were most commonly held in coffee shops and restaurants chosen by interviewees due to the close proximity of these locations to home, work, or other locations convenient to them. Interviews in these places were rarely interrupted by wait staff, probably because chatting for hours over a cup of coffee is a common social scene in Japan. The presence of two digital recorders on the table may also have defined the situation as one in which disturbances were

APPENDICES

unwelcome. Other interviewees prepared quiet meeting rooms at their work-places. Still others I met at their own apartments or houses, or at the homes of individuals who gave referrals. Privacy was strictly protected in all interviews, regardless of interview location. It is customary in Japan to bring gifts when vis-iting someone at home, to express gratitude by giving gifts, and to cover the cost of meals for guests. I spent about ten U.S. dollars per interviewee for such things, and expressed my appreciation in different ways that were appropriate to each meeting arrangement. These included giving interviewees a box of sweets or gift card, and/or by picking up the check at a restaurant.

I was initially concerned about the potential difficulties that could arise from arranging meetings with interviewees whose faces I did not know, and with completing the necessary number of interviews within a short time frame. These concerns turned out be non-issues. Meetings were scheduled and arranged with incredible smoothness thanks to the prevalence of cell phones and e-mail, as well as the punctuality and cooperativeness of all interviewees.

Sensitivity to power inequality between researcher and researched

Power inequality between researchers and researched is an important issue to consider and overcome.[7] Power inequality based on gender, race, and ethnicity was not an issue because I (a female) was to interview women, and the Japanese are largely homogeneous in terms of race and ethnicity. However, my being older than most interviewees posed a potential problem of power inequality, as age is one of the most important dimensions of status inequality in Japan. For instance, younger individuals are expected to show respect to older people by deferring more and speaking less.[8] I needed to take special precautions in order to minimize the influence of age inequality.

Interviewees in their late thirties and forties who did not know my age assumed that I was either equal or lower in age status – perhaps because of my student status. This was reflected in the level of speech and body language they used, and so it seemed clear that age differences between myself and them were not an issue. With younger interviewees, however, I made deliberate efforts to create a relaxed atmosphere. I dressed myself in relatively casual attire, such as jeans, unless I was visiting interviewees' workplaces, began our conversation in the casual form of Japanese language (which distinguishes levels of formality), told light jokes to make them laugh (which always helped them relax), and some-times explicitly told them that I expected no expressions of respect, joking that I would like to think of myself as being as young as they were. Even when some of my young interviewees themselves appeared to be outspoken and not afraid of initiating talk, I was mindful of managing the impression that I was not the kind of older woman who would frown upon or reprimand young individuals for not deferring to their elders. I sometimes gave compliments to them, for instance, that I admired them for being outspoken and expressive of their own views.

APPENDICES

Some qualitative researchers find certain levels of deception to be necessary, whereas others, especially those from feminist camps, recommend full disclosure as a way to establish genuine relationships.[9] My field research experience in Japan convinced me that research should be done strategically, taking cultural contexts into consideration. Concealment of my true age was important in encouraging younger Japanese interviewees to present their more honest selves. When I revealed my actual age to young interviewees at the end of interviews, they were apologetic and began to act with due respect, such as bowing to me and changing their speech level to the more polite form. Given the cultural context of Japan, I believe my strategically chosen "misrepresentations" of self worked well to create an atmosphere in which interviewees could relate more honest stories.

There was another status inequality I needed to be wary of: my married status in the context of interviewing unmarried women – especially those in older age groups. Singlehood at older ages is socially stigmatized and can be a sensitive issue for some. My married status could have made them feel marginalized or defensive when speaking of their life experiences. I decided not to reveal my marital status until the end of interviews, though I felt removing my wedding ring would be too deceptive and chose to leave it on.

Most interviewees paid little attention to my married status, but some women knew it (through their referrers). A few of them asked me, at the beginning of the interview, why I took interest in studying single women even though I myself was married. I gave the brief but honest explanation that I was single when I lived in Japan, married in the U.S. at age 30, and that many of my friends in Japan remained single. I told them that I wanted to understand the phenomenon because I felt I had a better grip on this issue as an insider. I felt they sensed my interest was genuine, as all the older, single interviewees comfortably and eagerly participated. My student status may also have helped to neutralize power differences between myself and interviewees. I am confident that my marital status posed no discomfort or threat to these participants.

Impact of my "foreign" status

My residence in the U.S. evoked a great many interesting questions, particularly by my single interviewees, ranging from whether I am happy in my marriage to an American, to whether American TV dramas accurately portray dating patterns there. Some questions made me realize how limited romantic opportunities were for them, and how invisible positive marriage role models were in Japan (this is discussed in Chapters 2 and 3).

Building rapport

As mentioned above, I prepared basic demographic questions (e.g., where they were from, number of siblings, jobs, residence, etc.) to open the interview, since this type of easy-to-answer questions often helps interviewees relax and allows the establishment of rapport. What I immediately learned about the Japanese interviewees was that many of them were humble and worried that they might not be able to contribute to my research because they were very "normal (*futsū*)." They thought they had nothing special to tell. It seemed that the opening of interviews with easy-to-answer demographic questions helped them realize, and feel relieved, that they actually had a lot to contribute. This humble attitude – "I am no one special" – was probably a reflection of Japanese culture, which emphasizes the virtue of humility. These questions not only helped establish rapport, but proved to be useful tools for convincing humble Japanese interviewees that their stories were worthy of attention.

Data analysis

The data (i.e., transcripts and field notes) were analyzed in the original language (i.e., Japanese), and only by me. No computer software was used for the analysis. Several steps were taken to analyze the data, both deductively and inductively, following strategies recommended by field researchers.[10] First, I carefully read transcripts and took notes on themes that were relevant to my theoretical framework (i.e., perceptions of ideal age for marriage, experience of pressure to marry, and conceptions of gender roles) and on other themes that emerged from the data. I assigned tentative categories to these emerged themes. There were several themes from the data that appear to be associated with interviewees' conceptions of gender roles (e.g., ideal and expected life courses, views towards the role of housewife, maternal employment, men's role, etc.), and thus I divided this category into several subcategories.

As an initial coding process, or in "open coding," I coded the data for each category (e.g., strong, ambiguous, weak, no interests in marriage). Several other themes emerged during the initial coding, and I wrote them down, categorized them, and coded the data under these new categories. Codes were then organized into analytic categories (i.e., "axial coding" in Glaser and Strauss's term). I read over the data several more times and repeated this process until I was satisfied with coding and categorization. I compared the findings among different age groups, and assessed and reassessed whether my cohort categorization was reasonable.

Limitations of my study

Like any other research, my study has limitations. First and foremost, my research is based on a small sample of 40 women, and thus the research findings are not generalizable to a large population. The sample was also drawn from the Greater Tokyo Area. For this reason, my research is not sensitive to potential regional differences and may not apply well to women in rural areas.[11] Tokyo has also been found to be more conservative – surprisingly for an urban area – than other regions when it comes to gender ideology. According to Ochiai, this is because the commute to work is typically long, and nuclear families (i.e., living away from extended kin) are more common in Tokyo. Both conditions require that one parent stay home to provide care for children.[12] Readers should be careful in generalizing my findings to other regions.

My study is also limited in terms of the impact of socioeconomic class. I was cognizant of recruiting interviewees with varying levels of education, occupation, and income, but I found that these were not necessarily good indicators of women's socioeconomic locations. For instance, it was normal for women to have high school or two-year college/vocational school education while coming from families with highly educated fathers with middle-class income/occupation. Sugimoto described how class status is often inconsistent in Japan.[13] Women's education, income, and occupation are not clearly associated with single status in Japan, but class differences in lifestyle and family practices have been observed.[14] Taking up the challenge of classifying women into social classes is beyond the scope of this study, but I recognize nonetheless that the absence of consideration of social class is a major limitation of my research.

In retrospect, I wished I had looked into the impact of gendered schooling. One of my interviewees, who went to a girl-only high school and two-year vocational school (with mostly female students), thought her schooling affected her life in the following way:

> I wish I had gone to college. Two years [of vocational schooling] were so busy and short.... They [four-year college students] were like between kids and adults.... They had lots of free time. There are more opportunities to meet different kinds of people in college. I went to English vocational school so most [students] were girls. I had to study hard and didn't have much time to play. I didn't have male friends.... If I had had male friends, I think I'd have understood men better.... I think I couldn't handle men well, dating and stuff because of that. I think I had a bad start [sad laugh].
>
> (Saori, 45 years old, never married)

It is common for Japanese youth to go to single-gender high schools, and Saori's gendered experience may well apply to other women – as well as to men.

According to Sugimoto, approximately 5 percent of Japanese residents are estimated to be ethnic minorities, including foreign workers from Asia, the Middle East, and Brazil, *Burakumin* (a discriminated-against group classified as the lowest caste during the Tokugawa feudal period), Resident Koreans, Ainu (indigenous population), Okinawan, etc. One of my interviewees was Okinawan, and the rest were ethnically Japanese – as far as I know. Unfortunately, one Okinawan interviewee's story could not provide enough data to assess the impact of ethnicity. This study, therefore, is limited to women of the ethnic majority.

APPENDICES

Notes

1 Glaser and Strauss 1967.
2 Ministry of Internal Affairs and Communications 2011.
3 For example, Berg 2007.
4 NIPSSR 1983, 1998, 2004.
5 Brinton 1993; Kelsky 2001.
6 Azuma 2001; Condon 1984; Lebra 1976.
7 Ardell 1997; McCorkel and Myers 2003; Ortiz 2005.
8 Condon 1984; Kerbo 2008; Kerbo and McKinstry 1995, 1998; Lebra 1976; Nakane 1970.
9 For example, Acker, Barry, and Esseveld 1983.
10 Berg 2007, Lofland et al. 2006.
11 L. Nakano, (2014) mentions that single women face more pressure to marry from friends, family, and neighbors in rural areas than in Tokyo, and Tokyo has a social environment that accepts singles. Nagase (2006) and Sasagawa (2006) discuss important urban/Tokyo–rural differences in women's views of gender roles.
12 Ochiai 2004/2006.
13 Sugimoto 2010.
14 D. Kondo 1990.

APPENDIX B
Interview guide (in English translation)

- Which part of Japan are you originally from?
- How old are you?
- What is the highest level of education you have attained? What year did you graduate?
- Do you have siblings? Are they married?
- What is your occupation? How many years have you been in your present job? Have you taken any (other) jobs in the past?
- What is your income?
- [To married women] What year did you marry? (Or how many years have you been married?) Do you have children? How old are they?
- Do you live with your parents, siblings, partner, spouse, in-law parents, children, or by yourself?
- Tell me about all the job(s) you have taken. How did you like your job(s)? Why? Please describe your job(s). Have you ever faced difficulties finding a job? How long are you planning to stay in your current job? [if unemployed] Are you planning to work? When?
- Tell me about other workers at your workplace(s). Were there many single women in your first workplace? How about single men? Were there any single female workers who were much older than you? What did you think of these women? How did other people at work view/treat these women?
- Tell me about your parents and siblings. Are they married? Was your mother employed when you were growing up? What was her occupation? What did you think about your mother's employment status? What is/was your father's occupation? Did he help around the house when you were growing up? What do/did you think of your parents' and siblings' marriages?
- Tell me about your residence (current or before marriage).

[if living alone] How long have you been living on your own? Do you own or rent your place? What are the benefits and costs of living alone?

[if living with parents/siblings] How would you describe your relationships with your parents/siblings? Do you do chores? What/how often? Do you

APPENDICES

pay some money to your parents? Do your parents tell you that you need to move out? Do you plan to move out? When/why/how?

[if living with a partner] How long have you been living with him/her? Do you plan to/did you marry your cohabiting partner? Why/why not?

- Tell me about your current and past relationships. How many romantic relationships have you had in your life? How long did each relationship last? How old are/were they? Where and how did you meet them? Did/do you think of marriage with any one of them? What kinds of persons are they? Were they unmarried or married? How long did you date/live with each of them? [to married women] When did you start thinking about marriage to your husband? What did you like about him? Is he the eldest son? How is the relationship between him and his parents?
- Have you ever had *miai*? What did you think of your *miai* partners? Why did you (not) consider them as possible future husbands? Why have you never used this system?
- [After explaining different life courses for women: housewife; returning to work full-time or part-time after staying home for a while; having it all; DINKS; singlehood living alone; singlehood living with someone; bread-winning with a househusband, unwed motherhood, and others] What type of life course do you think, or did you think in the past, is/was ideal? Why? What life course do you expect to have in your real life? Can you think of any women you look up to as role models? If so, what are/were they like? Why do you think other life courses are not ideal? If you could go back in time to when you were 20 years old, would you choose a life course different from the current one? How and why?
- Tell me what you think about marriage age. Have you ever thought that you want to, or should, marry by a certain age? How old? When did you think so? Why? Do you think there is such a thing as *tekireiki* (appropriate ages to marry)? Why/why not? Was there some time in your life when you began to think about marriage seriously? Has anyone ever said to you that you need to marry soon? Who were they and what did they say? How did you feel about it? Have you ever felt pressure to marry? How old were you?
- Would you like to have (more) children? Do you think you have to be married before having children?
- What are the merits of marriage? Merits of singlehood?
- Do/did you want to marry? Why/why not?
- [if she want(ed) to marry] Are there any characteristics of men you think are important in a marital partner? [To probe] How about men's level of education, income, occupation, attractiveness, height, weight, personality traits, hobbies, views regarding gender roles in marriage, attitudes towards women, region of origin, nationality, family composition (e.g., eldest son), relationship with their mother? Any other things that are, or used to be, important to you?

APPENDICES

- What do you expect from your (future) husband? How should a husband be? How about a wife?
- In your (future) marriage, who do you expect should take on the following tasks: cooking, laundry, cleaning, grocery shopping, discipline of children, physical care of young children, playing with children, care of elderly parents, household budgeting, decision-making on important family matters such as buying a house, education of children.
- How do you spend your free time, like weekends and after work hours?
- Tell me about your friends. How many friends do you regularly meet or talk with? Are they married or single? Do they have children? Are they male or female? What do you do with them?
- What do you think of your friends' marriages or your own marriage?
- [to married women] Do you have any complaints about your marriage?
- People often call unmarried women "Parasite Singles" or "Loser Dogs." How do you feel about such labels?
- Tell me about your future. What kind of life do you think you might be having 10, 20 years from now? Do you have any concerns regarding your current circumstances or your future? Feel free to talk about any concerns you wish to discuss. [to unmarried women] Do you ever feel you may remain single for life? Do you ever feel glad that you did not marry? Why? [to married women] When do you feel glad that you're married? Do you ever regret that you married?
- [to the recession cohort] Do you know any older women who never married? What do you think about them?
- [to unmarried women] Do you think that you have certain traits undesirable to a potential (male) marital partner? These do not need to be shortcomings. For instance, very smart or very tall women may not be taken well by some men. Please tell me if you feel you have any traits like that.
- [to married women] Do you know any single men around? Do you have any ideas as to why they remain single?
- [to the boom cohort] Do you have any advice to younger, never-married women?
- Do you have anything you wish to discuss with me?

At the end of interview:

- This is all I would like to ask you in this interview. Do you have anything you wish to discuss, or want to ask me? Please feel free to tell me anything you would like.
- This research is to identify why more Japanese women are remaining single. Can you refer me to a few women who have never been married and might be interested in participating in this research?
- May I contact you if I would like to ask you more questions later? What is the best way to contact you?

APPENDIX C

Interview participants

Name*	Age**	Marital status***	Education	Occupation	Income	Residence****	Relationships****
Izumi	46	Never-married	College	Marketing researcher	>$70,000	alone (owning)	no
Eri	46	Married (25)	College	Secretary (part-time)	<$20,000		
Kazuko	45	Never-married	M.A.	Artist/Instructor	"very small"	w/parents	no
Sumire	45	Never-married	M.S.	Pharmacist	$50,000	w/parents, sister	no
Kozue	45	Never-married	2-year college	Clerical worker	$60,000–70,000	alone (renting)	yes (two men)
Rumi	45	Never-married	2-year college	Advertising	>$70,000	alone (owning)	no
Saori	45	Never-married	Vocational	Clerical worker	"very small"	w/father	no
Tamami	45	Married (25)	College	Social worker (part-time)	$20,000–25,000		
Sonoko	45	Married (23)	2-year college	Store clerk (part-time)	<$20,000		
Chie	45	Married (24)	High school	Clerical worker (part-time)	<$20,000		
Seiko	43	Never-married	M.A.	Accountant	>$70,000	alone (renting)	yes (long distance)
Tsuneko	43	Never-married	College	Marketing consultant	$50,000–60,000	alone (renting)	no
Natsumi	43	Never-married	College	Illustrator (freelance)	$40,000–50,000	alone (renting)	no
Teruko	41	Never-married	College	Graphic designer (freelance)	Declined	alone (renting)	yes (married man)
Nozomi	40	Married (29)	Vocational	Housewife	N.A.		
Tomomi	39	Never-married	Vocational	Social worker	$30,000–35,000	w/parents, brother, niece	no
Harumi	39	Married (31)	High school	Housewife	N.A.		
Fujiko	38	Married (27)	College	Housewife	N.A.		
Mari	38	Married (29)	2-year college	Housewife	N.A.		
Midori	36	Never-married	College	Advertising	$35,000–40,000	w/male partner	yes (cohabiting)

Hitomi	36	Never-married	College	Marketing consultant	$50,000	alone (renting)	no
Yoko	36	Never-married	Vocational	Section manager	$55,000	alone (renting)	yes
Kei	35	Never-married	Vocational	Clerical worker	$25,000–30,000	w/parents	no
Shizuka	34	Never-married	Vocational	Clerical worker	$25,000–30,000	w/parents	no
Akane	34	Married (33)	College	Housewife	N.A.		
Honoka	32	Never-married	Vocational	Marketing consultant	$55,000	alone (renting)	no
Mutsumi	32	Never-married	Vocational	Clerical worker (temp)	$30,000–35,000	w/parents	yes
Yuri	32	Never-married	High school	Clerical worker	$35,000–40,000	w/parents	yes (engaged)
Megumi	31	Never-married	College	Clerical worker	$40,000–45,000	alone (renting)	no
Yayoi	31	Never-married	College	Clerical worker (temp)	$20,000–25,000	w/mother	no
Momoe	30	Never-married	College	Clerical worker	$40,000	w/parents	no
Ran	29	Never-married	M.D.	Medical researcher	$40,000	alone (renting)	yes (engaged)
Shoko	29	Never-married	2-year college	Homecare worker	$20,000–25,000	w/parents	yes
Rika	29	Married (24)	2-year college	Dental assistant (part-time)	<$10,000		
Kyoko	29	Married (28)	Vocational	Cook	$20,000–30,000		
Junko	27	Never-married	M.A.	Secretary	$30,000	w/roommate	yes
Ryoko	26	Never-married	College	Unemployed	N.A.	w/male partner	yes (cohabiting)
Maya	26	Never-married	College	Unemployed	N.A.	w/female partner	yes (cohabiting)
Yuki	26	Never-married	College	Receptionist (part-time)	<$10,000	w/male partner	yes (cohabiting)
Kimi	25	Married (25)	College	Bank teller	$35,000–40,000	w/male partner	yes (cohabiting)

Notes

* All the names are pseudonyms.

** The ages are as of the date I interviewed them in 2009.

*** The number in parenthesis indicates age at marriage.

**** The information is provided only for never-married women. All the never-married women who were sharing their residence with their partners were renting apartments. For those who were living with their parent(s), their residence was owned by the parent(s), except for Saori who co-owned her condominium with her father.

BIBLIOGRAPHY

Acker, Joan, Kate Barry, and Joke Esseveld. 1983. "Objectivity and Truth: Problems in Doing Feminist Research." *Women's Studies International Forum* 6(4): 423–435.

Allison, Anne. 1994. *Nightwork: Sexuality, Pleasure, and Corporate Masculinity in a Tokyo Hostess Club*. Chicago: The University of Chicago Press.

Ansari, Aziz (with Eric Klinenberg). 2015. *Modern Romance*. New York: Penguin Press.

Applbaum, Kalman D. 1995. "Marriage with the Proper Stranger: Arranged Marriage in Metropolitan Japan." *Ethnology* 34(1): 37–51.

Arudou, Debito. 2011. " 'Sexlessness' wrecks marriages, threatens nation's future." *The Japan Times,* September 6, 2011. Retrieved March 20, 2016 (www.japantimes.co.jp/community/2011/09/06/issues/sexlessness-wrecks-marriages-threatens-nations-future/#.VvnoouIrLIU).

Ato, Makoto. 1989. "*Mikon bankon jidai no tōrai* [The arrival of the age of non-marriage and late marriage]" *Kazoku kenkyū nenpō* [Annals of Family Studies] 15: 24–35.

Ato, Makoto. 1994. "*Mikonka bankonka no shinten: Sono dōkō to haikei* [The development of the non- marriage and late-marriage phenomenon: its trends and background]." *Kazoku shakaigaku kenkyū* [Japanese Journal of Family Sociology] 6: 5–17.

Ato, Makoto and Hiroshi Kojima. 1983. "*Gendai seinen no kekkonkan: Dai 8ji shussan-ryoku chōsa 'dokushinsha chōsa' no kekka kara* [Views of marriage among young adults: from the results of the 8th National Fertility Survey]." *Jinkū mondai kenkyū* [Journal of Population Problems] 168: 30–57.

Ato, Makoto, Shigesato Takahashi, Eiko Nakano, Yoshitoshi Watanabe, Hiroshi Kojima, Ryuichi Kaneko, and Fusami Mita. 1994. "*Dokushin seinensō no kekkonkan to kodomokan: Dai 10kai shusshō dōkō kihon chōsa (dokushinsha chōsa) no kekka kara* [Views of marriage and children among single young adults: from the results of the 10th National Fertility Survey]." *Jinkō mondai kenkyū* [Journal of Population Problems] 50(1): 29–49.

AtWiki. 2009. "*Josei sabetsu hatsugen: Mori Yoshiro, 'Kononai josei ha nenkin fuyo', 'Onna wa shiya ga semai'* [Discriminatory remarks against women: Yoshiro Mori, 'No need of pension for childless women' 'Women are short-sighted']." Retrieved February 13, 2016 (www14.atwiki.jp/joseisabetu/pages/18.html).

Azuma, Hiroshi. 2001. "Moral Scripts: A U.S.–Japan Comparison." Pp. 29–50 in *Japanese Frames of Mind: Cultural Perspectives on Human Development*, edited by H. Shimizu and R.A. Levine. Cambridge, UK: Cambridge University Press.

Banks, Ralph R. 2011. *Is Marriage for White People?: How the African American Marriage Decline Affects Everyone*. New York: Plume.

BIBLIOGRAPHY

BBC News. 2004. "Japan's Gaffe-Prone Politicians: Japan's Ruling Coalition Is Rueing the Latest Gaffe by One of Its Ministers." June 4, 2004. Retrieved February 27, 2016 (http://news.bbc.co.uk/2/hi/asia-pacific/3058189.stm).

Beck, Ulrich and Elisabeth E. Beck-Gernsheim. 2005. *Individualism: Institutionalized Individualism and Its Social and Political Consequences.* London:Sage.

Becker, Gary S. 1981/1991/1993. *Treatise on the Family.* Cambridge, MA: Harvard University Press.

Bentel, Brian M. and Akiko Yoshida. 2013. "Marriage in the Cultural Vacuum." *Sociological Imagination,* 49(2): 11–29.

Berg, Bruce L. 2007. *Qualitative Research Methods for the Social Sciences* (6th ed.). Boston: Pearson.

Blair-Loy, Mary. 2003. *Competing Devotions: Career and Family among Women Executives.* Cambridge, MA: Harvard University Press.

Blossfeld, Hans-Peter. 1995. "Changes in the Process of Family Formation and Women's Growing Economic Independence: A Comparison of Nine Countries." Pp. 3–32 in *The New Role of Women: Family Formation in Modern Societies,* edited by H.-P. Blossfeld. Boulder, CO: Westview Press.

Boling, Patricia. 2008. "Demography, Culture, and Policy: Understanding Japan's Low Fertility." *Population and Development Review* 34(2): 307–326.

Brinton, Mary C. 1992. "Christmas Cakes and Wedding Cakes: The Social Organization of Japanese Women's Life Course." Pp. 74–107 in *Japanese Social Organization,* edited by T. Lebra. Honolulu: University of Hawai'i Press.

Brinton, Mary C. 1993. *Women and the Economic Miracle: Gender and Work in Postwar Japan.* Berkeley: University of California Press.

Brinton, Mary C. 2007. "Gendered Offices: A Comparative-Historical Examination of Clerical Work in Japan and the United States." Pp. 87–111 in *The Political Economy of Japan's Low Fertility,* edited by F. M. Rosenbluth. Stanford, CA: Stanford University Press.

Brinton, Mary C. 2011. *Lost in Transition.* Cambridge, UK: Cambridge University Press.

Bumpass, Larry L. and Minja Kim Choe. 2004. "Attitudes Relating to Marriage and Family Life." Pp. 19–38 in *Marriage, Work and Family Life in Comparative Perspective: Japan, South Korea and The United States,* edited by N. O. Tsuya and L. L. Bumpass. Honolulu: University of Hawai'I Press.

Chang, Chin-fen and Paula England. 2011. "Gender Inequality in Earnings in Industrialized East Asia." *Social Science Research* 40: 1–14.

Charlebois, Justin. 2010. "The Discursive Construction of Femininities in the Accounts of Japanese Women." *Discourse Studies* 12(6): 699–714.

Cherlin, Andrew J. 2012. "Goode's World Revolution and Family Patterns: A Consideration at Fifty Years." *Population and Development Review,* 38: 577–607.

Collins, Patricia Hill. 1998. "It's All in the Family: Intersection of Gender, Race, and Nation." *Hipatia* 13(3): 25–46.

Condon, John C. 1984. *With Respect to the Japanese: A Guide for Americans.* Yarmouth, ME: Intercultural Press.

Connell, R. W. 1995. *Masculinities.* Berkeley: University of California Press.

Cook, Judith A. and Mary Margaret Fonow. 1986. "Knowledge and Women's Interests: Issues of Epistemology and Methodology in Feminist Sociological Research." *Sociological Inquiry* 56(1): 2–29.

BIBLIOGRAPHY

Creighton, Millie. 1996. "Marriage, Motherhood, and Career Management in a Japanese 'Counter Culture'." Pp. 192–220 in *Re-imaging Japanese Women*, edited by A. Imamura. Berkeley: University of California Press.

Dales, Laura. 2015. "Suitably Single? Representations of Singlehood in Contemporary Japan." Pp. 21–32 in *Configurations of Family in Contemporary Japan*, edited by T. Aoyama, L. Dales, and R. Dasgupta. London: Routledge.

Dasgupta, Romit. 2003. "Creating Corporate Warriors: The 'Salaryman' and Masculinity in Japan." Pp. 118–134 in *Asian Masculinities: The Meaning and Practice of Manhood in China and Japan*, edited by K. Louie and M. Low. London: RoutledgeCurzon.

Dasgupta, Romit. 2010. *Re-Reading the Salaryman in Japan: Crafting Masculinities*. Abingdon, UK: Routledge.

Durkheim, Emile. 1951/1979. *Suicide: A Study in Sociology*. Translated by J. A. Spaulding and G. Simpson. New York: The Free Press.

Edin, Kathryn and Maria Kefalas. 2005. *Promises I Can Keep: Why Poor Women Put Motherhood Before Marriage*. Berkeley: University of California Press.

Edin, Kathryn and Joanna M. Reed. 2005. "Why Don't They Just Get Married? Barriers to Marriage among the Disadvantaged." *The Future of Children* 15(2): 117–137.

Ehara, Yumiko. 2005. "*Jendā ishiki no henyō to kekkon kaihi* [Changing gender consciousness and marriage avoidance]." Pp. 27–50 in *Shōshika no jendō bunseki* [Gender analysis of fertility decline], edited by Y. Meguro and H. Nishioka. Tokyo: Keisoshobo.

Elder, Glen H., Jr. 1994. "Time, Human Agency, and Social Change: Perspectives on the Life Course." *Social Psychology Quarterly* 57(1): 4–15.

Elder, Glen H., Jr. 1995. "The Life Course Paradigm: Social Change and Individual Development." Pp. 101–139 in *Examining Lives in Context: Perspectives on the Ecology of Human Development*, edited by P. Moen, G. H. Elder, Jr., and K. Lüscher. Washington DC: American Psychological Association.

Elder, Glen H., Jr. 1999. *Children of the Great Depression: Social Change in Life Experience*. Boulder, CO: Westview Press.

Elder, Glen H., Jr., Monica Kirkpatrick Johnson, and Robert Crosnoe. 2003. "The Emergence and Development of Life Course Theory." Pp. 3–19 in *Handbook of the Life Course*, edited by J. T. Mortimer and M. J. Shanahan. New York: Springer.

Elder, Glen H., Jr. and Lisa A. Pellerin. 1998. "Linking History and Human Lives." Pp. 264–294 in *Methods of Life Course Research: Qualitative and Quantitative Approaches*, edited by J. Z. Giele and G. H. Elder, Jr. Thousand Oaks, CA: Sage Publications.

Faison, Elyssa. 2007. *Managing Women: Disciplining Labor in Modern Japan*. Berkley: University of California Press.

Federal Interagency Forum on Aging Related Statistics. 2016. Agingstats.gov. "Population." Retrieved March 22, 2016 (www.agingstats.gov/main_site/data/2012_documents/population.aspx).

Ferree, Myra Marx. 1990. "Beyond Separate Spheres: Feminism and Family Research." *Journal of Marriage and Family* 52(4): 866–884.

Friedan, Betty. 1963. *The Feminine Mystique*. New York: Norton.

Fujieda, Mioko. 2011. "Japan's First Phase of Feminism." Pp. 317–336 in *Transforming Japan: How Feminism and Diversity Are Making a Difference*, edited by K. Fujimura-Fanselow. New York: The Feminist Press.

Fukuda, Setsuya. 2009. "Leaving the Parental Home in Post-war Japan: Demographic Changes, Stem-Family Norms, and the Transition to Adulthood." *Demographic Research* 20: 731- 816.

BIBLIOGRAPHY

Fukuda, Setsuya. 2013. "The Changing Role of Women's Earnings in Marriage Formation in Japan." *The Annuals of the American Academy of Political and Social Science*, 646: 107–128.

Garon, Sheldon. 1997. *Molding Japanese Minds: The State in Everyday Life*. Princeton, NJ: Princeton University Press.

Gelb, Joyce. 2003. *Gender Policies in Japan and the United States: Comparing Women's Movements, Rights, and Politics*. New York: Palgrave Macmillan.

Genda, Yuji. 2005. *A Nagging Sense of Job Insecurity: The New Reality Facing Japanese Youth*. Tokyo: International House of Japan.

Gender Equity Bureau Cabinet Office. 2016. *Danjo kyōdō sankaku hakusho* [White paper on gender equality]. Retrieved February 12, 2016 (www.gender.go.jp/about_danjo/whitepaper/h25/zentai/index.html).

Giddens, Anthony. 1991. *Modernity and Self-Identity: Self and Society in the Later Modern Age*. Stanford, CA: Stanford University Press.

Glaser, Barney G. and Anselm L. Strauss. 1967. *The Discovery of Grounded Theory: Strategies for Qualitative Research*. Chicago: Aldine.

GNH Centre Bhutan. 2016. "The Story of GNH." Retrieved March 6, 2016 (www.gnh-centrebhutan.org/what-is-gnh/the-story-of-gnh/).

Haworth, Abigail. 2013. "Why Have Young People in Japan Stopped Having Sex?" *Guardian*, October 20, 2013. Retrieved February 12, 2016 (www.theguardian.com/world/2013/oct/20/young-people-japan-stopped-having-sex).

Hays, Sharon. 1996. *Cultural Contradictions of Motherhood*. New Haven, CT: Yale University Press.

Hertog, Ekaterina. 2009. *Touch Choices: Bearing An Illegitimate Child in Japan*. Stanford, CA: Stanford University Press.

Hertog, Ekaterina. 2011. "'I Did Not Know How to Tell My Parents, So I Thought I Would Have to Have an Abortion': Experiences of Unmarried Mothers in Japan." Pp. 91–111 in *Home and Family in Japan: Continuity and Transformation*, edited by R. Ronald and A. Alexy. London: Routledge.

Hidaka, Tomoko. 2010. *Salaryman Masculinity: Continuity and Change in Hegemonic Masculinity in Japan*. Leiden, NL: Brill.

Hidaka, Tomoko. 2011. "Masculinity and the Family System: The Ideology of the 'Salaryman' across Three Generations." Pp. 112–130 in *Home and Family in Japan: Continuity and Change*. R. Ronald and A. Alexy. London: Routledge.

Hiroshima, Kiyoshi. 1999. "*1970–1990 nen ni okeru joshi no mikonritsu jōshō no yōin bunkai* [A decomposition of causes of increased never-population rates among women from 1970 to 1990]." *Keizai kagaku ronshū* [Journal of Economics] 25: 1–25.

Hochschild, Arlie (with Anne Machung). 1989. *The Second Shift*. New York: Avon Books.

Holloway, Susan D. 2010. *Women and Family in Contemporary Japan*. Cambridge, UK: Cambridge University Press.

Honda, Yuki. 2002/2005. "*Shinguru raifu* [Single Life]." Pp. 56–64 in *JGSS ni miru ishiki to kōdō* [*Values and behavioral patterns seen in the Japanese General Social Survey*], edited by N. Iwai and H. Sato. Tokyo: Yuhikaku.

Imamura, Anne E. 1987. *Urban Japanese Housewives: At Home and in the Community*. Honolulu: University of Hawaii Press.

Iwama, Akiko. 1999. "*Bankonka to mikonsha no raifu sutairu* [Late marriage and lifestyle of never-married singles]." *Jinkō Mondai Kenkyū* [Journal of Population Problems] 55(2): 39–58.

BIBLIOGRAPHY

Iwao, Sumiko. 1993. *The Japanese Woman: Traditional Image and Changing Reality.* New York: Free Press.

Iwasaki, Kenji, Masaya Takahashi, and Akinori Nakata. 2006. "Health Problems due to Long Working Hours in Japan: Working Hours, Workers' Compensation (*Karoshi*), and Preventive Measures." *Industrial Health* 44(4): 537–540.

Iwasawa, Miho. 2007. "Boom and Bust in Marriages between Coworkers and the Marriage Decline in Japan." *Japanese Economy* 34(4): 3–24.

Iwasawa, Miho. 2010. "*Shokuen kekkon no seisui kara miru ryōen tsuikyū no airo* [A narrow path for the search of good matches: what the boom and bust of coworker marriages tell us]." Pp. 37–53 in *Kekkon no kabe: hikon bankon no kōzō* [Obstacles to marriage: structure of non-marriage and postponed marriage], edited by H. Sato, A. Nagai, and S. Miwa. Tokyo: Keiso Shobo.

Iwashita, Kumiko. 2001. *Ohitorisama* [Singleton]. Tokyo: Chuokoron-shinsha.

Izuhara, Misa. 2006. "Changing Families and Policy Response to an Ageing Japanese Society." Pp. 161–176 in *Home and Family in Japan: Continuity and Change.* R. Ronald and A. Alexy. London: Routledge.

Jansen, Marius. 2000. *The Making of Modern Japan.* Cambridge, MA: The Belknap Press of Harvard University Press.

Jolivet, Muriel. 1997. *Japan: Childless Society? The Crisis of Motherhood.* London: Routledge.

Jones, Gavin and Wei-Jun Jean Yeung. 2014. "Marriage in Asia." *Journal of Family Issues,* 35(12): 1567–1583.

Jung, EeHwan and Byung-you Cheon. 2006. "Economic Crisis and Changes in Employment Relations in Japan and Korea." *Asian Survey* 46(3): 457–476.

Kamano, Saori. 2005. "*Dokushin danjo no egaku kekkonzō* [Images of marriage held by never-married men and women]." Pp. 79–80 in *Shōshika no jendā bunseki* [Analysis of gender in fertility decline], edited by Y. Meguro and H. Nishioka. Tokyo: Keisoshobo.

Kaneko, Ryuichi. 1994. "*Mikon jinkō ni okeru kekkon no juyō yōin no doko: Dai 10kai shusshō dōkō kihon chōsa (dokushinsha chōsa) no kekka kara* [Trends regarding the demands of marriage among unmarried population: from the results of the 10th National Fertility Survey]." *Jinkō mondai kenkyū* [Journal of Population Problems] 50(2): 1–24.

Kaneko, Sachiko. 2011. "The Struggle for Legal Rights and Reforms: A Historical View." Pp. 3–14 in *Transforming Japan: How Feminism and Diversity Are Making a Difference,* edited by K. Fujimura-Fanselow. New York: The Feminist Press.

Kauchi, Nobuko. 1984. *Shiryō bosei hogo ronsō* [Sources: the debate over motherhood protection]. Tokyo: Domesu shuppan.

Kelsky, Karen. 2001. *Women on the Verge: Japanese Women, Western Dreams.* Durham, NC: Duke University Press.

Kerbo, Harold R. 2008. *Social Stratification and Inequality: Class Conflict in Historical, Comparative, and Global Perspective* (7th ed.). Boston: McGraw-Hill.

Kerbo, Harold R. and John. A. McKinstry. 1995. *Who Rules Japan?: The Inner Circles Of Economic and Political Power.* Westport, CT: Praeger Publishers.

Kerbo, Harold R. and John. A. McKinstry. 1998. *Modern Japan: A Volume in the Comparative Societies Series.* Boston: McGraw- Hill.

Kiernan, Kathleen. 2000. "European Perspectives on Union Formation." Pp. 40–58 in *The Ties That Bind: Perspectives on Marriage and Cohabitation,* edited by L. J. Waite. New York: Aldine de Gruyter.

BIBLIOGRAPHY

Kiernan, Kathleen. 2004. "Redrawing the Boundaries of Marriage." *Journal of Marriage and Family* 66(4): 980–987.

Kinsella, Sharon. 1995. "Cuties in Japan." Pp. 220–254 in *Women, Media, and Consumption in Japan*, edited by L. Skov and B. Moeran. London: Curzon Press.

Kitanaka, Junko. 2012. *Depression in Japan: Psychiatric Cures for a Society in Distress*. Princeton, NJ: Princeton University Press.

Klinenberg, Eric. 2012. *Going Solo: The Extraordinary Rise and Surprising Appeal of Living Alone*. New York: Penguin Books.

Kondo, Dorinne K. 1990. *Crafting Selves: Power, Gender, and Discourses of Identity in a Japanese Workplace*. Chicago: University of Chicago Press.

Kondo, Kazuko. 1995. "*Onna to sensō: bosei, kazoku, kokka* [Women and war: motherhood, family, and the nation]." In *Nihon joseishi saikō, V, semegiau onna to otoko: kindai* [Reconsideration of Japanese women's history, volume V, women and men to fight each other: modern period], edited by A. Okuda. Tokyo: Fujiwara Shoten.

Kotani, Satoshi. 2002. "Why Are Japanese Youth Today So Passive?" Pp. 31–45 in *Japan's Changing Generations: Are Young People Creating a New Society?*, edited by G. Mathews and B. White. London: Routledge.

Koyama, Shizuko. 1991. *Ryōsai kenbo toiu kihan* [*Norm called good wife, wise mother*]. Tokyo: Keisoshobo.

Kroska, Amy and Cheryl Elman. 2009. "Change in Attitudes about Employed Mothers: Exposure, Interests, and Gender Ideology Discrepancies." *Social Science Research* 38(2): 366–382.

Kubo, Keiko, Suemi Kawasaki, and Chizuru Hayashi. 1993. "*Dansei no kekkon chitai yōin no kentō: Denki mēkā P sha jūgyōin no baai* [Factors influencing marriage postponement of male workers: A case study of male employees in P electric company]. *Katei keieigaku ronshū* [Journal of Home Economics] 3: 31–40.

Kukimoto, Shingo. 2005. "*Tonai zaijū shinguru no genzai: Mikonsha no kekkon ikō, oyako kankei, sōdan nettowāku* [The current situation of singles living in Tokyo: Ideas on marriage, parent-child relationships, and advising network among unmarried people]. *The Now and the Future of Young Generation in Japan*: 14–32.

Kurotani, Sawa. 2005. *Home Away from Home: Japanese Corporate Wives in the United States*. Durham, NC: Duke University Press.

Kurotani, Sawa. 2014. "Working Women of the Bubble Generation." Pp. 83–104 in *Capturing Contemporary Japan: Differentiation and Uncertainty*, edited by S. Kawano, G. S. Roberts, and S. O. Long. Honolulu: University of Hawai'i Press.

Lareau, Annette. 2011. *Unequal Childhoods: Class, Race, and Family Life*. 2nd edition. Berkeley: University of California Press.

LeBlanc, Robin M. 1999. *Bicycle Citizens: The Political World of the Japanese Housewife*. Berkeley: University of California Press.

Lebra, Takie Sugiyama. 1976. *Japanese Patterns of Behavior*. Honolulu: The University Press of Hawaii.

Lebra, Takie Sugiyama. 1984. *Japanese Women: Constraint and Fulfillment*. Honolulu: University of Hawaii Press.

Lee, Kristen Schultz. 2010. "Gender, Carework, and the Complexity of Family Membership in Japan." *Gender & Society* 24(5): 647–671.

Lee, Kristen Schultz and Hiroshi Ono. 2008. "Specialization and Happiness in Marriage: A U.S.–Japan Comparison." *Social Science Research* 37: 1216–1234.

BIBLIOGRAPHY

Lee, Kristen Schultz, Paula A. Tufiş, and Duane F. Alwin. 2010. "Separate Spheres or Increasing Equality? Changing Gender Beliefs in Postwar Japan." *Journal of Marriage and Family* 72: 184–201.

Lesthaeghe, Ron. 2010. "The Unfolding Story of the Second Demographic Transition." *Population and Development Review*, 36(2): 211–251.

Lesthaeghe, Ronald and Lisa Neidert. 2006. "The Second Demographic Transition in the U.S: Exception or Textbook Example?" *Population and Development Review* 32(4): 669–698.

Lock, Margaret. 1996. "Centering the Household: The Remaking of Female Maturity in Japan." Pp. 73–103 in *Re-Imaging Japanese Women*, edited by A. E. Imamura. Berkeley: University of California Press.

Lofland, John, David Snow, Leon Anderson, and Lyn H. Lofland. 2006. *Analyzing Social Settings: A Guide to Qualitative Observation and Analysis* (4th ed.). Belmont, CA: Wadsworth/Thomson Learning.

Long, Susan Orpett. 1996. "Nurturing and Femininity: The Ideal of Caregiving in Postwar Japan." Pp. 156–176 in *Re-Imaging Japanese Women*, edited by A. E. Imamura. Berkeley: University of California Press.

Long, Susan Orpett. 2008. "Someone's Old, Something's New, Someone's Borrowed, Someone's Blue: Changing Elder Care at the Turn of the 21st Century." Pp. 137–157 in *Imagined Families, Lived Families: Culture and Kinship in Contemporary Japan*, edited by A. Hashimoto and J. W. Traphagan. Albany, NY: State University of New York Press.

Lorber, Judith. 1994. *Paradoxes of Gender*. New Haven, CT: Yale University Press.

Lunsing, Wim. 2001. *Beyond Common Sense: Sexuality and Gender in Contemporary Japan*. London: Kegan Paul Limited.

Macnaughtan, Helen. 2015. "Womenomics for Japan: Is the Abe Policy for Gendered Employment Viable in an Era of Precarity?" *The Asia-Pacific Journal* 13(12): 1–17.

Makita, Meiko. 2010. "Gender Roles and Social Policy in an Ageing Society: The Case of Japan." *International Journal of Ageing and Later Life* 5(1): 77–106.

Martin, Patricia Yancey. 2004. "Gender as Social Institution." *Social Forces* 82(4): 1249–1273.

Martin, Steven P. 2006. "Trends in Marital Dissolution by Women's Education in the United States." *Demographic Research* 15: 537–560.

Mason, Michele M. 2011. "Empowering the Would-be Warrior: Bushido and the Gendered Bodies of the Japanese Nation." Pp. 68–90. In *Recreating Japanese Men* edited by S. Frühstück and A. Walthall. Berkeley: University of California Press.

Mathews, Gordon. 2003. "Can 'A Real Man' Live for His Family? *Ikigai* and Masculinity in Today's Japan." Pp. 109–125 in *Men and Masculinities in Contemporary Japan: Dislocating the Salaryman Doxa*, edited by J. E. Roberson and N. Suzuki. London: RoutledgeCurzon.

Mathews, Gordon. 2004. "Seeking a Career, Finding a Job: How Young People Enter and Resist the Japanese World of Work." Pp. 121–136 in *Japan's Changing Generations: Are Young People Creating a New Society?*, edited by G. Mathews and B. White. London: Routledge.

Mathews, Gordon. 2014. "Being a Man in a Straitened Japan: The View from Twenty Years Later." Pp. 60–80 in *Capturing Contemporary Japan: Differentiation and Uncertainty*, edited by S. Kawano, G. S. Roberts, and S. O. Long. Honolulu: University of Hawai'i Press.

BIBLIOGRAPHY

Matsuda, Masaki. 2011. "My Life as a Househusband" (translated by Kimberly Hughes). Pp. 138–144 in *Transforming Japan: How Feminism and Diversity Are Making a Difference*, edited by K. Fujimura-Fanselow. New York: The Feminist Press.

McCorkel, Jill A. and Kristen Myers. 2003. "What Difference Does Difference Make? Position and Privilege in the Field." *Qualitative Sociology* 26(2): 199–231.

McCurry, Justin. 2007. "World News: Japanese Minister Wants 'Birth-Giving Machines', aka Women, to Have More Babies." *Guardian*, January 28, 2007. Retrieved February 27, 2016 (www.theguardian.com/world/2007/jan/29/japan.justinmccurry).

McLelland, Mark. 2010. "'Kissing Is a Symbol of Democracy!' Dating, Democracy, and Romance in Occupied Japan, 1945–1952." *Journal of the History of Sexuality* 19(3): 508- 535.

Miller, Laura. 2004. "You Are Doing *Burikko*!: Censoring/Scrutinizing Artificers of Cute Femininity in Japanese." Pp. 148–165 in *Japanese Language, Gender, and Ideology: Cultural Models and Real People*, edited by S. Okamoto and J. S. Shibamoto Smith. Oxford: Oxford University Press.

Ministry of Health, Labor, and Welfare. 2003. *"Kosei rōdōshō hakusho:katsuryokuaru kōreishazō to sedaikan no aratana kankei no kouchiku* [Ministry of Health, Labor, and Welfare White Paper: construction of energetic image of the elderly and new intergenerational relationship]." Retrieved March 20, 2016 (www.mhlw.go.jp/toukei_hakusho/ hakusho/kousei_roudou/2003/dl/04.pdf).

Ministry of Health, Labor, and Welfare. 2009. *Heisei 21nendo "rikon ni kansuru tōkei" gaikyō* [2009 summary of "statistics related to divorce"]. Retrieved February 20, 2016 (www.mhlw.go.jp/toukei/saikin/hw/jinkou/tokusyu/rikon10/).

Ministry of Health, Labor, and Welfare. 2010. *Kaisei ikuji kaigo kyūgyō seido no aramashi* [Summary of the revised childcare and family care leave law]. Retrieved March 10, 2016 (www.mhlw.go.jp/topics/2009/07/dl/tp0701-1o.pdf).

Ministry of Health, Labor, and Welfare. 2012. *Annual Health, Labour, and Welfare Report 2011–2012: Work Conditions; Labor Relations*. Retrieved March 11, 2016 (www.mhlw.go.jp/english/wp/wp-hw6/dl/04e.pdf).

Ministry of Health, Labor, and Welfare. 2013a. *Heisei 25-nen ban kosei rodo hakusho* (2013 White Paper on Health, Labor, and Welfare). Retrieved January 31, 2016 (www.mhlw.go.jp/wp/hakusyo/kousei/13/dl/1-02-2.pdf).

Ministry of Health, Labor, and Welfare. 2013b. *Heisei 25-nen ban hataraku josei no jitsujō* [2013 Conditions of working women]. Retrieved March 6 2016 (www.mhlw. go.jp/bunya/koyoukintou/josei-jitsujo/13.html).

Ministry of Health, Labor, and Welfare. 2014a. *Chingin kōzō kihon tōkei chōsa* [Basic statistics on distribution of earnings]. Retrieved March 6, 2016 (www.mhlw.go.jp/ toukei/itiran/roudou/chingin/kouzou/z2014/).

Ministry of Health, Labor, and Welfare. 2014b. *Jinkō dōtai tōkei* [Vital statistics]. Retrieved March 6, 2016 (www.mhlw.go.jp/toukei/list/dl/81-1a2.pdf).

Ministry of Health, Labor, and Welfare. 2016. *Ikumen purojekuto* ["Ikumen" project]. Retrieved March 10, 2016 (www.ikumen-project.jp/index.html).

Ministry of Internal Affairs and Communications. 2011. *Heisei 22 nen kokusei chōsa: jinkōtō kihon shūkei kekka: kekka no gaiyō* [2010 population census: report of population and other basic data: summary report]. Retrieved March 4, 2016 (www.stat.go. jp/data/kokusei/2010/kihon1/pdf/gaiyou1.pdf).

Ministry of Internal Affairs and Communications. 2014. *Kōreisha no jinkō* [Elderly population]. Retrieved March 22, 2016 (www.stat.go.jp/data/topics/topi721.htm).

BIBLIOGRAPHY

Ministry of Internal Affairs and Communications. 2015a. Statistics Bureau home page. www.stat.go.jp/english/index.htm. Accessed February 12, 2016 www.stat.go.jp/english/data/handbook/c02cont.htm.

Ministry of Internal Affairs and Communications. 2015b. Statistics Bureau Census Results. Retrieved March 2, 2016 (www.stat.go.jp/data/kokusei/2010/users-g/kako.htm).

Ministry of Internal Affairs and Communications. 2015c. Statistics Bureau *Rōdōryoku chōsa* [Labor force surveys]. Retrieved March 2, 2016 (www.stat.go.jp/data/roudou/2.htm).

Miyake, Yoshiko. 1991. "Doubling Expectations: Motherhood and Women's Factory Work Under State Management in Japan in the 1930s and 1940s." Pp. 267–295 in *Recreating Japanese Women, 1600–1945*, edited by G. L. Bernstein. Berkeley: University of California Press.

Mizukoshi, Kosuke, Florian Kohlbacher, and Christoph Schimkowsky. 2015. "Japan's *Ikumen* Discourse: Macro and Micro Perspectives on Modern Fatherhood." *Japan Forum* (published on-line, DOI 10.1080/09555803.2015.1099558).

Molony, Barbara. 1995. "Japan's 1986 Equal Employment Opportunity Law and the Changing Discourse on Gender." *Signs: Journal of Women in Culture and Society* 20(2): 268–302.

Molony, Barbara. 2005. "The Quest for Women's Rights in Turn-of-the-Century Japan." Pp. 463–492 in *Gendering Modern Japanese History*, edited by B. Molony and K. Uno. Cambridge, MA: Harvard University Press.

Nagahara, Kazuko. 1982. "*Ryōsai kenbo shugi kyōiku ni okeru 'ie' to shokugyō* ['House' and occupation within good wife, wise mother ideology education]." In *Nihon joseishi, vol. 4: Kindai* [Japanese women's history, vol. 4: Modern period], edited by H. Wakita, R. Hayashi, and K. Nagahara. Tokyo: Yoshikawa Kobunkan.

Nagase, Nobuko. 2006. "Japanese Youth's Attitudes towards Marriage and Childrearing." Pp. 39–53 in *The Changing Japanese Family*, edited by M. Rebick and A. Takenaka. London: Routledge.

Nakamura, Mayumi and Hiroki Sato. 2010. "*Naze koibito ni meguriaenai no ka?* [Why can't people encounter lovers?)." Pp. 54–73 in *Kekkon no kabe: hikon bankon no kōzō* [Obstacles to marriage: structure of non-marriage and postponed marriage], edited by H. Sato, A. Nagai, and S. Miwa. Tokyo: Keiso Shobo.

Nakane, Chie. 1970. *Japanese Society*. Berkeley: University of California Press.

Nakano, Eiko. 1994. "*Mikon joshi no kekkonkan: Raifu kōsu tono kanrende* [Views of marriage among never-married women: its Association with life courses]." *Jinkō mondai kenkyū* [Journal of Population Problems] 50(3): 42–51.

Nakano, Lynne. 2010. "Working and Waiting for 'Appropriate Person': How Single Women Support and Resist Family in Japan." Pp. 131–151 in *Home and Family in Japan: Continuity and Change*. R. Ronald and A. Alexy. London: Routledge.

Nakano, Lynne. 2014. "Single Women in Marriage and Employment Markets in Japan." Pp. 163–182 in *Capturing Contemporary Japan: Differentiation and Uncertainty*, edited by S. Kawano, G. S. Roberts, and S. O. Long. Honolulu: University of Hawai'i Press.

Nakano, Lynne and Moeko Wagatsuma. 2004. "Mothers and Their Unmarried Daughters: An Intimate Look at Generational Change." Pp. 137–153 in *Japan's Changing Generations: Are Young People Creating a New Society?*, edited by G. Mathews and B. White. London: Routledge.

BIBLIOGRAPHY

Nakatani, Ayami. 2006. "The Emergence of 'Nurturing Fathers': Discourses and Practices of Fatherhood in Contemporary Japan." Pp. 94–108 in *The Changing Japanese Family*, edited by M. Rebick and A. Takenaka. London: Routledge.

National Institute of Population and Social Security Research (NIPSSR). 1983. *Shōwa 57 nen dokushin seinensō no kekkonkan to kodomokan: Dai 8 ji shussanryoku chōsa* [Views of marriage and parenting among single young adults: The eighth National Fertility Survey of 1982]. Tokyo: *Jinkō Mondai Kenkyūsho*. Retrieved March 20, 2016 (www.dl.ndl.go.jp/view/download/digidepo_9280429_po_14192802.pdf?contentNo=1& alternativeNo=).

National Institute of Population and Social Security Research (NIPSSR). 1998. *Heisei 9 nen nihonjin no kekkon to shussan:Dai 11 kai shusshō dōkō kihon chōsa* [Japanese marriage and fertility: The eleventh National Fertility Survey of 1997]. Tokyo: *Jinkō Mondai Kenkyūsho*. Retrieved March 20, 2016 (www.ipss.go.jp/syoushika/bunken/DATA/pdf/122367.pdf).

National Institute of Population and Social Security Research (NIPSSR). 2004. *Dai 12kai shusshō dōkō kihon chōsa* [The twelfth National Fertility Survey]. Tokyo: *Jinkō Mondai Kenkyūsho*. Retrieved March 20, 2016 (www.ipss.go.jp/syoushika/bunken/DATA/pdf/129515.pdf).

National Institute of Population and Social Security Research (NIPSSR). 2007. *Dai 13kai shusshō dōkō kihon chōsa* [The thirteenth National Fertility Survey]. Retrieved March 20, 2016 (www.ipss.go.jp/syoushika/bunken/DATA/pdf/132542.pdf).

National Institute of Population and Social Security Research (NIPSSR). 2011a. *Dai 14kai shusshō dōkō kihon chōsa: dokushinsha chōsa no kekka gaiyō* [The fourteenth National Fertility Survey: Summary of survey of unmarried persons]. Tokyo: *Jinko Mondai Kenkyuusho*. Retrieved February 12, 2016 (www.ipss.go.jp/ps-doukou/j/doukou14_s/doukou14_s.pdf).

National Institute of Population and Social Security Research (NIPSSR). 2011b. *Dai 14kai shusshō dōkō kihon chōsa: fūfu chōsa gaiyō* [The fourteenth National Fertility Survey: Summary of survey of married couples]. Tokyo: *Jinko Mondai Kenkyuusho*. Retrieved February 12, 2016 (www.ipss.go.jp/ps-doukou/j/doukou14/doukou14.pdf).

National Institute of Population and Social Security Research (NIPSSR). 2012. *Heisei 22 nen wagakuni fuufu no kekkon katei to shusshoryoku* [Marriage Process and Fertility of Japanese Married Couples, 2010]. Retrieved February 12, 2016 (www.ipss.go.jp/syoushika/bunken/data/pdf/207616.pdf).

Nemoto, Kumiko. 2008. "Postponed Marriage: Exploring Women's Views of Matrimony and Work in Japan." *Gender and Society* 22(2): 219–237.

Nemoto, Kumiko, Makiko Fuwa, and Kuniko Ishiguro. 2012. "Never-Married Employed Men's Gender Beliefs and Ambivalence Toward Matrimony in Japan." *Journal of Family Issues* 34(2): 1673–1695.

New York Times. 2009. "The Opinion Pages: Scott's Vocab.'Soshokukei Danshi'" November 10, 2009. Retrieved February 21, 2016 (http://schott.blogs.nytimes.com/2009/11/10/soshokukei-danshi/?_r=0).

Nolte, Sharon H. and Sally Ann Hastings. 1991. "The Meiji State's Policy toward Women, 1890–1910." Pp. 151–174 in *Recreating Japanese Women, 1600–1945*, edited by G. L. Bernstein. Berkley: University of California Press.

North, Scott. 2009. "Negotiating What's 'Natural': Persistent Domestic Gender Role Inequality in Japan." *Social Science Japan Journal* 12(1): 23–44.

BIBLIOGRAPHY

Ochiai, Emiko. 2004/2006. *Nijuisseiki kazoku e: kazoku no sengo taisei no mikata koekata* [Towards the twenty-first century family: how to view and overcome the postwar family system]. 3rd edition. Tokyo: Yuhikaku sensho.

Ochiai, Emiko and Barbara Molony, eds. 2008. *Asia's New Mothers: Crafting Gender Roles and Childcare Networks in East and Southeast Asian Societies.* Kent, UK: Global Oriental Ltd.

Ogasawara, Yuko. 1998. *Office Ladies and Salaried Men: Power, Gender, and Work in Japanese Companies.* Berkley: University of California Press.

Ogino, Miho. 2006. "*Jinkō seisaku to kazoku: kuni no tame ni umukoto to umanu koto* [Population policy and family: to bear and not to bear children for the country]." In *Iwanami kōza 3: Ajia taiheiyō sensō: dōin, teikō, yokusan* [Iwanami seminar 3: Pacific War: mobilization, resistance, support], edited by A. Kurasawa, T. Sugihara, R. Narita, T. Morris-Suzuki, D. Aburai, and H. Yoshida. Tokyo: Iwanami Shoten.

Ohashi, Terue. 1993. *Mikonka no shakaigaku* [Sociology of non-marriage]. Tokyo: NHK Books.

Ohinata, Masami. 1995. "The Mystique of Motherhood: A Key to Understanding Social Change and Family Problems in Japan" (Translated by Timothy John Phelan). Pp. 199–2011 in *Japanese Women: New Feminist Perspectives on the Past, Present, and Future.* New York: The Feminist Press at The City University of New York.

Oki, Motoko. 1987. "*Ie to josei* [House and women]." In *Nihon joseishi* [History of Japanese Women], edited by H. Wakita, R. Hayashi, and K. Nagahara. Tokyo: Yoshikawa Kobunkan.

Oishi, Akiko. 2004. "*Jakunen shōgyō to oya tono dōbekkyo* [Youth labor force participation and residence with and away from parents]." *Jinkō mondai kenkyū* [Journal of Population Problems] 60(2): 19–31.

Ono, Hiromi. 2003. "Women's Economic Standing, Marriage Timing, and Cross-national Contexts of Gender." *Journal of Marriage and Family* 65(2): 275–286.

Oppenheimer, Valerie Kincade. 1988. "A Theory of Marriage Timing." *The American Journal of Sociology* 94(3): 563–591.

Oppenheimer, Valerie Kincade. 1994. "Women's Rising Employment and the Future of the Family in Industrial Societies." *Population and Development Review* 20(2): 293–342.

Oppenheimer, Valerie Kincade. 1997. "Women's Employment and the Gain to Marriage: The Specialization and Trading Model." *American Review of Sociology* 23: 431–453.

Oppenheimer, Valerie Kincade. 2000. "The Continuing Importance of Men's Economic Position in Marriage Formation." Pp. 283–301 in *The Ties That Bind: Perspectives on Marriage and Cohabitation*, edited by L. J. Waite. New York: Aldine de Gruyter.

Oppenheimer, Valerie Kincade, Hans-Peter Blossfeld, and Achim Wackerow. 1995. "United States of America." Pp. 150–173 in *The New Role of Women: Family Formation in Modern Societies*, edited by H.-P. Blossfeld. Boulder, CO: Westview Press.

Oppenheimer, Valerie Kincade, Matthijs Kalmijn, and Nelson Lim. 1997. "Men's Career Development and Marriage Timing During a Period of Rising Inequality." *Demography* 34(3): 311–330.

Oppenheimer, Valerie Kincade and Vivian Lew. 1995. "American Marriage Formation in the 1980s: How Important Was Women's Economic Independence?" Pp. 105–138 in *Gender and Family Change in Industrialized Countries*, edited by K. O. Mason and A.-M. Jensen. Oxford, UK: Clarendon Press.

BIBLIOGRAPHY

Organisation for Economic Co-operation and Development (OECD). 2015a. OECD Family Database: SF3.3. Cohabitation Rate and Prevalence of Other Forms of Partnership. Retrieved January 29, 2016 (www.oecd.org/els/family/SF_3-3-Cohabitation-forms-partnership.pdf).

Organisation for Economic Co-operation and Development (OECD). 2015b. OECD Family Database: SF2.4: Share of Births Outside of Marriage. Retrieved January 29, 2016 (www.oecd.org/els/family/SF_2_4_Share_births_outside_marriage.pdf).

Organisation for Economic Co-operation and Development (OECD). 2015c. OECD Gender Equity: Balancing Paid Work, Unpaid Work, and Leisure. Retrieved February 7, 2016 (www.oecd.org/gender/data/balancingpaidworkunpaidworkandleisure.htm).

Organisation for Economic Co-operation and Development (OECD). 2015d. OECD Gender Equity: Time Spent in Unpaid, Paid, and Total Work, by Sex. Retrieved February 7, 2016 (www.oecd.org/gender/data/timespentinunpaidpaidandtotalwork-bysex.htm).

Organisation for Economic Co-operation and Development (OECD). 2015e. OECD International Migration Outlook 2015. Retrieved January 31, 2016 (www.oecd.org/migration/international-migration-outlook-1999124x.htm).

Organisation for Economic Co-operation and Development (OECD). 2015f. OECD Family Database: SF3.1: Marriage and divorce rates. Retrieved March 22, 2016 (www.oecd.org/els/family/SF_3_1_Marriage_and_divorce_rates.pdf).

Ortiz, Steven M. 2005. "The Ethnographic Process of Gender Management: Doing the 'Right' Masculinity with Wives of Professional Athletes." *Qualitative Inquiry* 11(2): 265–290.

Piotrowski, Martin, Arne Kalleberg, and Ronald R. Rindfuss. 2015. "Contingent Work Rising: Implications for the Timing of Marriage in Japan." *Journal of Marriage and Family* 77(5): 1039–1056.

Population Reference Bureau (PRB). 2015. "2015 World Population Data Sheet." Retrieved March 22, 2016 (www.prb.org/pdf15/2015-world-population-data-sheet_eng.pdf).

Raymo, James M. 1998. "Later Marriages or Fewer? Changes in the Marital Behavior of Japanese Women." *Journal of Marriage and Family* 60(4): 1023–1034.

Raymo, James M. 2003a. "Educational Attainment and the Transition to First Marriage among Japanese Women." *Demography* 40(1): 83–103.

Raymo, James M. 2003b. "Premarital Living Arrangements and the Transition to First Marriage in Japan." *Journal of Marriage and Family* 65(2): 302–315.

Raymo, James M. 2015. "Living Alone in Japan: Relationships with Happiness and Health." *Demographic Research* 32: 1267–1298.

Raymo, James M. and Miho Iwasawa. 2005. "Marriage Market Mismatches in Japan: An Alternative View of the Relationship between Women's Education and Marriage." *American Sociological Review* 70(5): 801–822.

Raymo, James M., Miho Iwasawa, and Larry Bumpass. 2009. "Cohabitation and Family Formation in Japan." *Demography* 46(4): 785–803.

Raymo, James M., Hyunjoon Park, Yu Xie, and Wei-jun Jean Yeung. 2015. "Marriage and Family in East Asia: Continuity and Change." *Annual Review of Sociology* 41: 471–492.

Rebick, Marcus. 2006. "Changes in the Workplace and Their Impact on the Family." Pp. 75–93 in *The Changing Japanese Family*, edited by M. Rebick and A. Takenaka. London: Routledge.

BIBLIOGRAPHY

Retherford, Robert D., Naohiro Ogawa, and Rikiya Matsukura. 2001. "Late Marriage and Less Marriage in Japan." *Population and Development Review* 27(1): 65–102.

Rindfuss, Ronald R., Minja Kim Choe, Larry L. Bumpass, and Noriko O. Tsuya. 2004. "Social Networks and Family Change in Japan." *American Sociological Review* 69(6): 838–861.

Ripley, Will and Edmund S. Henry, CNN. 2014. "Outrage Follows Sexist Outburst at Tokyo Assembly Meeting" June 23, 2014. Retrieved March 20, 2016 (www.cnn.com/2014/06/20/world/asia/japan-assembly-sexist-outburst/).

Risman, Barbara J. 2004. "Gender as a Social Structure: Theory Wrestling with Activism." *Gender & Society* 18(4): 429–450.

Roberts, Glenda S. 2002. "Pinning Hopes on Angels: Reflections from an Aging Japan's Urban Landscape." Pp. 54–91 in *Family and Social Policy in Japan: Anthropological Approaches*, edited by R. Goodman. Cambridge, UK: Cambridge University Press.

Roberts, Glenda S. 2005. "Balancing Work and Life: Whose Work? Whose Life? Whose Balance?" *Asian Perspective* 29(1): 175–211.

Roberts, Glenda S. 2007. "Similar Outcomes, Different Paths: The Cross-National Transfer of Gendered Regulations of Employment." Pp. 141–161 in *Gendering the Knowledge Economy: Comparative Perspectives*, edited by S. Walby, H. Gottfried, K. Gottschall, and M. Osawa. London: Palgrave.

Ronald, Richard and Yosuke Hirayama. 2009. "Home Alone: The Individualization of Young, Urban Japanese Singles." *Environment and Planning* A, 41: 2836–2854.

Ronald, Richard and Lynne Nakano. 2013. "Single Women and Housing Choices in Urban Japan." *Gender, Place & Culture: A Journal of Feminist Geography* 20(4): 451–469.

Rosenberger, Nancy. 2013. *Dilemmas of Adulthood: Japanese Women and the Nuances of Long-Term Resistance*. Honolulu: University of Hawai'i Press.

Rossi, Giovanna. 1997. "The Nestlings: Why Young Adults Stay at Home Longer: The Italian Case." *Journal of Family Issues* 18(6): 627–644.

Sakai, Junko. 2006. *Make-inu no tōboe* [Distant howling of a defeated dog]. Tokyo: Kodansha.

Salamon, Sonya. 1975. " 'Male Chauvinism' as a Manifestation of Love in Marriage." *Journal of Asian and African Studies* X (1–2): 20–31.

Sasagawa, Ayumi. 2006. "Mother-Rearing: The Social World of Mothers in a Japanese Suburb." Pp. 129–146 in *The Changing Japanese Family*, edited by M. Rebick and A. Takenaka. London: Routledge.

Sato, Hiroki, Akiko Nagai, and Satoshi Miwa (eds). 2010. *Kekkon no kabe: hikon bankon no kōzō* [Obstacles to marriage: structure of non-marriage and postponed marriage]. Tokyo: Keiso shobo.

Sekiguchi, Toko. 2014. "Japan News: Abe Wants to Get Japan's Women Working: Prime Minister Holds Forum Friday to Discuss Working Women and Gender-Based Targets." *The Wall Street Journal*, September 11, 2014. Retrieved February 28, 2016 (www.wsj.com/articles/abes-goal-for-more-women-in-japans-workforce-prompts-debate-1410446737).

Settersten, Richard A., Jr. 2003. "Propositions and Controversies in Life-Course Scholarship." Pp. 15–45 in *Invitation to the Life Course: Toward New Understandings of Later Life*, edited by R. A. Settersten, Jr. Amityville, NY: Baywood Publishing Company, Inc.

Shinotsuka, Eiko. 1994. "Women Workers in Japan: Past, Present, Future." Pp. 95–149 in *Women of Japan and Korea: Continuity and Change*, edited by J. Gelb and M. L. Palley. Philadelphia: Temple University Press.

BIBLIOGRAPHY

Shioda, Sakiko. 2000. *Nihon no shakai seisaku to jendā: danjo byōdō no keizai kiban* [Social policy and gender in Japan: the economic foundation for gender equality]. Tokyo: Yomiuri Shinbunsha.

Shirahase, Sawako. 2005. *Shōshi kōrei-ka no mienai kakusa: jendā, sedai, kaisō no yukue* [The unseen gaps in an aging society: locating gender, generation, and glass in Japan]. Tokyo: University of Tokyo Press.

Smock, Pamela J. 2004. "The Wax and Wanes of Marriage: Prospects for Marriage in the 21st century." *Journal of Marriage and Family* 66(4): 966–973.

Smock, Pamela J., Wendy D. Manning, and Meredith Porter. 2005. " 'Everything's There Except Money': How Money Shapes Decisions to Marry among Cohabitors." *Journal of Marriage and Family* 67(3): 680–696.

Sugimoto, Yoshio. 2010. *An Introduction to Japanese Society* (3nd edition). Cambridge, UK: Cambridge University Press.

Sustainable Development Solutions Network, A Global Initiative for the United Nations. 2013. *Global Happiness Report, 2013.* Edited by J. Helliwell, R. Layard and J. Sachs. Retrieved March 6, 2016 (file:///G:/1PROJECT_BOOK%20MANUSCRIPT%20 SINGLE%20WOMEN/Stats%20sources/WorldHappinessReport2013_online.pdf).

Sweeney, Megan M. 2002. "Two Decades of Family Change: The Shifting Economic Foundation of Marriage." *American Sociological Review* 67(1): 132–147.

Tachibanaki, Toshiaki. 2006. *Kakusa shakai: Naniga mondai nanoka* [Unequal society: what is the real problem?]. Tokyo: Iwanami Shinsho.

Taga, Futoshi. 2003. "Rethinking Male Socialisation." Pp. 137–154 in *Asian Masculinities: The Meaning and Practice of Manhood in China and Japan*, edited by K. Louie and M. Low. London: RoutledgeCurzon.

Takeda, Hiroko. 2011. "Reforming Families in Japan: Family Policy in the Era of Structural Reform." Pp. 46–64 in *Home and Family in Japan: Continuity and Change.* R. Ronald and A. Alexy. London: Routledge.

Tamagawa, Masami. 2015. "Same-Sex Marriage in Japan." *Journal of GLBT Family Studies*, 0: 1–32.

Tamanoi, Mariko A. 1990. "Women's Voices: Their Critique of the Anthropology of Japan." *Annual Review of Anthropology*, 19: 17–37.

Tanaka, Keiko. 2003. " '*Parasaito shinguru*' kasetsu no kenshō: NFRJ98 dēta no bunseki kara [A test of the 'parasite single' hypothesis: from the analysis of NFRJ98 data]." *Kazoku kankei gaku* [Japanese Journal of Family Relations] 22: 95–105.

Tashiro, Sanae. 2015. "Is Being Single Better? An Analysis of Employment Structure and Wages of Japanese Female Workers." *Australian Journal of Labour Economics* 18(3): 239–264.

The Economist. 2011. "Briefing Asian demography: The flight from marriage." August 20, 2011. Pp. 21–24.

The Japan Times. 2007. "Yanagisawa calls women child-bearing machines." January 28, 2007. Retrieved February 13, 2016 (www.japantimes.co.jp/news/2007/01/28/ national/yanagisawa-calls-women-child-bearing-machines/#.Vr9f3fkrLIU).

Thornton, Arland. 2005. *Reading History Sideways: The Fallacy and Enduring Impact of the Developmental Paradigm on Family Life.* Chicago: The University of Chicago Press.

Tokuhiro, Yoko. 2010. *Marriage in Contemporary Japan.* London: Routledge.

Tomida, Hiroko. 2004. "The Controversy over the Protection of Motherhood and Its Impact upon the Japanese Women's Movement." *European Journal of East Asian Studies* 3(2): 243–271.

BIBLIOGRAPHY

Tsuya, Noriko O. and Karen Oppenheim Mason. 1995. "Changing Gender Roles and Below Replacement Fertility in Japan." Pp. 139–167 in *Gender and Family Change in Industrialized Countries*, edited by K. O. Mason and A.-M. Jensen. Oxford: Clarendon Press.

Tsuya, Noriko O., Karen Oppenheim Mason, and Larry L. Bumpass. 2004. "Views of Marriage among Never-Married Young Adults." Pp. 39–53 in *Marriage, Work, and Family Life in Comparative Perspective: Japan, South Korea, and the United States*, edited by N. O. Tsuya and L. L. Bumpass. Honolulu: University of Hawai'i Press.

Ueno, Chizuko. 1994. "Women and the Family in Transition in Postindustrial Japan." Pp. 23–42 in *Women of Japan and Korea: Continuity and Change*, edited by J. Gelb and M. L. Palley. Philadelphia: Temple University Press.

Ueno, Chizuko. 2009. *Ohitorisama no rōgo* (Retirement for the singleton). Tokyo: Hoken.

Ujikane, Keiko and Kyoko Shimodoi. 2014. "Business: Abe Funds Matchmaking to Ease Welfare Bill." *The Japan Times*, March 20, 2014. Retrieved March 6, 2016 (www.japantimes.co.jp/news/2014/03/20/business/abe-funds-matchmaking-to-ease-welfare-bill/#.VtyaXfkrLIU).

Uno, Kathleen. 1991. "Women and Changes in the Household Division of Labor." Pp. 17–41 in *Recreating Japanese Women, 1600–1945*, edited by G. L. Bernstein. Berkeley: University of California Press.

Uno, Kathleen. 2005. "Womanhood, War, and Empire: Transmutuations of 'Good Wife, Wise Mother' before 1931." Pp. 495–500 in *Gendering Modern Japanese History*, edited by B. Malony and K. Uno. Cambridge, MA: Harvard University Press.

van de Kaa, Dirk. 1987. "Europe's Second Demographic Transition." *Population Bulletin* 42(1): 3–57.

Wakakuwa, Midori and Kumiko Fujimura-Fanselow. 2011. "Backlash Against Gender Equality after 2000." Translated by M. Hara. Pp. 337–359 in *Transforming Japan: How Feminism and Diversity Are Making a Difference*, edited by K. Fujimura-Fanselow. New York: The Feminist Press.

West, Candace and Don H. Zimmerman. 1987. "Doing Gender." *Gender & Society* 1(2): 125–151.

White, Merry Isaacs. 2002. *Perfectly Japanese: Making Families in an Era of Upheaval*. Berkeley: University of California Press.

Yamada, Masahiro. 1999. *Parasaito shinguru no jidai* [The age of parasite singles]. Tokyo: Chikuma Shinsho.

Yamada, Masahiro and Momoko Shirakawa 2008. *Konkatsu jidai* [The age of marriage search]. Tokyo: Discover.

Yamaguchi, Tomomi. 2006. "'Loser Dogs' and 'Demon Hags': Single Women in Japan and the Declining Birth Rates." *Social Science Japan Journal* 9(1): 109–114.

Yoshida, Akiko. 2010. *Cultural Lag, Anomie, and Single Women in Japan*. Ph.D. dissertation. Department of Sociology, The University of Oklahoma.

Yoshida, Akiko. 2011. "No Chance for Romance: Corporate Culture, Gendered Work, and Increased Singlehood in Japan." *Contemporary Japan* 23: 213–234.

YouTube. 2014. "*Suzuki Akihiro togi shazai kisha kaiken* [Assemblyman Akihiro Suzuki, apology press conference], Part 2." June 23, 2014. Retrieved March 4, 2016 (www.youtube.com/watch?v=_VUoxgH7BDc).

BIBLIOGRAPHY

Yu, Wei-hsin. 2002. "Jobs for Mothers: Married Women's Labor Force Reentry and Part-Time, Temporary Employment in Japan." *Sociological Forum* 17(3): 493–523.

Zaiki, Kazuo. 2000. "*Bankonka mikonka to shōshika no dōkō* [Trend regarding late marriage, non-marriage, and birth rate decline]." Pp. 33–74 in *Kōrei shakai ron* [*The debate over aging society*], edited by M. Watanabe and T. Otani. Tokyo: Seibundo.

INDEX

Page numbers in *italics* denote tables, those in **bold** denote figures.

Abe, Shinzo 158, 159
aging population *see* population problems
anomie vii, 6–8, 9–10, 17, 18, 39–40,
    41n23, 150, *152*, 156–7, 166, 167n5
Article 14 of Constitution 84, 104n15,
    107

Banks, Ralph Richard 13n32, 15n39, 155
Becker, Gary 5, 13n33, 151, 154, 167n2
birth rate decline *see* population problems
birth-giving machine (*umu kikai*) 103,
    105n26, 159
Blair-Loy, Mary 16n55, 140, 142n17,
    143n30, 161
burikko 70n21

carnivorous women (*nikushoku-kei joshi*)
    71n31
causes of singlehood: deteriorated
    economic prospects due to recession
    15n52, 34, 41n21, 50–1, 61–2, 64, 67,
    71n33–71n34, 71n36, 126–7, 133–5,
    139, 142, 149, 154, 156–7; expanded
    opportunities for women 23–8,
    41n13–41n14, 41n19, 52–3, 58–61,
    66, 107, 109, 112, 141, 146, 156–7;
    gender segregation at work 33, 41n21,
    48–51, 54, 56, 60, 65–8,
    70n15–70n16, 70n18, 72n46, 147,
    149–50, *152–3*, 160–1; long work hours
    27–8, 40, 51–4, 55, 58, 60, 65–8,
    70n19, 72n45, 72n50, 88, 90–3, 96,
    100, 129–32, 137, 141, 147, 149, 150,
    152–3, 154, 158–60; men's beliefs in
    traditional gender roles 27, 53–6, 61–2,
    65, 67, 70n25, 71n38, 72n39, 72n45,

141–2, 147, 149, 150, *152–3*; parents'
    marriages 75–86, 93, 100–3, 104n19,
    119, 145, 147, 150, *152–3*, 157; peers'
    marriages 67, 86–103, 111–12, 116–17,
    120, 122, 124–5, 145, 147, 150, *152–3*,
    157, 164–5; problematic men 26–7,
    57–65, 67, 73n53, 103, 147, 150,
    152–3; views toward maternal
    employment 76–9, 81–2, 105n25,
    112–18, 120, 122–8, 132, 139–41,
    142n17, 143n22, 146, 148–9, *152–3*;
    weakened marriage age (*tekireiki*) norm
    17–25, 28–34, 38–40, 144–6, 148–50,
    152–3, 156–7; women's beliefs in
    women's traditional role 27–8, 29,
    55–6, 67, 78–9, 80, 89, 100, 108–27,
    129–31, 134–42, 145–9, 150, *152–3*,
    161; women's beliefs in men's
    traditional role 58–61, 67, 80, 119,
    121–2, 133–8, 140–7, 149, 150, *152–3*,
    161
Christmas cake 3, 8, 20, 22, 30, 146
chūto saiyō (hiring of non-new graduates)
    24
Civil Code 83, 84
cohort effects 7–8, 10, 15n49, 17–19, 39,
    43, 68, 85–6, 150, 156–7, 166
competing devotions 10, 16n55, 143n30,
    149
corporate practices; *see also* causes of
    singlehood: budget cuts 50, 66, 149;
    female worker retirement 70n23, 132;
    work devotion 51, 60, 66–7, 72n49;
    hiring freezes 41n21, 50–1, 64, 66,
    149; lifetime employment 64; *shanai
    ryokō* (company-sponsored trip) 49–50;

INDEX

shukkō (transfer to a smaller affiliated office) 50; supervisors as matchmakers 40n9, 50, 66, 72n47, 147, 156; *tanshin funin* (single-posting) 81, 90; *tenkin* (job relocation) 52; *undōkai* (company-sponsored sport event) 50
corporate warriors (*kigyō senshi*) 60

Dasgupta, Romit 60, 71n27, 73n51
deai (romantic encounter) 42, 43, 44
dekichatta kekkon (shotgun wedding) 30–1, 99, 125
demographic problem(s) *see* population problem(s)
developmental paradigm 13n33, 14n37
divorce: implied by married interviewees 90, 100, 111, 122; of interviewees' parents/acquaintances 11n7, 82, 84, 94, 98–9, 101–2, 127, 136, 137, *153*; rights 83, 104n11; scarcity of 75–8, 85, 98, 104n6, 110
doing gender 7, 55, 70n22, 167n4
drift into singlehood 1, 6, 7, 10, 28, 39, 66, 74, 133, 141, 145, 150, 156–7, 166
Durkheim, Emile 7, 10, 18, 39, 40, 150, 156–7, 166

economic boom and recession 1, 7, 8, 15n52, 19, 23–8, 50–1, 52–3, 60, 64, 107, 144, 146, 156–7; cohort definition 8, 9, 15n52; impacts on employment *see* causes of singlehood
Edin, Kathryn and Maria Kefalas 14n34, 71n36, 155
egalitarian gender ideology 112, 136–40, 148
empirical studies on singlehood in Japan 4, 5, 11n7, 12n9m 13n21, 13n26, 13n28–13n32, 13n33, 14n34, 14n38, 15n39, 15n41, 26, 41n14, 41n19, 42–3, 56, 64–5, 68n1–68n2, 68n3, 69n12, 70n24, 70n25, 71n29, 71n36, 71n38, 72n39, 72n45–8, 73n53, 143n20, 143n27, 154–5, 163, 167n2, 167n5, 168n13, 169n40–169n43, 169n46, 170n50
ethnic minorities 7, 166, 179
extramarital affairs *see* infidelity

Feminine Mystique 111
feminism/feminist movement (and absence of) 107, 111–12, 115, 142n4, 165–6, 170n50, 170n52

feminist perspective 6–8, 11, 166
fertility rate decline *see* population problems
Friedan, Betty 111
furītā 71n34, 121

gaijin (Westerners): interviewees' views toward 47, 69n10, 88, 96–7, 120
gender; *see also* causes of singlehood: definition/explanation 6–7, 151, 154–5; historical development of ideology regarding 73n51, 83–5, 104n12, 104n15, 106–7, 142n1, 168n36; ideal role of men/masculinity 60, 71n27, 83–5, 106, 121–2, 139, 150; ideal role of women/femininity 23, 70n20–70n21, 83–5, 89, 106–7, 109, 115, 139–42, 142n1, 142n7, 143n18, 143n27, 150, 165, 168n36
gō-kon (mixed-gender party for singles) 48
Gross National Happiness (GNH) 160

Hays, Sharon 140
heckling incident at Tokyo Assembly 1, 11n2, 11n4, 164
hegemonic masculinity 60, 71n27, 115, 121, *152*
herbivorous men (*sōshoku-kei danshi*) 64, 71n31
Hidaka, Tomoko 65, 71n27
Hochschild, Arlie 104n5, 137, 139, 140
housewifization *see* professional housewife

ie (house) ideology/system 83–4, 92, 100, 103, 147
infidelity 24, 43, 54, 60–1, 67, 71n29, 98, 99, 104n11, 147, 151
intersectionality 7, 167, 170n54

jinkō mondai (population problem) *see* population problems

kawaii (cute, feminine) 55, 70n21, 92
Kelsky, Karen 13n33, 26, 41n14, 170n50
King of Bhutan 160
konkatsu (marital partner search) 69n11

Lareau, Annette 140, 143n29
Liberal Democratic Party (LDP) 1, 11n4
life course theory 6, 7, 10, 15n49, 18–19, 39, 43, 74, 85–6, 100, 150, 157, 168n22
life expectancy *see* population problems

203

INDEX

linked lives 10, 15n49, 74, 85–6, 100, 150, 156–7, 166
Long, Susan O. 89, 115
Lorber, Judith 6, 151
loser dogs (*makeinu*) 4, 13n24, 183

McLelland, Mark 70n18, 84
marriage; *see also miai*: as a taken-for-granted life path 4, 6, 13n29, 14n33, 17, 146; democratization of 84–5; parents and peers *see* causes of singlehood; prewar period 83–4
miai (arranged marriage) 17, 29, 38, 40n3, 44–5, **45**, *46*, 47, 57, 72n47, 74, 79, 80, 83, 104n10, 156, 182; interviewee experiences of 57–9, 60, 119–20
mikonka (increased singlehood) 3

National Fertility Survey (s) (NFS) *4*, 11n7, 13n27, 42, 43, 45, **45**, *46*, 64, 68n2, 68n3, 71n38, 108, 142n9, 142n10, 149, 168n36, 174
Nemoto, Kumiko 13n33, 56, 65, 70n24, 70n25, 72n39, 72n45, 72n48, 167n2, 170n50

Ochiai, Emiko 73n51, 84, 109, 142n5, 170n52, 179
OL/Office Lady (female clerical worker) 23, 27, 33, 41n21, 47, 49, 66, 109, 110, 113
online dating services 47, 69n12
Oppenheimer, Valerie 5, 13n33, 154

Pacific War 103, 104n7
parasite single(s) 3, 4, 69n11, 183
parasite single hypothesis 3–4, 13n21, 167n2
patriarchy 3, 10, 72n45, 74–7, 79–85, 92–3, 97–8, 100, 103, 104n3, 104n4, 104n17, 133, 135, 137–8, 140, 141, 144, 147, 148, 150–1, *153*, 165; its toll on mother-daughter relationships 75–8, 103, 119, 165
period effects 85–6
population problems 3, 103, 105n27; aging population 3, 7, 159–60, 164, 165; association with singlehood 3, 12n19, 144, 145; birth/fertility rate decline 3, 12n10, 12n11, 12n13, 159–60, 168n36; dependency ratio 160; government policies, programs,

campaigning related to 3, 12n18, 103, 105n27, 131, 139, 143n25, 145, 158–60, 164, 165–6, 168n27, 168n36; life expectancy 3, 12n13; low level acceptance of immigrants 3, 12n14
professional housewife (*sengyō shufu*) 107, 109, 115, 142n7, 145–6

research method 6–9, 171–83; advantages and limitations of this study 6, 8, 166–7, 178–9; consideration of Japanese culture and statuses of researcher and the researched 9, 173–8; feminist methodology 6, 15n40, 15n41, 155, 157, 158, 166; grounded theory approach/data analysis/coding 9, 178; interview questions 9, 68n3, 69n8, 74, 103n2, 108, 110, 142n11, 173–8; life story interviews 6, 9, 145; limitations of quantitative research 6, 155, 174; sample/sampling methods 9, 166–7, 171–3, 178–9, *184–5*
Risman, Barbara 7
ryōritsu (having-it-all) 108, 112–18, 121, 126, 129, 130, 140, 142n17, 146, 149, *152*, 174, 182
ryōsai kenbo (good wife, wise mother) ideology 83–4, 104n12, 106, 107, 140–2, 142n1, 168n36

Sakai, Junko 4, 13n24
saishūshoku (return to work) 108–9, 114, 122–30, 133, 138–9, 174
salaryman (*saraî man*) 51, 57, 60, 65, 75, 115
salaryman masculinity 60, 71n27, 115, 121, 140
samurai masculinity 60
second shift 136, 137, 139
sexual minorities 4, 7, 13n29, 13n33, 69n9, 122, 139, 166, 167
Shiomura, Ayaka 1, 11n2, 11n4
single women: absence of agency/passivity observed among 22–3, 25, 34, 39, 68, 102–3, 131–3, 156–7, 165–6, 170; concern for future 148, 159–64, 169n40; coresidence with parents 2–3, 11n8, 13n30, 26, 29, 162; desires for children 31–3, 61, 69, 132, 147–50; desires for marriage 4, **4**, 6–9, 11n7, 13n26, 16n54, 19–23, 26–7, 31–3, 40, 43–4, 47–8, 51, 54, 56, 61–2, 69n5, 78–9, 85–6, 94, 99, 100–3, 104n10,

204

INDEX

110, 128–9, 141, 147–50, 155, 161–2; economic conditions 4, 25–6, 34–5, 41n11, 41n19, 159, 162–4, 169n40–169n41, 169n46; glorified images of 3–6, 144, 163–4, 169n42; health conditions 4, 13n30, 54, 162; living alone 2–3, 13n30, 29, 54, 162–3; negative treatments of/views toward 1–4, 12n20, 13n24, 20–1, 23, 35–8, 103, 105n26, 144, 146, 148, 162–3, 164; relationship histories 21–3, 25–8, 32, 34–5, 42–5, 47–8, 51–2, 54, 68n3, 69n13, 70n14

statistics related to singlehood: cohabitation 2–3, 11n7, 154–5; coresidence with parents and others 2–3, 11n8; divorce 104n6; higher rates among the disadvantaged 5–6; labor force participation 25, 41n10, 41n11, 70n15, 70n16; locations of romantic encounters 44–5, **45**, *46*; median age at first marriage 17, **18**, 148; never-married population 1–2, **2**, 147, 149–50, 154–5; reasons of singlehood 42, 68n2; relationship histories 42–3, 68n3; unwed motherhood 3, 12n9, 154–5

Taga, Futoshi 65
teishu kanpaku (authoritarian husband) 80, 82, 104n17, 137, 138
tekireiki (appropriate marriage age) norm; *see also* causes of singlehood 9–10, 17, 19–23, 25, 27, 28, 30, 33, 38, 40n9, 118, 145, 146, 148, *152*, 156, 182

theory of increased singlehood: assumption of human agency as a cause 3–6, 13n21–13n22, 13n33, 14n34, 14n37, 14n38, 144, 145, 151, 154–5, 169n43; cultural theories/second demographic transition theory 5, 13n33, 14n37, 154–5, 167n2, 168n10; neo-economic/rational choice theory/economic independence hypothesis 5, 13n33, 151, 154, 167n3; parasite singles hypothesis 3, 13n21, 167n2
Tokugawa Period 83, 104n9, 179
Tokuhiro, Yoko 13n33, 65, 72n47, 167n3, 170n50–2
torabāyu (to change jobs) 24, 41n13
total fertility rate (TFR) 3, 12n10–12n13

US Occupational Reform 83–4, 103, 107, 166

women's employment; *see also* causes of singlehood: pattern prior to economic boom 23, 38, 105n27, 106–7, 142n2, 142n5, 146, 156, 168n38
womenomics 159
work-life balance 3, 72n50, 131–2, 141, 158–61
World War II (WWII) 40n3, 70n18, 83, 104n7, 104n19, 106, 142n17, 161, 166

Yamada, Masahiro 3, 4, 13n21, 69n11, 72n47, 167n2